WAR, REVOLUTION, AND SOCIETY IN ROMANIA

THE ROAD TO INDEPENDENCE

Edited by

ILIE CEAUSESCU

SOCIAL SCIENCE MONOGRAPHS, BOULDER
DISTRIBUTED BY COLUMBIA UNIVERSITY PRESS, NEW YORK
1983

EAST EUROPEAN MONOGRAPHS, NO. CXXXV

BROOKLYN COLLEGE STUDIES ON SOCIETY IN CHANGE, NO. 34
WAR AND SOCIETY IN EAST CENTRAL EUROPE, VOLUME XV

Copyright © 1983 by Social Science Monographs, Inc.
Library of Congress Card Catalog Number 82-61911
ISBN 0-88033-023-6

Printed in the United States of America

TABLE OF CONTENTS

FOREWORD

The present volume is one of several of a series which, when completed, hopes to present a comprehensive survey of the many aspects of War and Society in East Central Europe. These volumes deal with the people whose homelands lie between the Germans to the west, the Russians to the east and north, and the Mediterranean and Adriatic seas to the south. They constitute a particular civilization, an integral part of Europe, yet substantially different from the West. Within the area there are intriguing variations in language, religion, and government; so, too, are there differences in concepts of national defense, of the characters of the armed forces, and of the ways of waging war. Study of this complex subject demands a multidisciplinary approach; therefore, we have involved scholars from several disciplines, from universities and other scholarly institutions of the USA, Canada, and Western Europe, as well as the East Central European socialist countries.

Our investigation focuses on a comparative survey of military behavior and organization in these various nations and ethnic groups to see what is peculiar to them, what has been socially and culturally determined, and what in their conduct of war was due to circumstances. Besides making a historical survey, we try to define different patterns of military behavior, including the decision-making processes, the attitudes and actions of diverse social classes, and the restraints or lack of them shown in war.

We endeavor to present considerable material on the effects of social, economic, political, and technological changes, and of changes in the sciences and in international relations on the development of doctrines of national defense and practices in military organization, command, strategy, and tactics. We also present data on the social origins and mobility of the officer corps and the rank and file, on the differences between the officer corps of the various services, and above all, on the civil-military relationship and the origins of the East Central European brand of militarism. These studies will, we hope, result in a better understanding of the societies, governments, and politics of East Central Europe.

Our methodology takes into account that in the last three decades the study of war and national defense systems has moved away from narrow concern with battles, campaigns, and leaders and has come to concern itself with the evolution of the entire society. In fact, the interdependence of changes in society and changes in warfare, and the proposition that military institutions closely reflect the character of the society of which they are a part have come to be accepted by historians, political scientists, sociologists, philosophers, and other students of war and national defense. Recognition of this fact constitutes one of the keystones of our approach to the subject.

Works in Western languages adequately cover the diplomatic, political, intellectual, social, and economic histories of these peoples and this area. In contrast, few substantial studies of their national defense system have yet appeared in Western languages.

The present volume consists of studies by Romanian and American historians and is designed to evaluate the political, social, and military dimensions of war and revolution in the process of unification of all the provinces inhabited by Romanians into the independent Greater Romania established at the end of World War I and, as such, it is a pioneer work in a Western language.

Of course, we have the duty of assuring the comprehensive coverage, cohesion, internal balance, and scholarly standards of the series they have launched. We cheerfully accept this responsibility and intend this work to be neither a justification nor a condemnation of the policies, attitudes, or activities of any of the nations involved. At the same time, our policy in this and in future volumes was and shall be not to interfere with the contributions of the various participants, but to present them as a sampling of the schools of thought and the standards of scholarship in the many countries to which the contributors belong.

Bela K. Kiraly
Editor-in-Chief

Mihnea Gheorghiu

I

INDEPENDENCE AND UNITY IN THE
HISTORY OF THE ROMANIAN PEOPLE

Independence and unity have always been the pillars of the national history of the Romanian people.

It is proper to emphasize the indestructible link of the people with ancestral lands. Such links explain the Geto-Dacians' wars waged against the Romans and, later, the wars waged by the Daco-Romans during the first waves of migratory peoples. The Dacian substratum, or the Roman stratum were preserved; the Daco-Romans became Romanians, the inhabitants of the land which they had defended against all enemies.

These links explain the Romanian people's steadfastness in defending the national being against numerous coveters and ill-willed, foes and invaders, steadfastness which first saved independence and internal autonomy, and later, after these had been gradually restricted, to regain them.

Four ideas—justice, social and national liberty, state independence and unity-have characterized the Romanian people's history; they constitute the permanent features of that history. One cannot imagine justice without liberty. At the same time independence cannot be conceived without justice and liberty just as unity cannot be achieved without liberty, justice and independence. The permanent elements of the history of the Romanian people: justice, liberty, independence and unity have been based on the consciousness of the ethnical, linguistic, cultural, economic unity of the entire Romanian people. The common origin of the Romanian people, the unity of language and culture, of customs, the

1

unbroken economic links during the Middle Ages and the modern epoch
gave rise to a consciousness of nation and then to an active national consciousness and that, in turn, to support unitary tendencies in the Romanian people's century-long struggle for independence.

⁎ Liberty and independence were defended by those "popular Romanias",
village communities and communities' unions during the migrations, by
Gelu and Menumorut, Glad and Athum in Transylvania, Tatos, Seslav
and Satza in Dobruja in the tenth and eleventh centuries; by the *bolo-
hoveni* and *brodnici* in Moldavia in the twelfth and thirteenth century;
Litovoi, Seneslau and Barbat in Wallachia in the thirteenth century;
Basarab I and Bogdan defended the independence of Wallachia and Moldavia in the first part and in the middle of the fourteenth century. The
liberty and independence of the Romanian countries were defended by
Mircea the Old, Stephen Muşatin and Dan II, Iancu of Hunedoara, Vlad
the Impaler and Stephen the Great, Pavel Chinezu, Radu of Afumaţi
and Peter Rareş in the battles carried on at Rovine and Hindău, at the
Danube, at Sibiu and Belgrad, at Tîrgovişte, Vaslui and Codrii Cosminului, Cîmpul Piinii and Feldioara and many other places. Similar efforts
and sacrifices, this time for regaining independence, were made by Ioan
Voivode the Brave at Cahul and Roşcani and especially by Michael the
Brave at Călugăreni-Giurgiu, Selimbăr and Suceava. Other names of
heroes and gallant fighters, of memorable and noteworthy places, are
recorded in the difficult road towards liberty and justice, independence
and unity. Horea in the Apuseni Mountains and their outskirts, Tudor at
Padeş and Bucharest, 1848—"the Daco-Romanian Revolution", 1859—
the Union of Principalities, 1877—Romania's independence, 1918—the
completion of the national unity.

Another characteristic of the struggle for justice and liberty, for independence and unity, was the participation of the Romanian people in all
Romanian historical provinces. The common ethnic basis, the consciousness of nation, and later the national consciousness explain the Romanian
people's solidarity and then, of the Romanian nation beyond the artificial political borders separating the Romanian countries, and later of
Romania from the Romanian territories which had been under foreign
domination: Transylvania, Bukovina, Bessarabia and Dobruja. This solidarity, manifest in territorial, cultural, linguistic, economic and psychical
problems led to complete national unity.

Old sources have ascertained the validity of this unity and solidarity. The papal bull of 1234[1], which mentioned that some people from Transylvania moved to Moldavia and merged with the Moldavian Romanians to the point of even accepting orthodoxy, the Diploma of Johannite Knights of 1247[2], which mentions the Transylvania peasants who fled beyond the Carpathians and the document of January 1383[3], which stated that peasants from Wallachia participated in the uprising of the peasants from southern Transylvania—are only a few of many documents attesting to unity and solidarity in those years.

Solidarity and unity were also evident during the battles for defending independence. During the rule of Voivode Mircea the Old, of the Transylvanian voivode Iancu of Hunedoara, of Vlad Dracul in Wallachia and of Bogdan II in Moldavia, the Transylvania voivode was considered "captain" of Wallachia, and the Voivode of Moldavia considered him, to be his "father" wishing the two countries "to be one". Likewise, during the time of Stephen the Great numerous Transylvanians were fighting together with the Moldavian soldiers, and the inhabitants of Braşov called the gallant Moldavian voivode "with heart and soul" for defending Transylvania against the Ottoman danger.

In all cases the multitudes were those that gave strength to this solidarity, either the solidarity appeared in the struggle for liberty and social justice, or for independence and political unity. The greater army, the army of country, made up of peasants taken from their ploughs, freemen—*moşneni* and *răzeşi*—and enslaved—serfs—, assured all the victories in the struggle for defending the independence gained at Rovine and Vaslui, and Sibiu and on the Ialomiţa. In accordance with the account of the humanist Antonio Bonfini[4], some years after the great revolt of the peasants of Bobîlna, Iancu of Hunedoara issued a general call to armies, gathering "soldiers from villages and towns", calling the Szeklers "to take up arms", ordering everybody, villagers and townspeople, to serve the army, "for everybody's liberation".

The example of the Romanian voivode, descending from the Knezes of Hunedoara, was followed by all the great commanders of armies. Vlad the Impaler recruited free peasants, serfs and townspeople for his army. The same social categories, supplemented by the forces of courtiers and boyars, made up the contingents of Stephen the Great who, according to a versed connoisseur of Moldavian realities, the Polish historian Jan Długosz, called to arms "not only the soldiers and boyars, but also the

peasants, teaching all how to defend the country"[5]. At Vaslui, the great
majority of the 40,000 soldiers was made up of peasants. The same
peasants contributed by their uprising against the noblemen and boyars
to the victory won by Michael the Brave at Selimbăr and Suceava and
thus, to the rule of Wallachia's prince over Transylvania and Moldavia,
and thus to the achievement of the first political union of the Romanian
countries under a single rule.

The century-old fight of the Romanian people for defending and later
for regaining independence and for achieving its national unity engendered
even from the fourteenth and fifteenth centuries an individual style of
military organization and of waging wars; this style was characterized,
inter alia, by the mobilization of everybody capable of bearing arms within a specific military establishment—"the greater army". It was, as a matter
of fact, a people's war presuming, on the one hand, the direct or indirect
military participation of the country's entire human potential, especially
of the peasantry, and on the other hand, the creation of a demographic-
economic vacuum on the route of enemy forces. This strategy which
presupposed rigorous discipline and moral qualities by the participants
in wars proved its strategic and tactical superiority vis-à-vis the traditional
military art of the feudal epoch. It compelled the Ottoman Empire to
recognize, following the establishment of Ottoman domination over the
Romanian countries by the end of the first half of the sixteenth century,
their autonomous status in relation to the Sublime Porte. Thus the
people's war proved to be the most valuable weapon against invaders
possessing overwhelming superiority in human and material resources.

This form of military action was to become again one of the essential
features of the modern Romanian army's organization in the nineteenth
century, which army contributed to the achievement of Wallachia's union
with Moldavia in 1859, to the winning of state independence as a result
of the War of 1877-1878, to the final victory in Romania's war of 1916-
1918 for the completion of the unitary Romanian national state. In the
battles fought against the foreign invaders for securing the unity and
liberty of the Romanian countries, the coinhabiting nationalities also
fought shoulder to shoulder with the Romanians. Romanians and others
worked together and fought together over the centuries. Thus, the Szeklers
took an active part in many battles fought by Michael the Brave. Likewise,
they fought alongside Stephen the Great, Petru Rareș, and other ruling

princes of Transylvania, Moldavia and Wallachia as have other inhabitants belonging to co-inhabiting nationalities on other occasions.

Such common action was indeed a logical requirement for the attainment of common aspirations and was evident also during the peasant revolts of Bobîlna, the peasant war of 1514 led by Gheorghe Doja, and later in the uprising of Horea, Cloşca and Crişan in 1784.

The echo of the uprising led by Horea was felt also in Moldavia and Wallachia. In fact, about 3,000 Moldavians and numerous Wallachians joined the rebels in Transylvania. And Horea's intention to unite Transylvania with "the country" were well-known, both by Gheorghe Rettegi and by ordinary people.[6]

The echo of the revolution of Tudor Vladimirescu in Moldavia and Transylvania was much greater. Peasants from many regions gathered, consulted and armed themselves inspired by the Proclamation of Padeş which they knew by heart. Tudor with his *pandurs* were impatiently awaited by Romanian peasants in Transylvania, too, who sought liberation from the oppression of the Hungarian noblemen.[7]

The stern measures taken by the authorities prevented the outbreak of the revolt in Transylvania but could not hinder the solidarity of the people in the Romanian provinces and could not suppress the idea of justice as it was formulated by Tudor Vladimirescu in the proclamation addressed to the "people" of Wallachia in March, 1821. That proclamation emphasized that his "best grounded decision" "joined by the people's voice" is that "in no case" would abandon "the demands for the country's rights", which if he failed to have adopted "those worthy words which had been noticeable until now everywhere it was proper", he would make certain "with all his heart and soul that they will be certainly obtained through bloodshed of any enemy who would try to violate those rights" which the people were to enjoy.[8]

No obstacle could impede the development the idea of unity because, as the *Organic Regulations* pointed out "the genesis, the religion, the customs and the common language of the inhabitants from these two principalities (Wallachia and Moldavia), as well as the common needs represent sufficient elements pleading for their union which was stopped and closed until now only by fortuitous circumstances."[9] (1832)

People with progressive ideas, identifying themselves with the people's aspirations and wishes whenever possible, tried to remove these "fortuitous circumstances". This happened about the middle of the fourth decade when leaders of the Romanian-Polish clandestine society of Sibiu, prominent intellectuals from Transylvania, Wallachia, Moldavia and Poland, united around the flag of the Revolution and of the "Marseillaise" adapted to the conditions of the Romanian society, had in view the peasants' emancipation from serfdom and the union of the three Romanian countries into an independent democratic republic.[10]

This idea was much more clearly expressed in combination with the other idea, of the union, in Wallachia in *"Declarația partidei nationale"* (The Declaration of the National Party) on November 1/13, 1838 titled: *Act de unire și independență* (Act of Union and Independence). The second point of this act clearly stated that it was necessary that new, political, public and civil laws be drawn up *"for the free* and *independent* Romanian people..*, and the elected ruling Prince had the duty of swearing that he "will make the Romanians happy, will win independence, will make friends and allies for the country."[11]

Such wishes became tendencies which won the minds and hearts of intellectuals and of the multitudes-peasants, workers, craftsmen—, and of the progressive bourgeoisie. Fully aware that liberty and justice, independence and unity represented the *sine qua non* conditions for socio-economic, political, cultural and organizational progress. And these tendencies were soon to be translated into programs and actions.

During the Revolution of 1848 identical plans were forged on all sides of the Carpathians concerning "the entire Romanian nation's union" into a "Daco-Romania" or "Romania" and the independence of the newly-created state. The program presented by A. T. Laurian to G. Bariț in April 1848 listed, as its first point, "national independence" in its comprehensive significance, namely "the Romanians to appear under their name, to have their representatives, to use their language in all their affairs"[12]. The creed and ideas of independence, conveyed by a letter, found an immediate echo in the mind and the heart of the man to whom he had addressed and who, only a few days earlier declared in writing in *"Gazeta de Transilvania"* that the Romanians "want full sovereignty, not a hermaphrodite one, want peace, with all their neighbors, alliance with their allies, in short internal and external liberty and fraternity". "These are the things they want and claim once in a life time and they won't rest until they gain them"[13]. From now on, no decision and no program was to be devoid of such ideas. These ideas were indeed not missing from the historic speech delivered by G. Bărnuțiu on May 2/14, who solemnly asked the Romanian nation to proclaim its liberty and independence. That idea was also included in *Protocolul* of Blaj, as the first of 16 points: "the Romanian nation relying on the principles of liberty, equality and fraternity claims in its own name the national independence from the political point of view.[14] " These plans did not confine themselves to a limited circle of revolutionaries and thinkers, but embraced the broad masses of people which convened on Cîmpia Libertății at Blaj on May 3/15, 1848 and called in unison, as a Magyar contemporary relates, "we want to unite with the country", "into a Romanian republic of Dacia". A correct understanding confirmed by the concrete actions and demonstrations in various parts of Transylvania; there were demonstrations and actions of ordinary people like those on the Tîrnave who asked to unite with Wallachia, or those on the Mureș who wished the union with Wallachia, and Moldavia, or those from Hunedoara and the Plain, who declared for all to hear that "Ardealul isn't Ardeal [Transylvania] from now on, it is Romania". Such a historic decision, "the union of the Romanians" was to be made at the "general Congress of all the Romanians" which was to convene in Bucharest in the summer of 1848.[15]

As a reflection of the society's needs at that stage of development, the problems of the union, autonomy and independence played an important part, too, in the *Program* of the revolution in Moldavia and Wallachia. "Administrative and legislative independence and non-interference by any foreign power in internal affairs", that was the contents of the first point of the *Proclamation-program* issued by the revolutionaries in Wallachia. The Moldavian revolutionaries proclaimed in their program entitled *Prințipii* (Principles), elaborated in Brașov, "the union of Moldavia and Wallachia into a sole independent Romanian state"; and in *Dorințele Partidei Naționale din Moldova* (Wishes of the National Party in Moldavia), drawn up in Cernăuți in August 1848, the same revolutionaries called for "administrative and legislative independence in all internal affairs without interference by any foreign power."[16]

In this context, Nicolae Bălcescu, the most progressive of the Romanian revolutionaries and thinkers of 1848, distinctly expressed some logical and fully-justified conclusions resulting from analysis of relations with the Porte concerning "the sovereign right" of the Romanian people.

That's why he proclaimed the duty to "defend our nationality and rights even to shed our blood if necessary."[17]

The romantic revolutionaries did not abandon these ideas even after the revolution had been suppressed by the Turkish and Tsarist armies. They directed their thoughts and hopes towards the revolution in Transylvania. Nicolae Bălcescu and the brothers Golescu, Barbu Iscovescu and Ionescu de la Brad left for the "Stone Fortress" of the Apuseni Mountains where Avram Iancu had organized his forces; they envisioned a united Romania, like a ring with a capital, which in Alecu Russo's vision "was to be called Rome", with large markets which were to be called: Piața Poporului (People's Place), Piața Traian (Trajans Place), Piața Ștefan (Stephen's Place), Piața Mihai (Michael's Place), Piața Moldovei (Moldavia's Place), Piața Banatului (Banat's Place), Piața Transilvaniei (Transylvania's Place).[18]

The extensive program of the Moldavian revolutionaries *Dorințele Partidei Naționale din Moldova*, a collective effort, but bearing the imprint of M. Kogălniceanu's thought, included the union of Moldavia with Wallachia regarded as "the keystone, without which the whole national edifice would break down", and the setting up of an independent state respecting "the rights created and guaranteed along hundreds of years which our ancestors have always known to preserve, even through cruel sacrifices and which we also want to leave to our great-grandchildren."[19]

The revolution was put down through the union of external repressive forces, Tsarist and Ottoman, with the internal reactionary ones. But the great ideas, the liberating ideals proclaimed by the Revolution: justice, liberty, unity and independence could not be suppressed. These ideas continued to live with the same vitality. They continued to be strong and alive not only in the minds and thoughts of the most progressive intellectuals of the times but also, in the minds and hearts of peasants, craftsmen and workers, progressive boyars and bourgeoisie. The Romanian revolutionaries in emigration predicted a "completed, free and inseparable" Romania, a Romanian democratic and social republic, relying on the truth that it is wished by the entire Romanian people.

From as early as 1850, analysing with much intuition the development of historic processes, N. Bălcescu foresaw that future revolutions seek national unity and liberty.[20] The far-sighted views of the great patriot were to be realized much earlier than the architects of the new national edifice had expected. The Union of the Principalities, namely of Wallachia with Moldavia, which had been contemplated by patriots for a long time, was achieved at the end of the sixth decade of the nineteenth century within the framework of the European diplomacy and over the opposition of some of the Great Powers. Union and independence had been sought by various constitutional organizations and bodies. The first and second points of *"Programul comitetului electoral din Moldova"* (The Program of the Electoral Committee in Moldavia), of *Programul unioniştilor* (the Program of the Unionists) in Moldavia, too, of *Comitetului central al Unirii din Bucureşti* (The Central Committee of the Union in Bucharest), of the Manifesto issued by the same committee, of the decisions took by the ad-hoc assemblies in Moldavia and Wallachia encompassed the same ideas: the observance of the autonomy and of our international rights and "the Union of the Romanian Country and Moldavia in a sole state".[21]

The result of these efforts and wishes, sacrifices and martyrdom was the Union of January 24, 1859 which meant the accomplishment of the "ruling" idea of the times, as contemporaries characterized it. The Union was prepared and supported by newspapers and leading cultural personalities such as Mihail Kogălniceanu, as publisher of a newspaper or as a professor at the Academia Mihăileană, Nicolae Bălcescu, as a persuasive speaker and writer, or Vasile Alecsandri, as a poet hailing the union in his verses and asking "the brothers of the same nation" to close "their hands together to the end of time," and also by the anonymous masses who waited and readied themselves for its achievement.

Under the circumstances, the representatives of the Great Powers, gathered at Paris, were obliged to acknowledge the reality that the inhabitants of the Romanian countries have always been "a sole people" they have "the same genesis, the same name, the same language, the same religion, the same history, the same civilization, the same institutions, the same laws and customs, the same fears and hopes, the same needs to satisfy, the same frontiers to guard, the same sorrows in the past, the same future to secure, and at least the same mission to accomplish", in the words of the Ad-hoc Assemblies in the Romanian Principalities.

The unavoidable conclusion to be drawn from these arguments could be none other than union, the Romanians' unanimous wish" which they wanted to be implemented as soon as possible."[22]

The Union seized the "thoughts and hearts" of patriots: peasants, workers, craftsmen, intellectuals, the progressive bourgeoisie and boyars. Neither the ambiguous attitude of some Great Powers, nor the opposition of others, nor the old conservatism of certain boyars could prevent its full realization. Colonel Alexandru Ioan Cuza, a participant in the 1848 Revolution, the prefect of Galatzi who resigned his commission in protest against the falsification of the elections, was unanimously chosen as ruling prince of Moldavia by Moldavia's elective assembly on January 5, 1859. This remarkable act, whereby deputies subordinated their own interests to those of the nation, was rooted in the firm belief that the union and national liberty will bring about also a union of thought and feelings as well as social justice and liberty for all. Of paramount significance in this respect was the attitude of the outstanding political and cultural personalities such as Koganiceanu, Alecsandri, Negri and others who withdrew their own candidacy in favor of Cuza.

On January 24, 1859 the Wallachians also elected Alexandru Ioan Cuza as their ruling prince. On December 11, 1861, in the proclamation to the nation the Prince of the United Principalities, Romania's Prince, officially stated that: "Union is achieved, the Romanian nationality is founded. Today your chosen ruler gives you a single Romania". The opening in Bucharest, Romania's new capital, of Romania's first Parliament represented an event of major historical significance not only for those times but also for the future. The Union paved the way to major reforms such as the secularization of monastic estates, the electoral law, the rural law, the law on instruction, the law for the organization of the armed forces, and others. The Union of 1859 can rightly be considered as the foundation of the edifice enriched and adorned by hardworking hands and clever minds, animated by a sincere love of their homeland.[23]

After the Union of the Romanian Principalities was achieved, another goal was sought by the Romanian people—the winning of independence.

The Romanian people could not ignore the Balkan Crisis which broke out in 1875 in Bosnia. From the beginning of 1876 Romania's rulers informed the European powers of the nation's determination to secure independence. The Memorandum of the Ministry of Foreign Affairs addressed to the Porte and the guaranteeing powers in June 1876 was, as a matter of fact, a declaration of independence. As Romania's official note was ignored alternate plans were devised and discussed at the Russian-Romanian meeting in Livadia (in the Crimea) in November 1876.

The winter of 1876-77 was one of preparations especially after the Porte rejected once again the proposals of the Powers contained in the London Protocol of March 1877.

On April 16, the legislative bodies validated the Romanian-Russian convention and on April 29 the same bodies acknowledged the state of war with the Ottoman Empire. Consequently, on May 9, 1877, the Assembly of Deputies passed a motion by which Romania's independence was proclaimed "the Assembly satisfied with the Government's explanations concerning the consequences of its vote of April 29 takes note that the war between Romania and Turkey, the breaking off of our relations with the Porte, as well as Romania's absolute independence received their official sanctioning."[24]

The entire country supported that decision, firmly determined to make any and all necessary sacrifices to implement it. The entire country meant Romania and all the Romanian provinces under foreign domination. The general enthusiasm on all sides of the Carpathians was indeed exciting and moving. The peasant turned soldier, the working masses support unstintingly the war effort—writers Vasile Alecsandri, Alex. Odobescu, I.L. Caragiale, George Coșbuc, Nicolae Gane, Duiliu Zamfirescu—immortalize the historical moment. So did painters—Nicolae Grigorescu, Carol Pap de Szatmari, Theodore Aman, Ioan Andreescu and many others. Many young men from Romania or the provinces subdued by big empires, from Brasov and Făgăraș, Sibiu and Hunedoara, from the valley of the Mureș and Tîrnave, from Banat and the Apuseni Mountains, from Bukovina—left their families and joined the forces defending Romania's independence.

Nothing could thwart such enthusiasm and solidarity. "Romanian men and women were firmly determined to go on—as declared Bariț in *"Gazeta Transilvaniei"*—with steady steps on the road showed by their hearts, national will and enlightened Europe's example, disdaining any troubles of the tyranny and selfishness killing the country."[25]

The independence was a strong supporting-pillar of the national edifice alongside its other strong pillar, the 1859 Union. For the edifice to be lasting, however, other pillars had to be erected. Outstanding writers in all the territories inhabited by Romanians collaborated in the same newspapers and magazines whose very titles contained a program of action. "Dacia viitoare" (Daciat to be), "Emanciparea" (The Emancipation), "Carpații" (The Carpathians), "Unitatea națională" (The national unity), "Naţiunea" (The nation), etc. At the same time progressive people, socialists and sympathizers with socialism, openly supported the goal of union of all territories inhabited by Romanians: "We want Dacia as it was—wrote Const. Mille—because history and right, tradition and plebiscite, the past and the present entitled us to aspire to a Roman Dacia. This land stained with our forerunners' blood and sweat, multiplied with their dust along the twenty centuries is ours. Then we want what is of the Romanians to belong to them, we want this unfair, inhuman domination of a nation over the other, an unworthy domination of the century we live in, to cease, we want all Romanians to be free and to form a state and not to groan under foreign and cruel dominations."[26]

The Memorandum-movement of the period 1882-1894 revealed once again the solidarity prevailing among Romanians of the Old Kingdom and of the subdued Romanian provinces. In fact, from a political and spiritual point of view the geographic frontiers were abolished. "The Cultural League" started its activity under those special circumstances and on a very significant date: January 24, 1891; during World War I it was transformed into the League for the Cultural Unity of all Romanians. It played an undeniably significant role in achieving the political union of all Romanians. Equally self-evident is the role played by progressive intellectuals who advocated the necessity of achieving the union, the complete independence. "A country, as a social organism—stated C. Dobrogeanu-Gherea in 1911—has to develop as a whole organism within its ethnical limits. Divided into more parts, like Poland or partially, Romania, its development becomes abnormal and pernicious to the highest degree". Underlining that national subjection is for the benefit of ruling classes and that, as a result, the working people are "making the chains heavier", C. Dobrogeanu-Gherea declared that social-democracy all over the world was fighting against injustice, oppression and enslaving of man by man, was fighting against all chronic diseases of the capitalist society, "against national oppression for the nations' liberation from foreign yokes."[27]

So step by step, with care and patience, with courage and responsibility, through the mature thinking of an entire people, one of the most important acts in the dramatic and heroic history of the Romanian people was achieved—the completion of national unity.

The completion of Romania's state unity in 1918 as a result of the objective necessities of the Romanian people's development and as a result of the struggle carried on by the people's masses all over the country created as pointed out by President Nicolae Ceauşescu, more favorable conditions for the struggle waged by revolutionary forces, for the general progress of Romanian society, contributed to the consolidation of national independence.

As is well known developments, internal and external, threatened the liberty, unity and national independence of Romania. The Program of the Romanian Communist Party pointed out "the policy of surrender and capitulation in the international field, in face of Germany, as well as the anti-national policy carried on by the most reactionary circles in Romania, the setting up of the military-fascist dictatorship in September 1940 opened the way to our country's complete enslavement by Hitler's Germany."[28] As it is also known, the re-establishing of the unity, independence and national sovereignty of Romania was paramount concern of the Communist Party. The Platform of the Romanian Communist Party of September 6, 1941 titled *"The People's Fight for Liberty and National Independence"*, the resolution of the Central Committee of the Romanian Communist Party of June 1943 concerning the establishment of the Anti-Hitler Patriotic Front, the Manifesto issued by the United Workers' Front on May 1, 1944, the Declaration of the National Democratic Bloc on June 20, 1944, the Declaration of the Central Committee of the Romanian Communist Party of August 24, 1944. All sought the union of all the forces deeply concerned with the regaining of national independence.

The independence, national unity and sovereignty regained after the defeat of Nazi Germany, was consolidated by the Romanian Communist Party and the Romanian socialist state in accordance with Romanian historical traditions and realities.

NOTES

1. *Documente privind istoria României, C. Transilvania* vol. I, sec. XI-XIII, p. 275.

2. *Ibid.*, p. 329-333.

3. Zimmermann-Werner-Müller, *Urkundenbuch zur Geschichte der Deutschen in Siebenbürgen*, vol. II, p. 565-566. cf. St. Pascu, *Răscoale tărăneşti în Transilvania*, vol. I, Cluj, 1947, p. 64-67.

4. Antonio Bonfini, *Historia Pannonica sive Hungaricarum rerum*

decares IV et dimidia, Köln, 1690, p. 311; cf. C. Mureșan, *Iancu de Hunedoara*, ed. a II-a, Bucharest, 1968, p. 75.

5.   I. Długosz, *Historia Polonica*, t. II, Leipzig, 1712, col. 417; cf. *Istoria României*, vol. II, p. 508.

6.   *Istoria României*, vol. III, București, 1964, p. 789-790; I. Ranca and L. Moldovan, *Contribuții privind răspîndirea răscoalei lui Horea în partea centrală și răsăriteană a Transilvaniei*, in "Studii", XXI, 1968, 2, p. 277-288.

7.   Hurmuzaki, *Documente privind istoria României*, seria mouă, vol. III, *Solidaritatea românilor din Transilvania cu mișcarea lui Tudor Vladimirescu*, publ. by A. Oțetea, p. 20-26; A. Oțetea, *Tudor Vladimirescu, și revoluția din 1821*, Bucharest, 1975, p. 278-284.

8.   *Documente privind istoria României. Răscoala din 1821. Documente interne*, I, București, 1959, p. 386.

9.   *Regulamentele organice ale Valahiei și Moldovei*, București, 1944, p. 341.

10.   Șt. Pascu, *Marea Adunare Națională de la Alba Iulia*, Cluj, 1968, p. 67.

11.   C. Bodea, *Lupta românilor pentru unitatea națională, 1834-1849*, București, 1967, p. 17-18, 216-218.

12.   *George Bariț și contemporanii săi*, ed. Șt. Pascu and I. Pervain, I, p. 145.

13.   *Apărarea patriei, a independenței și suveranității naționale*, Bucharest, 1975, p. 22

14.   T.V. Păcățian, *Cartea de aur*, I, p. 330.

15.   Șt. Pascu, *op. cit.*, p. 76-81.

16.   *Gîndirea social-politică despre Unire (1859)*, Bucharest, 1966, p. 39-45.

17.   Nicolae Bălcescu, *Drepturile românilor către Înalta Poartă*, in *Opere*, vol. I, Bucharest, 1953, p. 230.

18.   Șt. Pascu, *op. cit.*, p. 82-83.

19.   *Anul 1848 în Principatele Române*, Vol. IV, p. 109-136.

20.   N. Bălcescu, *Opere*, vol. IV, *Corespondență*, ed. G. Zane, Bucharest, 1964, p. 277-278.

21.   *Gîndirea social-politică*, p. 100-170.

22.   *Ibid.*, p. 149-150.

23.   C. C. Giurescu, *Viața și opera lui Alexandru Ioan Cuza*, București, 1966.

24. *Apărarea patriei, a independenţei şi securităţii naţionale*, p. 93.
25. G. Bariţ, *Scrieri social-politice*, Bucureşti, 1962, p. 89.
26. *Documente din istoria mişcării muncitoreşti din România, 1871-1892*, Bucharest, 1973, p. 165-167.
27. *Apărarea patriei...*, p. 120-121.
28. *Programul Partidului Comunist Român de făurire a societătii socialiste multilateral dezvoltate şi înaintare a României spre comunism*, Editura politică, 1975, p. 45.

II

THE "ENTIRE PEOPLE'S WAR: "
ITS HISTORIC SIGNIFICANCE

In its tumultuous history of over two millenia, during fierce battles waged almost without cessation against particularly strong aggressors, well-organized and distinctly superior militarily, the Romanian people learned and applied the lessons of history and devised tactics and strategies for defeating any and all aggression and, for safeguarding its own independence.

The adoption of the concept and practice of the entire people's struggle was essential for Romanians whose lands have always been threatened by rivalries among Great Powers seeking expansion of their spheres of influence.

Faced with invaders, usually superior in numbers and military technology, the Romanians were obliged to resort to various forms of actions which would allow them to nullify the enemy's superiority and to secure the conditions necessary for victory. In this way the concept and practice of the entire people's fight for defending the homeland developed.

The Geto-Dacians used the so-called "tactics of scorching the land", against foreign enemies. As it is known, the territory ruled by the ancestors of the Romanians was the target for conquests of numerous enemies. The permanent dangers faced by the Geto-Dacians enhanced their military skills, tactics, and technology.

The first aggressive action against the Geto-Dacian territories mentioned in the works of ancient historians was the expedition of the Persian King Darius I against the Scythians in 514 B.C. According to Herodotus, the only resistance facted by the Persians on their move toward the mouth of the Danube was from the Getae. As a result of the Getae's resistance, the Persians failed to establish their authority over the Geto-Dacian territories. In 335 B.C. Alexander the Great led an expedition against the Getae in the Wallachian Plain. According to Arrian, on the left side of the Danube there were about four thousand Getic horsemen and ten thousand foot soldiers. After several unsuccessful attempts to cross the Danube, Alexander, by altering his tactics, finally succeeded and began his offensive across "rich fields of wheat." Diversionary tactics used by the Getae did not result in victory but allowed their forces to withdraw in an orderly manner.

In 326 B.C. Strategus Zopyrion, governor of Thrace who was left by Alexander the Great as deputy commander at the Lower Danube area, staged an expedition against the Getae. After an unsuccessful attack against the city of Olbia, the Macedonian army was attacked and destroyed on its way back on the Buceag Plain by a large Getic army. The complete defeat of the Macedonian army consolidated Getic power in the Danube area.

About 291 B.C. Lysimachus initiated a new campaign against the Getae, led by Dromichaites, north of the Danube. Because of its numerical superiority, Lysimachus expected to easily defeat the Getae. After crossing the Danube, however, the army led by Lysimachus was pursued and ceaselessly harassed by the Getae. Encircled by the Getae, Lysimachus was forced to surrender and, together with his generals, became prisoners.

The difficulties of this campaign against the Getae were revealed in Diodorus' works according to which Dromichaites advised Lysimachus of the fact that the Getic fields were "fields on which no foreign army could escape under the open sky."[1]

The expansion of Rome toward the northeast in the 2nd century B.C., enhanced the Dacians' determination to strengthen their defense capabilities and develop the most suitable forms and methods of warfare. The establishment of the Dacian centralized and independent state, under Burebista at the beginning of the first century B.C. was a milestone in this respect. The military strategy developed by Burebista envisioned the participation of the entire population alongside an army of 200,00 men, and exploitation of the strategic advantages provided by a vast territory with a very diversified relief.

In 86 A.D. Decebalus became king of Dacia; he was endowed with exceptional military, political and diplomatic abilities and was one of the most illustrious personalities of ancient history. He was to become for the Romanian people a legendary hero, a symbol of courage and self-sacrifice in the defense of independence.

When he ascended Dacia's throne, the country was at war with the Roman Empire. Decebalus sued for peace but Domitian refused this request. Consequently in the summer of 87 A.D. Cornelius Fuscus crossed the Danube on a pontoon bridge and advanced toward Sarmizegetusa. After some harassing actions skillfully delployed prior to developing a surprise attack, Decebalus succeeded in destroying the greater part of the Roman army and in capturing the banners, war engines, arms and other materiel. In this memorable disaster for the Romans, the Dacian people, the army, Decebalus himself demonstrated the art of defeating an experienced enemy, superior in numbers and military equipment.

Domitian's reaction was not long in coming. A new army, larger than that of 87 A.D., was formed and put under the command of General Tettius Julianus who entered Dacia through the Banat and the Bistra Valley. Decebalus adopted harassing tactics. Thus, to restrict the Romans' advance he regrouped his forces and withdrew to the interior of the country. Concurrently, Decebalus organized surprise attacks which intensified the harassment of the Romans. Eventually, however, the Roman forces approached Sarmizegetusa And Decebalus, anxious to avoid a siege of his capital, sued for peace.

The peace of 89 because of its advantageous terms to the Dacians aroused deep discontent in Rome. The apprehensions over the Romans intentions unleashed their own military preparations particularly in the mountains around Sarmizegetusa. That is why as soon as Emperor Trajan ascended the throne in 97 he decided to suppress the Dacian state. In the spring of 101, the Romans declared war on the Dacians.

Trajan's forces and techniques were distinctly superior to Decebalus', however the Dacians had the advantage of knowing their own territory. Decebalus adopted a defensive strategy, he organized effective harassing actions. The 101-102 campaign ended in favour of the Romans and Decebalus was obliged to sue for peace pending the development of more favorable conditions for future action.

The peace lasted only two years. From 105 on the Roman garrisons in Dacia were subject to continuous attacks; thus, the second war between the Dacians and the Romans began. Several allies of Decebalus' allies concluded pacts of friendship with the Romans, which jeopardized the Dacians' cause. Despite Decebalus' heroic resistance, Sarmizegetusa, the capital of the Dacian state, was conquered in 106. The Dacians were defeated but not destroyed by the Romans.

The Roman conquest and the establishment of Roman rule over part of Dacia had, as any foreign conquest and domination, tragic consequences for the Dacian people. The dissolution of the independent and centralized Dacian state prevented the Dacians from organizing and developing their own army, not to mention the maintaining of their state independence and sovereignty.

However, during the 165 years of Roman rule, the Dacian people resisted, often forcibly, Roman rule. And resistance became more intense as interval crises in the Roman Empire intensified. The classic slave-owning system of exploitation was introduced in Dacia which led to aggravation of social antagonisms and of resistance by the Dacians. Resistance against the Roman domination assumed multiple forms ranging from tacit opposition to mass uprisings. From 107-108 until 271 the actions of the Dacians in Roman-occupied territories blended with those of the free Dacians proved to be among the main causes which forced Aurelianus' withdrawal south of the Danube in 271-275.

After 275, a new period began in the history of the Romanian people's resistance against foreign enemies; it was the period of resistance to the migratory peoples' invasion and temporarily settlement. The Romanian people were able to fight the often cruel invaders successfully and maintain their continuing existence on ancestral lands.

The entire people's resistance developed under very critical conditions because the Romanian people did not have an army of its own. The main forms of resistance were withdrawal to mountains and forests and accomodation to the invaders' tactics. The village and territorial communities the free peasants continued to exist in Dacia. They proved their viability under Roman domination and were used as a basis for territorial and political organization by the Romanian people. The waves of the migratory peoples helped consolidate the territorial communities since the conquerors were anxious to have the subdued population organized to better supply them with necessary goods. To turn the territorial communities joined and set up confederations to protect their own interests.

These confederations were situated in certain geographic locations, i.e., river valleys or closed areas, called *țări* (lands), from the Latin word terra (Țara Hațegului, Țara Lovistei, etc.). A "land" was ruled by a duke or voivode whose main function was military, to defend the voivodeship or the land.

On Transylvanian territory such state formations were set up even before the end of the first millenium. When Magyar tribes began their expansion into Transylvania they were opposed by these early Romanian state formations. It is known from chronicles that the Romanians in Transylvania, under the leadership of Glad, Gelu and Menumorut, resisted expansion of Magyar tribes. Later, Magyar feudal lords, led by the Hungarian King Stephen I, waged an unsuccessful war both against the voivode of Transylvania, Gyula (1002-1003) and against Ahtum, voivode of the Banat. After the death of King Stephen I, the Romanian voivodeships in Transylvania and Banat taking advantage of the weakness of the Magyar kingdom ranked by internal crises, consolidated their sovereignty. That is why in the twelfth century the so-called domination of Magyar lords stopped for a long time at Poarta Mezeșului. This fact is also verified by the Szecklers' settlements on the borders of Bihor. Toward the end of the eleventh century and the beginning of the twelfth Magyar invaders resumed their expansion into Transylvania which lasted until the beginning of the thirteenth century. The expansion was resisted by the Romanian population and the Magyar kingdom had to acknowledge the existence of the Transylvanian voivodeship which had been established in earlier times. The voivodeship of Transylvania was an autonomous political entity which recognized the suzerainty of the Magyar kingdom.

The Tatars' devastating invasion occurred while the Romanian state formations were in the process of consolidation and temporarily delayed the Romanians the formation of a single feudal state. The subdued Romanian people were able to organize a successful resistance movement and to contribute to the breakdown of the apparently invincible Tatar power. Local Romanian leaders exploiting internal and external conditions, were able to consolidate their efforts against their enemies. In the end, Basarab I became the ruler of Wallachia.

Following extended battles with the Magyars, Wallachia won its independence. The other independent Romanian state, Moldavia was formed east of the Carpathians by the union of existing political organizations

following military and political actions similar to those which had occurred in Wallachia. The unification of political entities on Moldavian
territory was facilitated by the successful struggle waged against foreign
invaders, particularly the Tatars. Dragoş, voivode of Maramureş, who had
distinguished himself in the battles against the Tatars became the ruler
of the territories east of the Carpathians. Taking advantage of the fact
that Hungary was engaged in war with Venice, Bogdan of Maramureş,
removed Dragoş's successor throne from the Moldavian and achieved
the independence of the Moldavian state in 1359. Under Bogdan, Moldavia
extended its territories, incorporating other Romanian political organizations east of the Carpathians and eventually secured the acquiscence
of the Hungarian king.

It was also in the fourteenth century that Dobrudja, an old Romanian
region, became an independent state. In 1388 a great Turkish expedition
threatened to turn the territory between the Danube and the Black Sea
into a *pashalik*. The energetic intervention of Mircea the Old saved
Dobrudja from Turkish domination and united it with Wallachia.

Concurrently with the organization of state formations on the entire
territory inhabited by Romanians, the people's resistance against foreign
invaders assumed the new advanced stage of total participation by the
entire population in defense of Romanian lands against often stronger
enemies.

From the very beginning of the Middle Ages our forerunners were
compelled to assume and implement the Dacians' so-called "tactics of
scorching the land", to use varying and ingenious forms and strategies of
warfare consonant with advantages offered by the terrain, to engage
in constant harassment to nullify the enemies' numerical and technological superiority, all with a view to driving the enemy beyond the
country's boundaries. The domination of the great neighboring empires
(Ottoman, Hapsburg, Tzarist) which through war, plunder and tribute
improverished the Romanian Countries throughout the centuries, left
the Romanian people in a state on constant military readiness in defense
of their ancestral lands.

In the Middle Ages the participation of the people in the struggle
against aggression was usually through the institutionalized, "greater
army" which comprised all social categories. Strategically, at the beginning of an armed confrontation the enemy would be harassed, deprived

of food supplies and, thus demoralized, he would be lured inside the country, to narrow places, where he could not deploy his forces and take advantage of his numerically superiority in numbers there he would be attacked by surprise and defeated in a decisive battle. The escaping forces would be pursued by horsemen and chased beyond the country's borders. "The Romanians never loved wars of conquest"—Nicolae Bălcescu pointed out—"and their wars were defensive politically but offensive militarily."[2]

Referring to the medieval Romanian "entire people's struggle," Nicolae Bălcescu wrote: "Any time an aggressor invaded our country, all the inhabitants of the fields laid their towns and villages to waste and took with their flocks and provisions to the mountains . . . The old men, the women and the children rested in the mountains and the young men took up their arms and organizing themselves into groups harassed the aggressors. The country's army hid in the woods avoiding facing the enemy's general battle, being satisfied with harassing him, breaking off his communications, taking his provisions . . . and compelling him to abandon the country empty handed or trapping him in unfamiliar, difficult terrain where he paid dearly for his boldness to have invaded Romanian land."[3]

In the wars fought by the Romanian people in defense of their ancestors' land, the great commanders took skillful advantage of the mountainous terrain. Thus, in 1330 at Posada, Basarab I with his small army succeeded in defeating, through a surprise attack, Magyar forces distinctly superior in number and materiel. Stephen the Great scored brilliant victories, masterpieces of military art, through the judicious use of the terrain, at Baia, Vaslui, Războieni (Valea Albă), Codrii Cosminului and many other places.

The entire people's war was also successfully pursued at night. The Romanian princes often fought battles after dark against superior enemy forces. Vlad the Impaler used this method in 1462, when he defeated Sultan Mohammed II who invaded Wallachia and with an army vastly superior in size and equipment.

The Romanian armies displayed much ability and ingenuity in battles waged in the forests. In the battle of 1377 fought in the woods of Șepeniț, the Moldavian army used, as chronicler J. Dlugosz related, used tilted trees as weapons against the enemy. A similar method was used by Stephen the Great in the battle of Codrii Cosminului on October 26, 1497.

Wallachian and Moldavian princes resorted under critical situations to the so-called "scorched earth tactics," as a very efficacious method of harassing the aggressor. Careful selection of battle grounds was also an important factor in scoring military victories. Romanian leaders sought to fight the enemy in places sufficiently distant from the country's borders in order to take on an exhausted, harassed, and weakened foe.

Equally important in the Romanian countries' general system of defenses in the context of people's war, were military fortifications and constructions of various types. These constituted strategic points at the country's borders and in the interior as well and allowed the princes sufficient time to muster their troops and engage the harassed enemy in battle at the proper moment. The population of the villages near fortresses and other fortified points, inhabitants of the villages, towns and cities of Wallachia, Moldavia and Transylvania participated in contructing, maintaining and defending these fortifications. A powerful system of defensive fortifications was built by Stephen the Great in Moldavia. During his reign, he completed the system of fortifications through the addition of newly-built fortresses and consolidated the existing fortifications both at the borders and the interior of Moldavia. He was the first Romanian prince to provide fortresses with cannons. Moldavia was circled with such fortifications at Teţina, Hotin, Soroca, Tighina, Cetatea Albă Chilia and Crăciuna (on the river Milcov) and three fortresses were found inside the country at Suceava, Roman and Cetatea Neamţului. Moldavia's fortifications formed part of a strong unitary system which played an important role in the defense of the country's independence. In Wallachia, Mircea the Old and, later Vlad the Impaler built and fortified the fortresses of Giurgiu, Turnu Poenari, Bucureşti, Comana, Tîrgşor, Tîrgovişte. In Transylvania fortresses were successively built at Bran, Braşov, Făgăraş, Deva, Alba-Iulia, Arad, to name a few.

In the Romanian Countries' military defensive system a remarkable part was also played by the temporary fortifications; here can be mentioned the wooden and earthen fortresses with stockades, moats and defensive walls. Designed to provide shelter for the inhabitants of certain regions, these fortresses were often situated at high altitudes to insure better reconaissance of the enemies' movements.

The fortified towns and cities such as Braşov, Mediaş, Sibiu and others played an important part in the defensive system; defenders were recruited preferably from their natives. Numerous towns in Moldavia and Wallachia were fortified with moats (trenches), earthern walls and stockades. On the hills located on the enemy's offensive lines or around the churches and monasteries "peasant fortresses" surrounded by walls and cannons and provided with supplies and provisions by the local population were often built.

As a result of the entire people's participation in the defense the ancestral land, of the utilization of varying strategies and methods, of the harassment tactics, of judicious choice and use of the terrain, of fortifications and constructions, the Romanian voivodes won brilliant victories in wars fought against superior enemies.

Ideas on the entire people's war included the programs and decisions related to the 1848 Revolution in Moldavia, Wallachia and Transylvania entailed common features such as arming the masses, setting up national guards and the like. The idea to establish a national guard was expressed in Wallachia in the Proclamation of Islaz which stated that "every Romanian is born a soldier, is a guardian of public happiness, a guarantor of the public liberty."[4] The national guard was considered at that time to be the most efficient method of defending revolutionary achievements and ancestral lands.

The foreign intervention which suppressed the Romanian Revolution underlined the necessity of arming the masses. As stated in the Programme of the Romanian Communist Party, "the main forces of the 1848 Revolution in all the Romanian Countries were the masses firmly determined to fight for a better, free and independent life."[5]

In the War of Independence the militias were mobilized to join the standing army. The mobilized militias comprised thirty-one infantry battalions and a cavalry regiment with four squadrons whose strength came to 33,000 men. The people's militia were assigned the mission of assuring the territory's security. They contributed to the war with their sanitary corps. The people's broad masses, especially the peasantry played a decisive role in 1877-1878; they made the greatest sacrifices in men and monies required by the war effort.

After the War of Independence, Romania's political and military leaders were concerned primarily with the consolidation of the standing army and with the masses' ability to fully and directly participate in the defense of our homeland. During the battles of 1916-1918, the people's masses contributed decisively in harassing, exhausting and expelling the enemy. The

masses formed the core of the military units engaged in the campaigns of
1916 and of the summer of 1917. President Nicolae Ceauşescu rightly
stated that "under those dramatic moments of the country's destiny, the
patriotic forces rose up in arms, mustered all their strength and decided
to resist the invading armies at all costs."[6]

During World War I, under the prevailing historical conditions, the
struggle of the armed masses assumed other forms as well. In 1918, units
of the Romanian national guard were established throughout Transylvania. They consisted of former members of the Austro-Hungarian army,
of workers, of peasants, of intellectuals and of other social categories.

After World War I, the problems of the entire people's struggle for defending the homeland continued to be a major concern to political and,
particularly military leaders. "The war is the work of the entire people.
So, the entire nation must be prepared for war. . . together with its entire
material and spiritual capability, it will prepare and wage war by its own
forces, will secure the victory in the future. . . . The war of the future
will be waged by armed nations. . . . "[7] In 1934 the General Staff defined the concept on the armed nation as follows: "Under today's social,
political and technological conditions the army represents only one of
the elements included in the fighting and resistance forces, the entire
nation being everything. . . but to achieve an armed nation is neither
easy nor possible at once."[8]

These ideas were elaborated under changing historical conditions, by
the Romanian Communist Party, into a comprehensive military doctrine
of the entire people's war for the defense of the homeland since World
War II. That doctrine, in harmony with our country's historic realities
and experiences is in fact a synthesis of the experience of the military
struggle of the Romanian people for the defense of its homeland against
numerically and technologically superior forces.

NOTES

1.   Diodorus Siculus, Biblioteca Historica, XIX, 73, 1-6, XXI, 11, 1-
2, 1-6, Trogus Pompeius, *Istoria lui Filip*, XVI, 1.

2.   Nicolae Bălcescu, *Opere alese*, vol. 1, Editura de stat pentru
literatură şi artă, Bucureşti, 1960, p. 53.

3.   Ibid., pp. 25-26.

4.   *Anul 1848 în Principatele Romăne. Acte și Documente*, vol. IV, București, 1902, pp. 492, 496.

5.   *Congresul al XI-lea al Partidului Comunist Român*, p. 622.

6.   Nicolae Ceaușescu, *România pe drumul desăvîrșirii societătii socialiste*, Editura politică, București, 1968, p. 469.

7.   Colonel G. Vizanti and Major Scarlat Urlățeanu, *Strategia românească în viitorul război*, București, 1932, p. 67.

8.   Arhivele M.Ap.N.-M.St.M., fond 332, dos.no.29, f.350-351.

III

THE ASYMMETRICAL CONFLICT IN THE MILITARY
HISTORY OF THE ROMANIAN PEOPLE

The scrupulous reconstitution of battles has ceased to be the single concern of military history; moreover, to place the research of Middle Age history in the purview of such reconstitutions is regarded today as obsolete. The current trend so evident in contemporary military historiography is to analyze the military phenomenon from more than one point of view. Two approaches are particularly noticeable: (1) investigation of the relationship between the military phenomenon (in the broadest meaning of the word, namely military structures and conflicts) and the society and (2) investigation of the relationship between the military phenomenon and politics.[1] The research program "War and Society in East Central Europe" focuses on these problems and methods of analysis.

In light of these new orientations we shall try to analyze the asymmetric conflict in the Romanian people's military history with special reference to the Middle Ages and the Modern Epoch. Our approach, however, requires some preliminary explanations. The very term of assymmetric conflict was used for the period after World War II in connection with the conflicts which occurred in Southeast Asia, Indonesia, Algeria and elsewhere, where "local nationalist forces gained their objectives in armed confrontations with industrial powers which possessed an overwhelming superiority in conventional military capability."[2] Thus, the issue is of a military conflict opposing enemies whose economic and military capacities were obviously in disparity, whence the characterization of "asymmetry of this conflict."[3] The cases studied by Andrew Mack concern big industrial powers, therefore the question arises whether it is justified to use his methodology to answer the fundamental question posed by his work—"why big nations lose small wars?"[4]

Without engaging in an ample theoretical debate on this problem, suffice it to say that the asymmetric war (conflict), by which we understand a confrontation between two enemies with widely varying military capabilities has existed in all stages of mankind's history. F. Engels justly pointed out that "the armies' entire organization and fighting manner and simultaneously, victory and defeat proves to be dependent on material conditions, i.e., on economic conditions, on human resources and on armament, that is to say on the quality and size of the population and on technology."[4] It is necessary to take into account the fact that the weight of these determining factors of military power has varied in history and consequently, that any analysis of any given epoch must take into consideration the specific features of that epoch. Asymmetric conflicts have assumed varied forms and it would be a mistake if one were to apply a sole methodology to their analysis.

As we do not intend to develop either a new general methodological principles for the study of asymmetric conflicts[5] or of world history, we shall confine our investigation to concrete cases of asymmetric conflict in the history of the Romanian people.

A brief overview reveals that the overwhelming majority of the wars in which the Romanian people were engaged have had—given the enemy's superiority in numbers and equipment—an asymmetric character. Noteworthy from this point of view is the fact that the oldest military conflict in Romanian history was of an asymmetric type. The first written documents refer to the Getae, the Romanian people's forerunners, shows that they were attacked by the Persian king Darius I in his campaign against the Scythians. At that time the Persian Empire was a genuine "super-power" of antiquity and Herodotus, who offered us the above mentioned information, calls the Getae's decision to resist—instead of following the example of other Tracians who surrendered to Darius without battle—"foolish,"[6] taking into account the disparity in numbers between the opposing forces. "The Father of history," who also mentions the quite unfavorable end of this confrontation fro the Getae, noticed on this occasion that they (the Getae) lost the battle "in spite of their being the most valiant and righteous of the Thracians."[7]

Numerous asymmetric conflicts after 514 B.C., the date of the confrontation between Darious and the Getae,[8] were successful such as the Geto-Dacians' fights with the Roman Empire,[9] the conflicts of the Daco-Roman population north of the Danube and later, of the Romanian population with some migratory peoples who invaded the Carpatho-Danubian-Pontic area,[10] the battles carried on by the Romanian knezates and viovodes in Transylvania and the Banat against Hungarian invaders during the tenth and eleventh centuries[11] to name a few instances. Even the very establishment of the feudal states, Wallachia and Moldavia, represented an effort of political emancipation through asymmetric conflicts with the Magyar kingdom, ruled by Charles Robert and then by Ludovic of Anjou, which ended with the Romanians' victory in the battles of 1330 (Posada, Wallachia) and 1364-1365 (Moldavia),[12] and which brought international recognition of the existence of the two Romanian states south and east of the Danube.

But the typical asymmetric conflict in the Romanian people's history was represented by the nearly five centuries of warfare carried on by the Romanian Countries (Wallachia, Moldavia, Transylvania) against the Ottoman Empire. By the end of the fourteenth century, the rapidly expanding Ottoman power reached the Danube and thus threatened the very existence of the three Romanian Countries. The Romanian Countries, however, succeeded in arresting the forces of the Ottoman "super-power" and engaged in long-term conflict during which, unlike the South-Danubian regions or central Hungary, they were able to retain their autonomy, their own political structures and at the end of the protracted struggle to gain their independence.

To fully grasp these achievements, it is necessary to refer again to Andrew Mark's comments on contemporary asymmetric conflicts: "For students of strategy the importance of these wars lies in the fact that the simplistic but once prevalent assumption—that conventional military superiority necessarily prevails in war—has been destroyed. What is also interesting is that although the metropolitan powers didn't win militarily, neither were they defeated militarily. Indeed the military defeat of the metropolis itself was impossible since the insurgents lacked an invasion capability. In every case, success for the insurgents arose not from a military victory on the ground—though military success may have been a contributory cause—but rather from the progressive attrition of their opponents' political capability to wage war. In such asymmetric conflicts, insurgents may gain political victory from a situation of military stalemate or even defeat."[13]

To understand the secret of the Romanian victory it is enough to change in this quoted passage the word "metropolis" with the "Ottoman Empire" and "the insurgents" with the "Romanian Countries." Before analyzing the evolution of the Romanian-Ottoman asymmetric conflict, it is necessary to emphasize the military endeavors of Romanian medieval society.

In the absence of a universally accepted typology of feudalism, which would allow the placing of the Romanian case in a general framework, it seems fair to say that the political-military non-pulverization of power, given by the kingship to the higher feudal lords or extorted by these from the kingship, as well as the preservation, throughout the entire Middle Ages, of large areas inhabited by free peasants[14] who played an important role in the Romanian armed forces of the Middle Ages have singled out Romanian feudal society from the classic forms of feudalism of Western Europe. If in Western Europe, the organization of the military forces have the imprint of feudal-vassal relationships and thus bestowed on the armies a seigniorial character,[15] in the Romanian Countries, particularly in Wallachia and Moldavia (in Transylvania, the Hungarian conquest modified or replaced certain political-military institutions of the autochtonous Romanians), the military organization mirrored the specific features of Romanian feudalism: besides the boyars' bands and the prince's "court" —which formed the so-called lesser army—the entire male population capable of fighting ("the greater army") was called to arms in times of great danger. That is why the extensive military actions deployed for defending the countries' independence have had such a profound popular character. The military historian Radu Rosetti correctly emphasized this feature of the war waged by the Romanians: "The Romanians' military art from the most ancient times until the end of the fifteenth century was of a small-sized people, of a people defending its poverty, and needs and nation. It was the art of a people of răzeşi, (free peasants) stubborn defenders of the land which was feeding them as it has fed their parents and forerunners. These good răzeşi did not seek war for the sake of war itself, but they defended their goods, defended their loved ones, and defended their lives with the tools used in everyday life."[16] The Romanian feudal society was not and could not be devoid of social and political strains and stresses so characteristic of the medieval world.[17] There were indeed social antagonisms between boyars and peasants, struggles for power between princes and boyars. These social cleavages and political divisions notwithstanding, whenever the political existence of the Romanian Countries was threatened, in other words, whenever the threat of the establishment of direction Ottoman administration, that is the introduction of the *pashalik* regime could be seriously envisioned, all the social-political forces of the Romanian society fought against it and the opposition became *the entire people's war*.[18] This consensus of will and action allowed the mobilization of all demographic-military and logistical resources of the Romanian Countries in a common effort and compelled the enemy to abandon the political objectives of its military actions. The disparity in the military strength of the Romanian Countries and of the Ottoman Empire was too great for Moldavia, Wallachia and Transylvania—even when their forces were combined as was the case during the rule of Iancu of Hunedoara, the prince of Transylvania and later on, governor of Hungary (1441-1456), Stephen the Great, Moldavia's prince (1457-1504), or Michael the Brave, Wallachia's prince (1593-1601)—to enable them to defeat the Ottoman Empire. However, using once more the terminology of the contemporary asymmetric conflict, if the Romanian Countries did not dispose of the capabilities required to invade the aggressor's territory and to annihilate his forces, they had the capability of preventing attainment of the enemy's political objectives —complete domination of Romanian territories.

It has been said that the Ottomans did not transform the Romanian Countries into pashaliks because they were not on the main route of the Ottoman offensive toward Central Europe.[19] But in fact, as a well-informed authority, Michael Bocignoli of Raguza, pointed out, Suleiman the Magnificent wanted to introduce the pashalik regime into Wallachia as an Ottoman base of military action against Hungary.[20] The Porte, however, had to abandon this plan because of Romanian military resistance. An analysis of the character of the successful military riposte which allowed the retention of the Romanian Countries' statute of autonomy is now in order.

The entire people's war made use of the classical tactics of "scorched earth" thereby depriving the enemy of the customary local sources of supply. Physical weakness due to poor nourishment was accompanied by

psychic exhaustion resultant from the lack of security created by a permanently harassing foe.[21] But if during the campaign the Ottoman army would score military victories, those could not be exploited politically and eventually the invaders would be compelled to withdraw. In this respect a convincing example is the campaign of Mohammed II, the conqueror of Constantinople, against Moldavia in 1476. As soon as he reached the Moldavian land the Sultan was shown a distressing sight: "we have found"—wrote the Italian Giovanni Maria Angiolelo, the Sultan's treasurer—"all the villages and settlements abandoned and the fields on fire because Count Stephen, realizing that he could not hold out against the Sultan, sought to win otherwise. So, he ordered the inhabitants of his country to flee beyond the mountains and to pass into Poland . . . he also ordered all the crops to be cut, even the reed from the swamps, and after the grain and weeds had been cut, he ordered everything scorched, so that the Sultan was deceived because he thought he would find the country filled with grain and grazing fields, as in fact it really is, but he found it abandoned by the people and everywhere a dust of coal was raising that it filled the sky with smoke and whenever we were making a halt everybody had black faces and our clothes, from the bottom up had also to endure the black dust. Even the horses had to suffer because the dust entered their nostrils. That is why the Sultan never dismounted his horse and the watching bands never deployed their lines until the camp was set up and the guard secured on all sides."[22] Under such conditions the advance of the Ottoman army entailed gradual exhaustion; although Mohammed scored a victory in the battle of Valea Albă (on July 26, 1476)—where Moldavia's ruling prince could not oppose more than 10,000 men[23] much less the 100,000 soliders of the Sultan—Mohammed II failed to conquer any of the country's fortresses (Suceava, Hotin, Neamţ, Chilia, Cetatea Albă) so, on August 10 he ordered the retreat. The Ottoman's withdrawal took place under the blows delivered by the Moldavian army, mustered through mass recruiting (as the chronicler Grigore Ureche noted Stephen completed his army "with shepherds from the mountains and servants").[24] The political objective of the Ottoman campaign ended in failure: Stephen the Great continued to retain power in an independent country.

The events of the summer of 1476 are typical of the Romanian-Ottoman asymmetric conflict: a serious disparity in forces between the fighting armies, the enemy's advancing into a country laid to waste, the invading forces' exhausting themselves for lack of resources for both men and horses, the utilization of harassing actions, the victory scored by the Ottoman army over the Moldavian army on the open battlefield, the Sultan's inability to conquer the country because of fierce resistance by the fortresses, the retreat under the incessant harassing actions of the Moldavian army. Thus, in such an asymmetric conflict, even if the lesser combatant (Moldavia) suffers a military defeat (Valea Albă), the final result is the political defeat of the great combatant (the Ottoman Empire).

The failure of Mohammed II in 1476 belongs to a series of defeats suffered by the Ottoman army on Romanian territory, either through the exhaustion of the Ottoman army as it advanced into a zone of "demo-economic vacuum," or, by the Romanians' scoring victories in so-called classice battles (i.e., the battle of Vaslui in 1475). The Ottoman army's inability to crush the Romanian resistance compelled the Porte to abandon its plans to transform the Romanian Countries into pashaliks and to acknowledge their statute of autonomy. In turn, Wallachia, Moldavia and Transylvania, unable to eliminate the Ottoman threat, accepted Ottoman suzerainty on condition that their autonomy would be respected and stipulated in written documents ("capitulations"). The Italian humanist Filippo Buonaccorsi—Callimachus, while in the service of the Polish king, correctly depicted—as one directly aware of the Romanian realities —Romanian-Ottoman relations. Evoking the battles fought by Vlad the Impaler against the Ottomans and the death of Wallachia's ruling prince,[25] he noted that after the death of the heroic voivode, the Wallachians "submitted but retained all their institutions, their wealth, even their liberty." With regard to the Moldavians the Italian humanist noted that even after they had lost the fortresses of Chilia and Cetatea Albă seized by the Ottomans in 1484 they "still watched over the rest of their country and often inflicted on the Sultan so heavy losses, for many times in the preceding years, that he was compelled at least to name Stephen, the Moldavian's ruling prince, as his ally and friend . . . Stephen did not yield to arms but to certain conditions . . . and the Romanians after they had repelled the armies and its attempts, they were subdued by agreements not as a vanquished people, but as vanquishers."[26] This text has an exceptional value for grasping the final issue of the asymmetric conflict: the Romanians accepted Ottoman suzerainty "not as vanquished, but as vanquishers." The wording may seem intentionally paradoxic, for the sake of stylistic effect; in fact, however, the wording discerned the essence of Romanian-Ottoman relations. The repeated failures recorded by the Ottoman Porte in the attempts to crush Romanian resistance forced the Ottoman Empire to acknowledge Romanian autonomy.[27]

The observance of the statute of autonomy of the Romanian Countries was, of course, the expression of a given balance of forces: whenever the Ottoman Porte discovered or thought, that the Romanian resistance diminished in intensity, it violated this statute through interference in the country's political life, through increasing the local material obligation, through annexing parts of Romanian territory or, during the Ottoman Empire's declining years, by ceding certain Romanian territories to foreign powers.

At the end of the sixteenth century—in connection with the transformation which occurred in the Mediterranean basin following the discovery of the New World—a large increment of the Romanian Countries' tributary obligations to the Porte occurred. Significant socio-economic mutations took place within the Romanian society itself, through the expansion of the boyar's estates to the prejudice of the free peasants, and through the strengthening of the power of the boyars, who sought to set up a genuine nobiliary regime.[28] The enslaving of the free peasantry decreased the power of the "greater army"[29] during a period when, in fact, a reorganization of the power hierarchy was taking place on the entire European continent. The spreading of fire arms imposed a fundamental alteration of military technology which entailed major expenditures for securing such arms and for employing specialists who could handle these weapons. States with ample financial resources required for military modernization retained or acquired the status of "Great Power."[30] The Romanian Countries, which were under Ottoman domination did not dispose of the financial means required for the modernization of their arsenals. Moreover, the peasantry subjected to increasingly more burdensome financial obligations and to the loss of their free status could not supply the effectives of a professional army well trained in handling fire arms. Despite these unfavorable conditions, as the totality of material obligations to the Porte reached its peak at the end of the sixteenth century,[31] the Romanian military response gained in intensity through the common military action of Wallachia, Transylvania and Moldavia which, during this new episode of the Romanian-Ottoman asymmetric conflict, were united for the first time in 1600 under the rule of Wallachia's prince Michael the Brave (1593-1601). The military actions of the Romanian ruling princes, particularly those of Michael the Brave, faced the Porte with the possibility of the emancipation of the Romanian Countries from Ottoman domination. The solution of a pashalik briefly attempted after the Ottoman invasion of Wallachia in the summer of 1595,[32] was soon abandoned. Fear of the repetition of the military and political actions identified with Michael the Brave acted as a deterent to the Porte. The retention of the Romanian Countries' autonomy was due, in large measure to the anti-Ottoman war waged by the Romanians at the end of the sixteenth century.

Following the unsuccessful attempt made by Wallachia, Moldavia and Transylvania in 1658-1662 to repeat the anti-Ottoman war of Michael the Brave, a long period of quiet reigned until the campaign of Peter the Great and his ally Dimitrie Cantemir, Moldavia's ruling prince in 1711. The struggle for national emancipation was henceforth to be integrated into the so-called "Eastern Question" as the Romanians' efforts to rid themselves of the Ottomans became a function of Great Powers' rivalry for settling the inheritance of the "Sick Man of Europe" to their advantage. If the conflict limited to the Romanian Countries and the Ottoman Empire retained an asymmetric character, albeit less seriously given the decline of Ottoman power, the international context, modified through the interference of the Great Powers, such as the Habsburg and Russian empires, both anxious to control the Romanian territories, changed the essential data of the asymmetric confrontation.

A few conclusions are in order:

1. Asymmetric conflicts do not represent a specific phenomenon of the contemporary era;

2. The Romanian people's history recorded numerous asymmetric conflicts among which the most important and of longest standing was that with the Ottoman Empire;

3. Marked by military victories and defeats, the Romanian-Ottoman asymmetric conflict ended with the Romanians' political victory embodied in the Romanian Countries' statute of autonomy in the fifteenth-nineteenth centuries until the proclamation of state independence in 1877;

4. The military-political-formula which assured success in the asymmetric conflict was the entire people's war.

NOTES

1. Cf. Andre Martel, *Le renouveau de l'histoire militaire en France,* in "Revue historique," 95, t. CCXLV (1971), pp. 107-126. See also Piero Pieri, *Sur les dimensions de l'histoire militaire,* in "Annales," XVIII (1963), no. 4, pp. 625-638 and Jean Delmas, *L'histoire militaire contemporaine et ses problemes,* in "Revue historique de l'armee," XXXI (1970), no. 2, pp. 101-109.

2. Andrew Mack, *Why Big Nations Lose Small Wars? the Politics of Asymmetric Conflict,* in "World Politics," vol. XXVII, no. 2, January 1975, p. 175.

3. The term also encompasses the peaceful relations between two countries with disparate demo-economic capabilities. For instance, see the paragraph "Asymmetric relations" in the study by Hong-Koo Lee and Chong wook Ching, *Foundations of Future U.S.-South Korean Relations, Toward a Community of Mature Partners,* in "Journal of Northeast Asian Studies," vol. I, no. 1, March 1982, pp. 58-59; the authors also use the term of "asymmetric influence."

4. F. Engels, *Opere militare alese,* vol. I, Bucharest, Editura Militară, 1962, p. 17.

5. Cf. *Note on methodology,* in Andrew Mack, op. cit., pp. 195-199.

6. Herodot, IV, 93 (Herodot, *Istorii,* vol. I, Bucharest, Editura științifică, 1961, p. 345).

7. Ibid.

8. For the expedition's dating and causes, Ibid., p. 496. Cf. and Mircea Petrescu-Dîmbovița, *Scurtă istorie a Daciei preromane,* Jassy, Editura Junimea, 1978, pp. 111-112.

9. H. Daicoviciu, *Dacii,* Bucharest, Editura științifică, 1965, p. 201 and the foll.

10. Eugenia Zaharia, *Populația românească în Transilvania în secolele VII-VIII,* Bucharest, Editura Academiei, 1977, p. 111: "The socio-economic and military organization of communities and the community unions prove that the Romanians were organized very well during the peoples' migrations; they couldn't resist otherwise. The idea according to which

the Romanians saved themselves by hiding in the mountains, woods or swamps must be changed, in the sense that they carried on such actions in face of danger and they carried on these actions being well-organized as we know they did, later on, in the face of the Tatars and Turks."

11. Ștefan Pascu, *Voievodatul Transilvaniei*, vol. I, Cluj-Napoca, Editura Dacia, 1971, p. 19ff.

12. See the studies collection *Constituirea statelor feudale românești*, Bucharest, Editura Academiei, 1980; Victor Spinei, *Moldova în secolele XI-XIV*, Bucharest, Editura Științifică și Enciclopedică, 1982, pp. 290ff.

13. Andrew Mack, op. cit., p. 177.

14. For the existence and the organization of the free peasants see H. H. Stahl, *Contributii la studiul satelor devălmase*, 3 vol., Bucharest, Editura Academiei, 1958, 1965; idem, *Les anciennes communautes villageoises roumaines*, Bucharest, Paris, Acad. Roum. and C.N.R.S., 1969; Daniel Chirot, *Social Change in a Peripheral Society*, New York, Academic Press, 1976.

15. See in detail Ph. Contamine, *Le guerre au Moyen-Age*, Paris, *P.U.F.*, 1980.

16. General Radu Rosetti, *Istoria artei militare a românilor pînă la mijlocul veacului al XIII-lea*, Bucharest, Imprimeria Națională, 1947, p. 558.

17. Friedrich Heer, *The Medieval World*, New York, 1962, pp. 32-55; Guy Fourquin, *Les soulevements populaires au Moyen-Age*, Paris, *P.U.F.*, 1972.

18. Major General Ilie Ceaușescu, *Războiul întregului popor pentru apărarea patriei la români*, Bucharest, Editura militară, 1980.

19. P. P. Panaitescu, *Interpretări românești*, Bucharest, Editura Universul, 1947, p. 158.

20. *Călători străini despre tările române*, vol. I, Bucharest, Editura științifică, p. 178.

21. Major General Ilie Ceaușescu, *Hărtuirea în actiunile de luptă duse în războiul integrului popor pentru apărarea patriei*, Bucharest, Editura militarș, 1981, p. 45 and the foll.

22. *Călători străini despre tările române*, quoted edition, pp. 135-136; for the similar tactics used by Vlad the Impaler, Wallachia's ruling prince against the same sultan during his campaign against Wallachia in 1462 see the account of Michael Bocignoli, ibid., pp. 176-177. The traveler

from Ragusa gave a fine description of the harassing actions launched by Vlad the Impaler against the Ottoman army: Vlad "preparing some horsemen, very often at night or in the day time, for most times came out of the woods by devious ways and known paths and unexpectedly was killing many Turks either looking for food, or wandering too far from their army; sometimes he was attacking their main force when they did not expect this at and after he killed many of them and before they could regroup to fight, he fled again into the woods and did not let the enemy fight under equal conditions."

23. An attack carried on by the Crimean Tartars compelled Stephen to permit the peasants from his army to go for two weeks to defend their households. *Istoria României*, vol. II, Bucharest, Editura Academiei, 1962, pp. 520-521.

24. Ibid., p. 523.

25. About them see in detail, N. Stoicescu, *Vlad Țepeș*, Bucharest, Editura Academiei, 1976, pp. 85-119 and Ștefan Andreescu, *Vlad Țepeș (Dracula)*, București, Editura Minerva, 1976, pp. 91-146.

26. Șerban Papacostea, *Politica externă a Moldovei în timpul lui Ștefan cel Mare. Puncte de reper*, in "Revista de istorie," t. 28 (1975), nr. 1, pp. 16, 26.

27. For the statute of autonomy of the Romanian Countries see Ion Matei, *Quelques problemes concernant le regime de la domination ottomane dans les Pays roumains*, in "Revue des etudes sud-est europeennes," X (1972), no. 1, pp. 65-81 and XI (1973), no. 1, pp. 81-95; Donald Edgar Pitcher, *An Historical Geography of the Ottoman Empire*, Leiden, 1972, pp. 131-132, 138-139.

28. Daniel Chirot, op. cit., pp. 37ff. uses even the term of seignorial state.

29. N. Stoicescu, *Oastea cea mare în Țara Românească și Moldova (secolele XIV-XVI)*, in vol. *Oastea cea mare*, Bucharest, Editura militară, 1972, pp. 48-51.

30. For all these changes see the classic work by Fernand Braudel, *La Mediterranee et le monde mediterraneen a l'epoque de Philippe II*, 2 vol., (ed. a 2-a), Paris, 1966.

31. Mihai Berza, *Haraciul Moldovei și Țării Românești în secolele XV-XIX*, in "Studii și materiale de istorie medie," II (1957), pp. 16, 32-33î N. Beldiceanu, *La crise monetaire ottomane au XVI-eme siecle et son*

influence sur les Principautes roumaines, in "Sudost-Forschungen," Bd. XVI (1957), pp. 70-86.

32. Aurel Decei, *Istoria Imperiului ottoman,* Bucharest, Editura ştiinţifică şi enciclopedică, 1978, p. 277.

Nicolae Stoicescu

MILITARY ASPECTS OF THE DEFENSE OF ROMANIAN TERRITORIES IN THE FOURTEENTH, FIFTEENTH AND SIXTEENTH CENTURIES

Located in a geographic area where the political interests of some great powers confronted each other over the centuries, the Romanians moulded, in often dramatic circumstances and with an amazing steadfastness, a distinct political personality of their own, and ensured the continuity of their state life. Their love for independence and freedom, a leitmotif of the Romanian people's entire history, was interwoven with a feeling of sympathy with the fight for liberty of other peoples in this part of Europe.

The first major moment in that centuries-old struggle was marked by the establishment, in the fourteenth century, of the Romanian feudal states of Wallachia and Moldavia, a fact which had considerable bearing on the organization of the fight against the expansionist tendencies of the neighboring states.[1]

The establishment of two Romanian feudal states—the so-called state pluralism—has not been a phenomenon specific to the history of the Romanian people, having been experienced by other peoples as well (see the German, Italian, Russian peoples to name a few). The fact that during the Middle Ages the Romanians lived in separate states does not justify in any way the opinion of some foreign scientists according to whom the Moldavians would be a different people—speaking a Moldavian language—from the Wallachs who inhabited Wallachia. According to the same logic, it would mean that the Bavarians or the Saxons are not Germans for the mere reason that they lived in separate states, or that the Milanese, the Venetians, or the Genoese are different people as well, just because they, too, inhabited separate states before the unification of Italy.

The establishment of the Romanian independent feudal state was achieved through military action against foreign expansion by those who sought to dominate the lands to the south and east of the Carpathians. Sensitive to the transformations occurring in Europe at the time and making a lucid analysis of the consequences of some political mutations Voivodes Bessarab in Wallachia (c. 1317-1352), and Bodgan in Moldavia (1359-c.1365) knew how to turn to good advantage the various difficulties encountered by the rulers of neighboring states, to shake off foreign encroachment and to organize the Romanian states.

An important moment in Romanian history, the battle called Posada (1330), initiated a series of fierce battles that were to preserve and consolidate the Romanian countries, attacked by the great neighboring powers which were pursuing expansionist aims. Posada was followed by other equally important battles such as Rovine (1394), Podul Inalt or Vaslui (1475), Războieni (1476), Roșcani (1574), Călugăreni (1595).

Voivodes Bessarab and Bogdan, both whose names are linked with the establishment of self-dependent Romanian states, set the targets of Romanian policy and defined the means for their achievement. The victories scored by Bessarab and Vlaicu (1364-c.1377), in Wallachia, and those of Bogdan and Stephen I (c.1394-1399), in Moldavia, ensured the independence of their countries from the expansionism of the Magyar Kingdom, while strengthening their position in international relations in the second half of the fourteenth century. During a subsequent period, this allowed them to withstand the strong offensive which the Ottoman Empire initiated late in the century.

The founders of the Romanian independent states realized that state survival required far reaching foreign relations. As the Romanian states asserted themselves in the European political constelation, through their military deeds, the understood—and their descendants were to learn from their political experience—that state independence cannot be a lasting one if there is no concern for organizing the military means to protect it. The course of events had demonstrated that alliances could serve, under certain conditions, the idea of liberty, but that one could not leave to them alone the task to protect it. Convinced of that truth, the Romanian state leaders tried to make the "country's host" or the "greater host"[2] guarantee of their countries strength and liberty.

Vlad the Impaler was to formulate in classical terms the need for military strength as a prerequisite of independence—"Don't you ever forget"—

he wrote to the inhabitants of Brașov in 1456—"That when a man or a prince is strong (at home), then he can obtain the peace he looks for, but when he is weak, then someone stronger will come against him and do whatever he wishes to."[3] The Romanian historical experience was to confirm the reality of that principle. When external events seriously jeopardized the fate of the Romanian people, brilliant commanders emerged.

Having a large free peasantry, a distinct feature when compared to the other European state, and not too heavy forms of dependence for the oppressed peasants, the Romanian states asserted themselves in the international political life through a military organization which permitted, in case of great danger, the mobilization of the entire "country", and thus to muster up to 40,000 soldiers each of the defense of territorial integrity.

The assistance of the entire population made it possible for Mircea the Old (1386-1418)—at a moment when powerful states south of the Danube were engulfed by the Ottoman expansion—to save the country and gain international renown. The "common people" made up the bulk of the feared army of Vlad the Impaler. With an army of peasants, "taken almost directly from the plough," Stephen the Great scored his great victories. As shown by the Polish chronicler I. Dlugosz, the great prince "summoned to the army not only the military or the noblemen, but also the peasants, teaching each of them to keep guard for the homeland's defense."[4]

Independence was ensured as long as there was any army of the country, recruited from people closely tied to the land, and representing their interests. The decline of the country's army and the emergence of contigents of mercenaries had grave consequences by the sixteenth century.

The princes and voivodes of the Romanian countries tried to secure the support of neighboring states in the face of the Ottoman danger. However, they received effective assistance only in a few battles, thus generally bearing the brunt of war alone. Stephen the Great is credited with one of the most beautiful appeals to solidarity in the fight against the Porte, addressed to the European Powers; drawn up after the battle of Vaslui, on January 10, 1475, the appeal invited the state leaders in Europe to organize a general fight "on sea and on land, after we cut off his (the enemy's) right hand, by the help of the Almighty God."[5]

Unfortunately, in spite of the admiration of the European Powers for the military prowess of Moldavia's prince, his appeal remained unanswered and he received, in his own words "nothing." Stephen revealed his disappointment through the messenger he sent to Venice, following the war with the Ottomans of 1476: "Quite true, what followed would not have happened to him, had he know that the Christian and neighboring princes would behave as they did. For, although there had been agreements and oaths between them, they betrayed him and that is why he went through all this. The agreements and the oaths between them said that all of them had to be ready and help any place that prince against when they (the Turks) would have gone. . . . But they left me alone, and things happened as I said before."[6]

Deprived of foreign help, the leaders of the Romanian countries were forced to secure help only from their own inhabitants. A major feature of the policy of the Romanian princes was the coordination of the military endeavours of all Romanian lands, with a view to defending the historic national being. The social-economic structures characteristic of feudalism and the external conditions prevented the formation of one state on Dacia's territory during the Middle Ages. However, tendencies to restore the former ethnical-political unity existed all the time, nurtured by one or the other Romanian province, and they were gradually achieved as soon as economic conditions and international factors would allow.

Thus, from the political-military alliance of the Romanian countries of the fourteenth and fifteenth centuries, a genuine confederation was established in the mid-fifteenth century, under the leadership of Iancu of Hunedoara and Stephen the Great. By the sixteenth century, the idea of remaking Dacia under a sole leader was formulated.

Just as Iancu of Hunedoara—who was considered "Chieftain" of Wallachia and "father" of Moldavia's prince, who wished that his country and Iancu's Transylvania be "one country"—Stephen the Great pointed out, through his political and military actions, the significance of the alliance of the Romanian countries against the Ottomans. Stephen helped Wallachia and Transylvania militarily and left the impression among his contemporaries that he effectively ruled in both sister-provinces of Moldavia. During his reign, Stephen the Great was considered the leader of all Romanians' struggle against Ottoman expansion. This accounts for the fact that on February 26, 1478, the representatives of the city of Brașov addressed Moldavia's prince by the following relevant words: "it seems that God Himself hath chosen and sent thee to rule over and defend Transylvania."[7]

Both Wallachia and Moldavia sought the support of Transylvania, which, in its turn, based her security on political rapprochement with Wallachia and Moldavia. Faced with foreign danger, especially the Ottoman, the military efforts of the three Romanian countries were often coordinated under the command of one of their voivodes. Indeed, the numerous anti-Ottoman campaigns during which soldiers from all Romanian provinces fought, sometimes shoulder to shoulder, contributed to enhancing their awareness of their unity as a people.

The political and military relations between the Romanian countries were so close that true interdependence was reached. Thus, Alexandru Aldea, Prince of Wallachia, wrote to the Transylvanians in 1432: "if this country (Wallahica) were to die, you would die, too."[8] Later, before the union of Wallachia and Transylvania, Michael the Brave thought that the two Romanian countries "are so much subordinated to each other, and so much tied together, that the fall of one of them entails the fall of the other, whereas its maintenance keeps the other in being as well."[9]

Foreigners, too, were aware fo this reality. In 1538, Suleiman the Magnificent voiced his fear that the Romanian countries might unite and jointly resist the Ottomans should the Turks try to occupy one of them. Almost similar fears were expressed by the *mufti* of Sultan Murad III (1574-1595), who spoke of the disappearance of Transylvania's messenger to the Porte, which might have entailed military action by the prince, and "if Transylvania rises in arms, the same will happen in Wallachia and Moldavia." For these reasons, the *mufti* urged that military preparations be undertaken by the Porte to prevent common military action by the three Romanian countries.

The alliance of the Romanian countries helped them withstand foreign dangers. Expressing some older realities, in 1652 Matei Basarab viewed the strength of his relations with Transylvania as follows: "whom shall we fear if our countries (Wallachia and Moldavia) keep the good understanding of until now? Nobody, except the Almighty God."[10]

Another major factor which ensured the success of the fight for independence was the military prowess of Romanian voivodes and princes so admired by contemporary observers. Thus, Mircea the Old was called "the bravest and most quick-minded of all Christian princes," because of the victories he had scored aginst the Ottomans.[11]

About Vlad Dracul, Prince of Wallachia (1436-1447, with interruptions), chronicler A. Bonfini said that he was "that righteous and unde-feated man, who was the strongest and bravest adviser in every battle, because, with a small army, but a great heart and mind and through the virtues of his soldiers which went beyond what everybody expected, and without nay help from outside, he waged a long war with the Turks, a war all Christians put together could have hardly fought."[12] A similar opinion was shared by chronicler Wavrin of Burgundy, who met Vlad the Impaler during the campaign the latter led against the Ottomans in 1445, when he became convinced that the prince of Wallachia was "very famous for his bravery and wisdom" (*moult fame de vaillance et de sagesse*).[13]

Iancu of Hunedoara, the Voivode of Transylvania, a Romanian by birth, who won brilliant victories by cooperating with the Romanian forces in Transylvania and with the extra-Carpathian Romanian countries, for which reason he was considered "capitain des Valaques," was called by Pope Calixtus III "The most powerful champion of Christ" (*qui ab unico Christi fortissimo athleta Johanna Vavvoda*), and on his death was praised as being "*illum Pugilem invictum, formidabilem defensorem hostibus.*"[14] After the victory of Belgrade in 1456, the Milanese Jacopo Calcaterra considered "illustrious" Ianuc "*como uno deli piu gloriosi homini che treicento anni havessero ho al presente vivano al mondo*"; his name had to be praised "*fin de sopra le stelle.*"[15]

A continuator of the fight of Iancu, the famous Vlad the Impaler—Dracula, Prince of Wallachia (1456-1462), also aroused by his gallentry the admiration of both his contemporaries and some writes of past centuries. One of the most beautiful eulogies were brought to him by the Italian humanist Filippo Buonaccorsi-Callimachus—then at the court of the Polish king Casimir IV Jagiello, who compared the brave prince with another anti-Ottoman fighter, the famous Scanderbeg: "*caesi a magno etiam illo Epirota Scandrabeo nec a minori out viro aut imperative Dracula valacho.*" Bemoaning the death of the hero, Callimachus called him "*maximum illum Imperatoreum, et Ducem Valdislaus Draculam.*" Early in the sixteenth century, M. Bociognoli of Ragusa considered Vlad the Impaler a "clever man, most skilled in soldierly matters," who defended "his country extremely well." During the same century, the humanist A. Verancsics said that "Dracual" was "too brave" a prince. Finally, in the eighteenth century, military history specialists considered Vlad the Impaler "*un des plus grands Capitaines de son siecle, comparable a Sertorius,*" this being mainly due to the "*tres memorable*" night attack.

No doubt, the most illustrious Romanian voivode was Stephen the Great, Prince of Moldavia (1457-1504), who scored some of the most

outstanding victories in the fight against Ottoman expansion. "Your feats
. . . have brought so much fame to your name, that it is now on everyone's
lips and you are higly praised by everybody without the least exception,"
Pope Sixtus IV wrote to the prince after the great victory of Vaslui
(1475).[16] In their turn, the Venetial Senate acknowledged that "there
isn't anybody who does not realize the extent to which Stephen can influence the development of events, both in one direction and in the
other."[17]

There is no doubt, however, that the most beautiful homage was paid
to him by the Polish chronicler I. Dlugosz, who exclaimed in full admiration: "Oh, thou wonderful man, in no respects less deserving than the
great heroes of Antiquity we all praise so much, thou, who first of all the
world's princes has now won such a brilliant victory against the Turks."
In Dlugosz's opinion, Stephen was the "most worthy of being entrusted
the command and leadership of the world, particularly the role of commander against the Turks, with the common advice, agreement and decision of the Christians, for the other kings and princes are idling away their
time in pleasures and civil strife."[18]

Unfortunately, these beautiful remarks about the brave Romanian
voivodes were not supplemented with effective assistance in the fight
against foreign aggression which the Romanian countries had to face
alone.

Known for their bravery were not only the princes and voivodes, but
also other Romanian fighters. About Vlad the Impaler's soldiers, the
Byzantine dignitary Torzelo said that they ranked with the bravest men
of the world."[19]

The sixteenth century recorded numerous testimonies about the gallantry of the Romanian soldiers, a fact acknowledged by all the foreigners
who knew them. Matteo Muriano, the Italian physician of Stephen the
Great, showed in 1502 that the Moldavians "are all brave and clever men,
used not to sitting between pillows, but to go to war, on the battlefield."[20]
Later, under the reign of Petru Rareş, a Saxon from Transylvania called
G. Reicherstorffer, considered that the Moldavians were "good enough at
soldierly matters and also very clever," or "highly skilled in soldierly affairs and warfare."[21] The same opinion was shared by the Polish chronicler I. Bielski, according to whom the soldiers of Rareş were "brave,
skilled in handling the spear and the shield."[22] Another Italian, A. M.

Graziani, considered in his turn that the Romanians "engage in battle with so much boldness, with so much disdain for the enemy and self-confidence, that they often defeated, with rather small forces, the strong armies of their neighbors."[23]

To the acknowledged bravery of the Romanian soldiers, one should add as an important element the tactics and strategy adopted by the princes of the Romanian countries. The accurate understanding of the forces they represented in comparison with the danger threatening their country made them adopt those forms of fighting and resistance which wore down the aggressors before the decisive battle, to select as battle grounds places which would not allow the deployment of entire enemy forces and thus minimize the numerical superiority and armament of the enemy.

To prevent the supplying of the invading armies—achieved as a rule from the households of the inhabitants of the areas they were crossing— the Romanian princes had the villages evacuated and everything laid waste in front of the enemy advance. As a result, famine affected the invaders and their horses and the ensuring disarry enhanced the chances of the Romanian military forces. The military tactics of the Romanians involved the destruction of material goods, long wanderings and great privations for the native population, reflected the Romanians' determination to defend their civilization. Indeed, unlike their stronger neighbors, who oftend encroached upon the independence and territorial integrity of the Romanian countries, the Romanians waged only just, defensive wars. "That is why, of all Romance languages, it is only in the Romanian that the popular word designating the force which defends the country derives from the Latin word *hostis* (foreign, enemy)," which meant that the "host was the force defending the country against an enemy."[24]

Until the end of the sixteenth century two stages can be observed in the history of the Romanian people's fight for independence in close correlation with internal socio-political changes and external circumstances.

The first stage in the emancipation and development of an international strategy evolved with the establishment of self-dependent Romanian states in the fourteenth century. That stage ended in the mid-sixteenth century with the Romanian countries falling under the domination of the Ottoman Porte. The second stage evolves during the second half of the sixteenth century ending with the regaining of liberty and the union of the Romanian countries under the scepter of Michael the Brave.

During the first stage, the Romanian leaders watched closely the development of Magyar-Polish relations and the changes occurring in the Balkan Peninsula as a result of the rapid Ottoman advance, and sought solutions in alliances for the consolidation of the Romanian feudal states. Defense needs led to a rapprochement of Transylvania, Wallachia and Moldavia and the corollary evoltuion of common foreign policies. For this reason, Mircea the Old interfered in Moldavia in order to help a prince—Alexander the Good—ascend to the throne, and Iancu of Hunedoara and Stephen the Great repeatedly sought to rally the Romanian countries into forming a joint anti-Ottoman front.

The brilliant victories won by the princes and voivodes of the Romanian countries of that period—Mircea the Old, Iancu of Hunedoara, Vlad the Impaler, Stephen the Great, Radu of Afumați, Petru Rareș ensured the independence of the Romanian countries at a time when neighboring states like Bulgaria, Serbia and Hungary had been turned into *pashaliks*. The Romanian anti-Ottoman resistance, ensured state continuity and provided a protecting wall for Central and Western Europe.

Defense of the country and of European civilization was achieved at the cost of many losses and sacrifices of human lives. However, for lack of external support and because of defections within the system of anti-Ottoman Christian coalitions, the Romanian princes were left with no alternatives other than to reach an understanding with the Ottoman Porte. Because of the tradition of armed resistance by Romanians, the Porte had to grant the Romanian countries a large measure of autonomy which, as a matter of fact, ensured their independent historical development. To quote a contemporary, the Romanians submitted through treaties, "not as if defeated, but as victors," thus managing to preserve their "settlements, wealth and even their freedom."[25] In exchange for a tribute paid by the Romanian countries, the Porte pledged not to attack them, to observe their state integrity and not to interfere with their internal organization. Whenever the Ottoman Porte tried to violate the obligations it had assumed through the "old treaties," a military response was to be anticipated. Nevertheless, the establishment by the mid-sixteenth century of Ottoman domination in the Romanian countries increased the latter's dependence on the Porte.

Turned after the fall of Hungary, into an autonomous principality under the suzerainty of the Porte, in 1541, Transylvania was also subjected, albeit to a lesser degree, to the same regime as Wallachia and Moldavia. Still,

Transylvania's leaving the feudal Magyar kingdom facilitated the evolution of ever closer ties with the Romanian countries south and east of the Carpathians.

During the Ottoman rule, the economy of the Romanian countries was predominantly channelled toward the Ottoman Empire. They gradually lost part of their rights sanctioned by the Porte in the "old treaties" (capitulations); despite the stipulation of the "capitulations," Turks or representatives of Ottoman interests settled in the Romanian countries.

During the second half of the sixteenth century, as a result of the transformations wrought in the social-economic structure of the Romanian countries, the free peasantry, who had formed the main military force, entered a process of decay, while the number of the dependent peasants increased, and their juridical status worsened. Obviously, that process led to a lessening of the peasants' interest in the country's defense, to a weakening of the military capacity of the Romanian countries. In addition to improvements in military technology—the wide use of firearms, requiring special training on the part of the soldiers—the changes that occurred in the status of the peasantry led, to an ever greater extent, to the replacing of the country's host by troops of mercenaries. The establishment of Ottoman rule in Wallachia after 1529 (the greater host is mentioned for the last time in 1533), and in Moldavia in 1538, was both a cause and an effect of the decay of the greater host. Afraid of possible uprisings, the Porte severely limited the size and scope of Romanian armies and assumed the role of defender of the Romanian provinces against external foes and attacks. The fortifications lost their importance and some were even dismantled by the order of the Porte.

As Ottoman rule became more onerous, anti-Ottoman actions such as the revolt of voivode John, who entered history under the nickname of "the Terrible" (1572-1574), did occur. However, after John's heroic fall, Ottoman domination and exploitation became even more severe triggering off, in the late sixteenth century, the military reaction led by Michael the Brave.

The wars of Michael the Brave compelled the Ottoman Porte, fearful of the emergence of yet another Michael, to relax its exploitation of the Romanian countries.

What was the European significance of the wars waged by the Romanian people? As the outstanding Romanian historian P. P. Panaitescu emphasized, by stopping Ottoman expansion on the Danube until the sixteenth century, the Romanian people offered the West the necessary respite to build up their defenses against the Ottoman danger. If at Nicopole, in 1396, the crusade army of the Western knights was defeated by the Turkish light cavalry and infantry, in 1529, during the siege of Vienna, the imperial army proved superior, in terms of equipment (particularly firearms), to the Ottoman troops. "The delay caused by the Romanian resistance meant not only an attrition war for the Turkish forces; it was decisive in that it allowed the adjustment of the (Western) armies for the defeat of the invaders. It gave Western Europe time to engage in battle in a stage that was much more to her advantage, with different arms and a different military organization."[30]

NOTES

1. For the general framework of that battle, see: Ilie Ceauşescu, *Războiul Întregului popor pentru apărarea patriei la români* (The Romanians' Entire People's War for the Defense of the Homeland), Bucureşti, 1980.

2. See: N. Stoicescu, *"Oastea cea mare" în Ţara Românească si Moldova (secolele XIV-XVI)* (The "Greater Host" in Wallachia and Moldavia in the 14th-16th Centuries), in vol. *Oastea cea mare* (The Greater Host), Bucureşti, 1972, pp. 25-51; Ştefan Ştefănescu, *Oastea Ţării şi epopeea românească a secolelor XIV-XVI* (Wallachia's Army and the Romanian Epic of the 14th-16th Centuries), in vol. *România şi tradiţiile luptei armate a întregului popor*, (Romania and the Traditions of the Entire People's Armed Struggle), Bucureşti, 1972, pp. 25-32.

3. Hurmuzaki, *Documente* (Documents), XV/1, p. 46.

4. I. Dlugosz, *Historia Polonica*, II, Lipsiae, 1712, col. 345. In a similar way acted Iancu of Hunedoara, of whom chronicler A. Bonfini said: "he gathered soldiers from towns and villages, ordered the Szeklers to take up arms, and all of them, villagers and townsfolk alike, were bound, by a public decree, to serve in the army, for the benefit of each and every one." (C. Mureşan, *Rolul lui Iancu de Hunedoare în mobilizares maselor populare împotriva expansiunii otomane* (The Role of

The European importance of Romanian resistance to Ottom[a]
pansion in the fourteenth, fifteenth and sixteenth centuries cann[ot]
underestimated.

Many Romanian princes and voivodes realized that they were fig[hting]
not only for the defense of their own countries, but also for that o[f]
neighboring countries and of European "Christendom" in general. [For]
instance, on February 11, 1462, before the battle against the Turks, [Vlad]
the Impaler, ruler of Wallachia wrote to Matthias Corvinus, King of [Hun-]
gary and his ally: "If this little country perished, this would be of no [bene-]
fit or help to your Highness, but a loss for all Christendom." The Vene[tian]
ambassador in Buda, in his turn, warned the West as to the serious c[on-]
sequences that the fall of Wallachia to the Turks mgiht have: "*Vene[ndo]
il Turcho, per il primo succedera la diffectione di Valacho a poi qu[ella]
di questo Regno (Hungary), over ignominisos accordo a tutti christiani.[*"]

Before the battles with the Ottomans of 1475, Stephen the Gr[eat]
showed his resolve "to fight with all his stamina for Christendom," at t[he]
same time expressing his hope that he would not be left alone in front [of]
that powerful enemy. After the victory scored at Vaslui on January 1[0,]
1475, the prince called to the attention of the European countries th[e]
fact that Moldavia was the "gate to Christendom" and warned that "if th[is]
gate, which is our country, is lost—God forbid!—then the whole of Christ[-]
endom will be in great peril." The valliant prince considered the victor[y]
of Vaslui as belonging not only to him, but to the "entire Christendom,["]
in the name of which he was fighting. Stephen's idea on the role of Molda[-]
via as a "gate to Christendom" was shared by the Senate of Venice and by
Sultan Bayazid II as well.

Another brave man, Prince John of Moldavia, wrote, in turn, to the
councillors of Poland on July 28, 1572: "if it were not for our country,
the Turks would have perpetrated terrible pillage and slaughter in the
country of Your Majesty, but as such, our Moldavian country being located right in front of her, the country of Your Highnesses, my good
Lords, has been left in peace by the enemy."[28]

Michael the Brave too spoke in terms similar to those used by Stephen
the Great a century before him, when writing to I. Potocki, on July 15,
1595, before the battle of Călugăreni: "I embarked upon this difficult
undertaking with this poor country of ours, to be a shield for the entire
Christian world." The prince was convinced of the fact that Transylvania
and Wallachia were the "bulwark and defense of the entire Christendom."[29]

The European importance of Romanian resistance to Ottoman expansion in the fourteenth, fifteenth and sixteenth centuries cannot be underestimated.

Many Romanian princes and voivodes realized that they were fighting not only for the defense of their own countries, but also for that of the neighboring countries and of European "Christendom" in general. For instance, on February 11, 1462, before the battle against the Turks, Vlad the Impaler, ruler of Wallachia wrote to Matthias Corvinus, King of Hungary and his ally: "If this little country perished, this would be of no profit or help to your Highness, but a loss for all Christendom." The Venetian ambassador in Buda, in his turn, warned the West as to the serious consequences that the fall of Wallachia to the Turks mgiht have: *"Venendo il Turcho, per il primo succedera la diffectione di Valacho a poi quella di questo Regno (Hungary), over ignominisos accordo a tutti christiani."*[26]

Before the battles with the Ottomans of 1475, Stephen the Great showed his resolve "to fight with all his stamina for Christendom," at the same time expressing his hope that he would not be left alone in front of that powerful enemy. After the victory scored at Vaslui on January 10, 1475, the prince called to the attention of the European countries the fact that Moldavia was the "gate to Christendom" and warned that "if this gate, which is our country, is lost—God forbid!—then the whole of Christendom will be in great peril." The valliant prince considered the victory of Vaslui as belonging not only to him, but to the "entire Christendom," in the name of which he was fighting. Stephen's idea on the role of Moldavia as a "gate to Christendom" was shared by the Senate of Venice and by Sultan Bayazid II as well.

Another brave man, Prince John of Moldavia, wrote, in turn, to the councillors of Poland on July 28, 1572: "if it were not for our country, the Turks would have perpetrated terrible pillage and slaughter in the country of Your Majesty, but as such, our Moldavian country being located right in front of her, the country of Your Highnesses, my good Lords, has been left in peace by the enemy."[28]

Michael the Brave too spoke in terms similar to those used by Stephen the Great a century before him, when writing to I. Potocki, on July 15, 1595, before the battle of Călugăreni: "I embarked upon this difficult undertaking with this poor country of ours, to be a shield for the entire Christian world." The prince was convinced of the fact that Transylvania and Wallachia were the "bulwark and defense of the entire Christendom."[29]

What was the European significance of the wars waged by the Romanian people? As the outstanding Romanian historian P. P. Panaitescu emphasized, by stopping Ottoman expansion on the Danube until the sixteenth century, the Romanian people offered the West the necessary respite to build up their defenses against the Ottoman danger. If at Nicopole, in 1396, the crusade army of the Western knights was defeated by the Turkish light cavalry and infantry, in 1529, during the siege of Vienna, the imperial army proved superior, in terms of equipment (particularly firearms), to the Ottoman troops. "The delay caused by the Romanian resistance meant not only an attrition war for the Turkish forces; it was decisive in that it allowed the adjustment of the (Western) armies for the defeat of the invaders. It gave Western Europe time to engage in battle in a stage that was much more to her advantage, with different arms and a different military organization."[30]

NOTES

1.   For the general framework of that battle, see: Ilie Ceauşescu, *Războiul Întregului popor pentru apărarea patriei la români* (The Romanians' Entire People's War for the Defense of the Homeland), Bucureşti, 1980.

2.   See: N. Stoicescu, *"Oastea cea mare" în Ţara Românească si Moldova (secolele XIV-XVI)* (The "Greater Host" in Wallachia and Moldavia in the 14th-16th Centuries), in vol. *Oastea cea mare* (The Greater Host), Bucureşti, 1972, pp. 25-51; Ştefan Ştefănescu, *Oastea Ţării şi epopeea românească a secolelor XIV-XVI* (Wallachia's Army and the Romanian Epic of the 14th-16th Centuries), in vol. *România şi tradiţiile luptei armate a întregului popor*, (Romania and the Traditions of the Entire People's Armed Struggle), Bucureşti, 1972, pp. 25-32.

3.   Hurmuzaki, *Documente* (Documents), XV/1, p. 46.

4.   I. Dlugosz, *Historia Polonica*, II, Lipsiae, 1712, col. 345. In a similar way acted Iancu of Hunedoara, of whom chronicler A. Bonfini said: "he gathered soldiers from towns and villages, ordered the Szeklers to take up arms, and all of them, villagers and townsfolk alike, were bound, by a public decree, to serve in the army, for the benefit of each and every one." (C. Mureşan, *Rolul lui Iancu de Hunedoare în mobilizares maselor populare împotriva expansiunii otomane* (The Role of

Iancu of Hunedoara in Mustering the People's Masses against the Ottoman Expansion), in "Studii" IX, 1956, nr. 4, p. 61; idem, *Iancu de Hunedoara* (Iancu of Hunedoara), 2nd ed., Bucureşti, 1968, p. 75).

5. Ion Bogdan, *Documentele lui Ştefan cel Mare* (The Documents of Stephen the Great), II, p. 321. A similar appeal had been made on November 29, 1474, before the battle of Vaslui, this one too without any result whatsoever (ibid., p. 319).

6. I. Bogdan, op. cit., vol. II, p. 348.

7. N. Iorga, *Indreptări şi întregiri la istoria românilor*, (Corrections and Additions to the History of the Romanians), in "Anale Acad. Române. Memoriile Secţiei istorice," S.II, t. XXVII, 1905, p. 118.

8. *Documenta Romaniae Historica*, B, vol. I, p. 296.

9. *Călători străini despre tările române*, (Foreign Travellers' Accounts on the Romanian Countries), IV, p. 159.

10. I. Lupaş, *Istoria Unirii românilor* (A History of the Romanians' Union), p. 162.

11. Leunclavius, *Historiae musulmanae Turcorum*, col. 418.

12. A. Bonfini, *Rerum Hungaricarum decades IV*, Lipsiae, 1771, p. 470.

13. N. Iorga, *Cronica lui Wavrin şi românii* (Wavrin's Chronicle and the Romanians), in "Buletinul Comisiei istorice a României," VI, 1927, p. 61.

14. G. Lăzărescu, N. Stoicescu, *Ţările române şi Italia pînă la 1600* (The Romanian Countries and Italy until 1600), Bucureşti, 1972, p. 79.

15. Ibid., p. 78. As Aeneas Silvio Piccolomini, Iancu's contemporary showed, he brought more fame to the Romanians, from among whom he had been born, than to the Magyars (*non tam Hungaris, quam Valachis, ex quibus natus erat, gloriam auxit*).

16. Hurmuzaki, *Documente*, II/1, p. 14.

17. I. Bogdan, op. cit., II, p. 348.

18. I. Dlugosz, op. cit., vol. II, col. 528.

19. Bertrandon de la Broquiere, *Le voyage d'outre mer*, p. 265; *Istoria României* (A History of Romania), II, Bucureşti, 1962, p. 428.

20. *Călători străini despre române*, I, p. 149.

21. Ibid., p. 196.

22. "Arhiva istorică a României," I/1, 1865, p. 168.

23. E. Legrand, *Deux vies de Jac! ues Basilikos*, pp. 172-173. A. Verancsics, in turn, maintained that Petru Rareş boasted an "amazingly

numerous cavalry and so skilled a peasant army and so stubborn when attacking the enemy in the most difficult places that those who did not see this would hardly be made to believe it" (*Călători străini*, I, p. 418). We likewise mention the opinion of Polish chronicler Stanislas Orichovius, who stated that the Moldavians are very brave men, and taking account of their fame in war and gallantry, though their country is small, there is not any other people able to face them" (D. Cantemir, *Descrierea Moldovei* (A Description of Moldavia), București, 1973, p. 125).

24.   Ștefan Pascu, *"Oastea de șară,"* *oaste populară în țările române în secolele XIV-XVI* (The "Country's Host," a Popular Host in the Romanian Countries in the 14th-16th Centuries), in *Armata Republicii Socialiste Române, Traditii și contemporaneitate* (The Army of the Socialist Republic of Romania. Traditions and Contemporary Features), București, 1975, p. 21.

25.   N. Stoicescu, *Vlad Tepeș* (Vlad the Impaler), București, 1979, pp. 140-141.

26.   N. Stoicescu, *Vlad Tepeș*, București, 1976, p. 97. Chronicler L. Chalcocondil recorded in a different way the appeal launched by the prince of Wallachia "if (the Turks) invade and occupy Dacia, you should realize that they will not rest, but will soon start war against you, and the inhabitants of your countries will be inflicted great suffering by them. Therefore, it is not timw that, while helping us, you help yourselves, stopping that army as far as possible from your country" (*Expuneri istorice* [Historical Lectures], V. Grecu Ed., pp. 286-287).

27.   I. Bogdan, *Documentele lui Ștefan cel Mare*, II, pp. 323, 348-349. See also p. 347 where the prince showed that Moldavia was "a wall of defense for the Hungarians' country and the Poles' country."

28.   "Romanoslavica," 1965, p. 301. Several decades before the messenger of voivode Stefăniță spoke to the same effect: "If God allows this country and Prince to be destroyed, Your Majesty must know that the same will happen to other Christian princes as well," M. Costăchescu, *Documentele moldovenesti de la Ștefănită Voievod (1517-1527)* (Moldavian Documents Belonging to Voivode Ștefaniță 1517-1527), Iași, 1943, pp. 543, 544, 548.

29.   N. Iorga, *Documente nouă, în mare parte românesti, relative la Petru Șchiopul și Mihai Viteazul* (New, Mostly Romanian Documents about Petru Șchiopul and Michael the Brave), București, 1898, p. 456.

30.   P. P. Pansitescu, *Interpretări românesti. Studii de istoria economică şi socială* (Romanian Views. Studies in Economic and Social History), Bucureşti, 1947, pp. 150-151.

Ştefan Ştefănescu

DEFENSE OF THE INTEGRITY OF THE ROMANIAN STATE IN THE SIXTEENTH AND SEVENTEENTH CENTURIES

The establishment of the feudal states, Wallachia and Moldavia, in the fourteenth century was of decisive importance for the Romanian people's future; its organization in independent states saved it from the danger of being absorbed by the neighboring powers and provided its own framework for development and assertion. The emergence of the new political organizations stimulated demographic-economic development, as well as social and military organization. The internal cohesion, enhanced through the new state organization, permitted the two countries to withstand the permanent tendencies of expansion of the big neighboring states, especially of the Ottoman Empire and ot preserve their political existence.

The first part of the century-long anti-Ottoman war because of the military achievement of the Romanian army headed by Mircea the Old (1386-1418) ended with a diplomatic settlement of the military conflict. Wallachia, while acknowledging the Porte's suzerainty, remained an independent state with its own social organization, its own army and institutions, its entire political hierarchy. At the same time, the political-military developments proved the urgent necessity of cooperation among the three Romanian Countries.

In the following period ended by the rule of Vlad the Impaler (1448, 1456-1462, 1476) in Wallachia, the Wallachian policy alternated between anti-Ottoman war and long-term agreement with the Porte; this policy, as a matter of fact, mirrored the relative military balance of the powers involved in that conflict.

In 1455 the Ottoman Empire began to directly exert pressure against Moldavia, too, thus initiating the third stage of the Romanian's anti-Ottoman war, now headed by Stephen the Great (1457-1504).

The tradition of heroic battles fought by Stephen the Great was continued by other Romanian ruling princes after the defeat of the Magyar army at Mohacs (1526), in which Louis II of Hungary was killed. After the defeat of the Hungarians, two pretenders emerged for securing the Hungarian crown: Ferdinand of Habsburg, bother of Emperor Charles V and John Zapolya, the voivode of Transylvania. Zapolya was supported by Petru Rareş, the voivode of Moldavia (1527-1538, 1541-1546), who sought to exploit the conflict between Ferdinand and Zapolya to extend his own influence in Transylvania. There, military expeditions of Moldavian armies into Transylvania culminated in the battle of Feldioara (on June 22, 1529) in which Ferdinand's supporters were defeated.

Encouraged by that victory, Petru Rareş sent his army into Poland, but suffered a severe defeat at Obertyn (1531). As the Porte disavowed the Polish campaign, Petru Rareş approached the Habsburgs. The agreement concluded on April 4, 1535 with Ferdinand, however, referred only to mutual obligations in case of joint anti-Ottoman actions; it did not obligate the Moldavian ruler to support Ferdinand's aims in Transylvania. In fact, the Moldavian voivode offered only to use his entire army against the Turks. That was an attractive offer as may be deduced from the contemporary opinion of the humanist G. Reicherstorffer who considered Moldavia to be "a genuine defensive wall of Christendom."[1]

The new political orientation of Petru Rareş asserted itself when the Venetian adventurer Aloisic Gritti, supported by the Porte, sought to ascend the throne of Hungary himself and his sons the thrones of the Romanian Countries. Faced with such a threat, Petru Rareş reentered Transylvania and captured Gritti. The alliance concluded with Ferdinand of Habsburg (1535) was of no use for the Moldavian prince, however when Suleiman the Magnificent decided to intervene against "the rebel." In the summer of 1538, a Turkish army of 200,000 men invaded Moldavia while the Polish feudal lords attacked from the north and the Tatars from the east. Rareş could not be helped by Ferdinand or by Charles V because the emperor was engaged in a sea battle at Prevesa where—as Paolo Paruta stated—"partisse dal conflitto rotta & vinta."[2] Nevertheless, Petru Rareş decided to resist, but, betrayed by the great boyars he was forced to abandon the war and leave the country; he fled to Transylvania. The Sultan set up a garrison in the country's capital, annexed Bugeac (the southern part of Bessarabia) and transformed the territory surrounding the fortress of Tighina into the *rayah* of Bender. Moldavia was subdued by the Ottoman Empire.

Two facts are worthy of further notice: the establishment of the autonomous principality of Transylvania and of Ottoman rule in Buda (1541). The acknowledgement of Transylvanian autonomy by the Porte augured well for the continuing retention of autonomy by Wallachia and Moldavia. On the other hand, the extension of Ottoman domination as evidenced by the transformation of the Banat into a pashalik facilitated the exerting of Ottoman pressure against the Wallachian and Moldavian voivodes and the Transylvanian ruling prince as well.

Under these circumstances, as the Porte encircled the three Romanian Countries from the east, south and west as a result of the creation of the pashalik of Buda, the wars waged by the Turks and the Imperial Court provided the Romanian voivodes an opportunity to form an anti-Ottoman alliance initiated by the Habsburgs. On March 1, 1542, Petru Rareş signed a secret convention with Margrave Joachim of Brandenburg according to which the former lent to the latter the huge sum of 200,000 ducats for financing anti-Ottoman actions which, however, woefully ended in failure in front of the Buda fortress.[3] But the alliance concluded with Joachim of Brandenburg revealed the voivode's determination to regain Moldavia's autonomy.

The second part of the sixteenth century was characterized by political decline in Moldavia and Wallachia because of the Ottoman domination and of struggles among they boyar's parties; that decline was arrested, however, by Ioan Voivode the Brave and Michael the Brave.

This time also, the burden of the wars waged on a "front fortifié"—as historian Ferdinand Braudel said[4]—in the Balkan area fell upon the Serbians, Romanians, Bulgarians and Albanians. The Romanians engaged in continuous warfare with the Ottomans to regain their independence. The Polich chronicle by Bielski mirrored the Romanians' attitude: "The Moldavians have already risen against Peter Voivode (the Lame)"—said the chronicler in 1576—"because they suffered many injustices both from him and the Turks', whom he loved and housed at his Court."[5]

The heroic battles fought by Ioan Voivode the Brave, Moldavia's ruling prince, are within this purview. In the battle of Jiliştea of April 1574, supported only by a small detachment of Cossacks voivode Ioan defeated the Turks and in his pursuit of the enemy, the voivode seized the city of Burcharest. The Turks, however, launched a counterattack and in the battle of Iezerul Cahulului he was betrayed by the boyars and after the battle of Roșcani he was forced to surrender and eventually was killed.

All this notwithstanding, the echo of Ioan's heroic deeds was far reaching. Thus, Leonard Gorecki, in his work *Descriptio Valachiae* (Moldaviae), compared the Moldavian voivode to the greatest army commanders of his time such as the king of Sweden, Gustavus Adolfphus. Another humanist, Lasiecki, stated that Ioan Voivode the Brave gained by his gallant deeds both the respect and love of his people. In France, his battles were known through *L'histoire* by Popeliniere.[7]

After the death of the Moldavian voivode, when the dreaded Sinan Pasha became Grand Vizir for the third time, the Porte predicted that "from now on, the Christians and the Turks will enjoy few moments of peace." As a matter of fct, the Turks, in alliance with the Crimean Tatars, succeeded in defeating the Persian kingdom and Poland which, torn by internal dissension could not oppose the anti-Polish plans of the Turks. In the autumn of 1593 Sinan Pasha seized the fortresses of Sissek (1593)— an important strategic point situated at the confluence of Sava, Culpa and Oder—of Vesprim and of Palata. In the face of such losses, the imperial victory gained at Szekesfehervar (Alba Regală) was worthless. In that atmosphere of general panic when the Spanish Don Guillen was waiting in Vienna for the Turkish armies, Michael the Brave was elected as the ruling prince in Wallachia (1593).

Michael the Brave entered the consciousness of the Romanian people as "the Unifier," having achieved, for a short time, the bringing together under the same rule, the Romanian territories. The 1600 Union of Wallachia, Transylvania and Moldavia was the expression of the close economic, political, cultural and military relations among the three Romanian countries, relations, grounded on the joint consciousness of the unity of the nation.

When Prince Michael came to the throne of Wallachia (1593) the international situation was extremely complicated. Treaties that had given rise to hopes of at least temporary peace were undone, unexpected changes occurred in the system of alliances. Ever more insistent external pressures and internal political and economic difficulties were prejudicing the political status of autonomy of the Romanian Countries and were fore-boding their imminent incorporation into the body politic of the con-tending neighboring powers: the Ottoman Empire, the Habsburg Empire and the Polish Kingdom.

Aware of the ongoing political changes, Michael the Brave evinced extraordinary ingenuity in his strategy of alliances, designed to strengthen his power at home and Wallachia's role in international affairs.

In line with these goals, Michael the Brave organized a powerful intel-ligence and executive apparatus and pursued a ceaseless struggle against the all-powerful boyars. His successes in that struggle facilitated the achievement of one of his principal political aims—Wallachia's freedom, threatened in the first place by the Ottoman Empire.

In foreign affairs, Michael the Brave tried to conclude a system of al-liances which would free him for action against the Porte. His primary tactic of dividing and immobilizing his enemies was, however, not entirely successful as Wallachia's neighbors were more interested in deposing him than in assisting him.

Michael the Brave ascended the throne of Wallachia at a time when in-ternational circumstances seemed favorable for action against the Turks. While the liberation movements of the Balkan peoples intensified, com-pelling the Porte to use important military forces to subdue them, several European states joined together in the "Holy League," established at the initiative of the House of Austria and under the patronage of the Holy See.

The interests of Wallachia determined Michael the Brave to break with the Ottomans and become a supporter of the idea of an anti-Ottoman struggle. Michael adhered to the "Holy League" and took steps to free the country from the Ottoman economic system. On November 13, 1594, the unpopular Ottoman creditors and traders present in Wallachia were annihalated. This action was regarded as a declaration of war. This was followed by military actions, first on the left and then on the right bank of the Danube. The attack on Giurgiu was followed by the sacking of Cetatea de Floci, Hîrşova and Silistra. At the beginning of 1595 (Janu-ary 14-16) the Romanian armies fought fierce, but victorious battles against the Tatars at Putinei and Stăneşti (near Giurgiu). At Şerpăteşti, *paharnicul* (Cupbearer) Manta defeated important Ottoman and Tatar forces which were pursued by Michael the Brave. Michael then crossed the Danube and won a major victory at Ruschuk against two pashas, Hassan and Mustapha, who had orders to depose Michael and replace him with Bogdan, the son of Prince Iancu.

The Ottoman attempt to send armies to Moldavia through Wallachia in order to dethone Prince Aron, who had also moved against the Turks, determined Prince Michael to send a part of his army, under the command of Ban Mihalcea, across the Danube to attack Silistra, the point from which the Ottomans intended to force their advance on the left bank of the Danube. Moreover, Michael devised a plan of simultaneous attacks against the Ottoman positions in Brăila, Chervena (in northern Bulgaria, not far from Turtucaia), Turtucaia and Nikopol. Michael the Brave's victories alarmed the Porte as rumors circulated that he was nearing Adrianopole and that he had proclaimed himself "king" or even "emperor."

The Porte decided to put down the rebellion north of the Danube and to reintegrate Wallachia into the Ottoman economic system. In the spring of 1595, the Turkish army headed by the Grand Vizier and commander-in-chief of the Ottoman armies, Ferhad Pasha moved toward the Danube. Upon reaching Ruschuk, where the plan for Wallachia's conquest was to be finalized, the Ottoman army became unruling largely because of the conflict between Ferhad Pasha and Sinan Pasha. Taking advantage of the situation, Michael sought to prevent the Ottoman army from crossing the Danube and even attacked Nikopolis to force the Ottoman army to disband. At the beginning of July, Ferhad Pasha was replaced by Sinan Pasha, who had the reputation of being the best army commander in the Ottoman Empire. Sinan Pasha crossed the Danube at Giurgiu, heading a large army; Michael retreated to Călugăreni where he scored a remarkable victory on August 13/23, 1595. Aware, however, that he could not withstand for any lenght of time renewed attacks launched by Sinan Pasha, Michael decided to withdraw toward the mountains, hoping to receive support from Transylvania, Bucharest and Tîrgoviște fell to the Ottomans. A powerful resistence movement emerged, however, in the regions in which the Ottoman armies were advancing as armed peasants made surprise attacks on the invading forces.

With help received from Sigismund Bathory (the Prince of Transylvania), from Archduke Maximilian, from the Prince of Moldavia, Ştefan Răzvan, and from the Grand Duke of Tuscany, Michael the Brave forced the Ottoman army to withdraw. Tîrgoviște was freed on October 6, Bucharest on October 12 and Giurgiu on October 20. The Ottoman army left behind north of the Danube many prisoners and the rich booty plundered from Wallachia. In November 1595 the Wallachian territory was liberated of Ottoman armies. The ports on the Danube, including Brăila were returned to Wallachia after many years of Ottoman rule. The southern border of the country was again on the Danube.

The year 1596 marked the transition from the purely "military" to the "political and military" stage of the independence war. In 1596 the Ottoman Empire was engaged in battle with the Habsburg Empire which ended in the defeat of the latter at Eger and Keresztesz (October 26, 1596). The Habsburg-Ottoman war facilitated the attainment of Michael's goals. Victories of the Wallachian army were registered in a number of places south of the Danube: Pleven was burnt down by the groups led by Baba Novac, who advanced toward Sofia; other groups attacked Vidin and Babadag. In the autumn of 1596 devastating Tatar hordes again raided Wallachia. After burning a number of towns—Buzău, Gherghiţa and Bucharest—they were driven away by Prince Michael, who then attacked Turnu and the Nikopolis fortress on the right bank of the Danube.

The news of Michael the Brave's victories quickly spread all over Europe, the name of the Romanian prince being uttered with esteem and with great expectations. The Greek population, under Ottoman rule, regarded Michael as a possible emperor of Byzantium.

At the request of the Ottomans and upon realizing from his discussions with Sigismund Bathory, the Prince of Transylvania, that cooperation among the states engaged in the struggle against the Ottoman Empire was difficult to attain. Michael the Brave concluded peace with the Porte at the end of 1596 and received the princely banner from Constantinople.

Two years later, in 1598, the war resumed; Prince Michael again defeated the Ottomans in a number of localities south of the Danube: at Cladova, Vidin, Nikopolis. In March 1598, after the Ottoman attack on Wallachia and their defeat at Obluciţa (Isaccea) the hostilities ended (October 6, 1598). Although suspicious of the Porte, Michael was even more concerned over the plans devised against him by the rulers of Transylvania and Moldavia, who were supported by Poland. He took steps to increase his military strength and engaged in intensive diplomatic activities. A detailed plan, combining diplomatic and military action was implemented and it brought about the joining together of Transylvania, Wallachia, and Moldavia.

Michael the Brave entered Transylvania when Cardinal Andreas Bathory, a partisan of pro-Polish and pro-Ottoman policy, became its ruler
in 1599. In the autumn of 1599, Michael had no alternatives but to resort to military action, coupled with skillful diplomacy, and he succeeded
in both. Pressures were exerted upon him not only by the Ottomans, but
also by the Prince of Moldavia, Ieremia Movilă, enthroned by the Poles
in 1595. The latter, with the army poised against Wallachia, sent a special
messenger to Michael the Brave asking him to leave the country and cede
the throne to Simion Movilă, his brother. Andreas Bathory, in turn, also
sent messengers to Michael asking him to cease the fight against the Ottomans and surrender Wallachia to him. In a report sent by Valentin Walawski, a Polish commander in Michael's army, to Andrew Taranowski, it
was stated that Michael "soon sent back the messengers of the Cardinal
saying that he would not cease the struggle against the Ottomans till his
eyes were covered by earth, because he had pledged support to the Christian emperor against the Ottomans. With regard to surrendering the country,
he shall surrender his country and homeland to nobody until he is dragged
by the feet from there." Walawski said that the information received by
Prince Michael from his trusted people with regard to the preparations
made against him, on the one hand, by Andreas Bathory and, on the other
by Ieremia Movilă with the support of the Polish chancellor Jan Zamoyski
—while the Ottomans themselves waited poised to cross the Danube—
determined him to make the decision to intervene first in Transylvania.

To prevent an Ottoman attack against the country during his campaign
in Transylvania, Michael entered into negotiations with them and, following the union of Transylvania and Wallachia wrote that if they were not
hostile he would observe in respect to the Porte "the rules established in
the past."[11] He also wrote to Emperor Rufolf II as if his assuming authority in Transylvania had been done on the advice and on behalf of the
House of Austria.[12]

So as not to incur the wrath of the emperor before he could consolidate his rule in Transylvania and also secure the support of the Saxons,
who were favorable to the Habsburg cause, Michael designated himself
as a deputy of the emperor in Transylvania. In the documents issued by
his chancellery in Transylvania, he called himself: "We, Michael, Prince of
Wallachia, adviser to His Holy Imperial and Royal Majesty, his Deputy in
Transylvania and commander-in-chief of his armies in the adjacent provinces subordinated to Transylvania."[13]

This title was in fact obscuring the actual position which Michael sought to acquire gradually in Transylvania. These intentions were perceived by contemporary diplomats who stated in their reports that he insisted on being called "Highness" (Altezza) and "Prince" *(Principe di Transilvania)* and that he had no intention of surrendering Transylvania to Emperor Rudolf. The chancellory of Wallachia referred to Michael as "Prince of Transylvania,"[15] "Prince of the whole of Transylvania"[16] or "great king of the whole of Transylvania."[17] For the people living south of the Carpathians, it was clear that, through the defeat of Cardinal Adreas Bathory, Michael the Brave "conquered the entire of Transylvania and sat as king on the throne of Alba Iulia and of the whole of Transylvania."[18]

In Michael's view, the union of Transylvania and, later, that of Moldavia with Wallachia was based on the necessity to establish a broader political organism in the struggle against the Ottoman Empire. In this respect, a role that cannot be underestimated was played by the ethnic community, stemming from the identity of origin, language and religion of the inhabitants of the three countries. Contemporary sources show that in adversity Michael encouraged his soldiers "to behave bravely, both for the glory of Christ, in whose name they were fighting, and for that of their nation, and of the Romans, from whom they professed to descend *(per la gloria della lor natione, et di que romani da cui facevano professione di discendere)*."[19] In this testimony, as well as in the proclamation addressed thirty years earlier by Iacob Heraclid Despot to the Moldavians, there was proof of consciousness and pride in the Roman origin by the Romanian people.

Michael the Brave's entering Transylvania entailed manifestations of solidarity by the Romanian population when at Şelimber on October 18, 1599, the new political status of Transylvania was decided. Burdened by taxes and obligations, politically oppressed, the Romanian peasant masses in Transylvania rose against the landowners on hearing of the victory of Michael the Brave. Having confidence in a prince of their own nationality and urged, it seems by the priests and monks sent from Wallachia by Michael, who knew and wanted to exploit to his political advantage the state of mind of the Romanians in Transylvania, the peasants sought to removed with the help of this prince of their nationality, the yoke of serfdom.

Political reaons determined Michael the Brave the sacrafice the interests of the peasantry; to ensure his rule in Transylvania, he tried to attract the nobility, the only class which, in the juridical context of the time, had a constitutional position, had the administrative and political power and was of military value.

The measures taken by Michael the Brave in favor of the Romanians in Transylvania—exemption of the Romanian priests from labor duties and the decision to grant free pastures to the Romanian villages on the big estates of the nobles and Saxons caused no changes in the social-economic structure. However, his measures evinced a significant concern for improving the situation of the great majority of the population of Transylvania.

Of particular interest for the way in which Michael the Brave conceived of his position in Transylvania are his negotiations with Emperor Rudolf II. The essence of Michael's demands was the recognition by the Emperor of the lasting, hereditary character of his rule in Transylvania, as well as in Wallachia, of his founding a dynasty in those countries. Michael also asked that the borders of Transylvania be those existing at the time of Emperor Maximilian II and Prince Johannes Sigismundus; that there should be restored to Transylvania Oradea and the Bihor area, Hust with the land of Maramureş, the lands of Crasna, Solnoc, Zărand, Baia Mare with Baia de Sus and the other lands that had belonged to it previously; that he should have the right to grant villages and lands to whom he chose; that he should have supreme juridicial power; that he should be given the same ruling title which the emperor had granted to Sigismund Bathory;[20] and finally all territories which had previously belonged to Transylvania and Wallachia which were recaptured from the Turks, should revert to the two countries.[21] In another version, Prince Michael demanded "that the fortresses and provinces that we might gain from the Ottomans be left to us, to join with the two countries."[22]

During his rule in Transylvania, Michael the Brave maintained the organization, the autonomy of the country, her governing bodies, but he tried to use officials brought him from Wallachia. The Princely Council, for instances, acquired a mixed character; it consisted of Magyar nobles and Wallachian boyars. Above and alongside the old administrative organization of Transylvania, Michael also set up a Wallachian administration; he also took steps to strengthen Transylvania militarily. He preserved the army of the nobility but also expanded the size of his own army and secured the funds for its maintanence primarly from the towns. The principal fortresses were manned by his own captains. Michael the Brave maintained and even extended the privileges of the Magyar nobility, but he also made grants and public offices available. He maintained the official languages in Transylvania (Latin and Magyar) but he himself and his officials also used the Romanian language in documents. Michael the Brave tried to elevate the position of the Romanian church in Transylvania and secured imperial recognition for the Orthodox religion as a constitutional religion.

The union of Transylvania with Wallachia achieved by Michael the Brave and the administrative, socioeconomic and religious measures he imposed in Transylvania greatly alaramed all his neighbors and even the Habsburg emperor, whose interest was to establish a purely German administration in Transylvania. The most concerned over the growing power of Michael was the king of Poland, Sigismund III, and the prince of Moldavia, Ieremia Movilă, who felt directly threatened by the consolidation of Michael's position in Transylvania and by his alliance with Tsar Boris Godunov and with the Cossacks from Moldavia became the center of intrigues against Michael, the place from where Sigismund Bathory voiced new claimed to the throne of Transylvania and Simion Movilă to that of Wallachia. At the beginning of 1600, Michael had decided to intervene in Moldavia, and informed Rudolf II of his plans. The emperor replied: "It is not the time now to fight with Moldavia, when he have had the Ottomans on our back, and if we fight against Moldavia, we (will have to) leave aside the Ottomans." But Michael did not abide by Rudolf's wishes. On May 6-7, his army was at Bacău and on May 8 he wrote from Roman to Rudolf, who was in Prague, that he had entered Moldavia to punish Ieremia Movilă, who slandered him and even the House of Austria, and who was scheming to remove Transylvania from imperial authority. Through Pezzen, a high official of the emperor, Prince Michael informed Rudolf that if he were to receive proper support for his actions he would take from the Ottomans all the land from the Black Sea to Buda so that he would be remembered "for a hundred years by everybody."[23]

Michael's troops entered Moldavia and in a single month, Moldavia was united with the other Romanian countries. On May 27, 1600, in a charter issued at Iaşi, Michael assumed the title: "Prince Michael, by Grace of God Prince of Wallachia and of Transylvania and of the whole of Moldavia."[24]

Fears were expressed in Poland that Michael the Brave even intended to attack that country, as it offered shelter to may fugitives from Wallachia, who were dissatisfied with his policies. In a letter written by a Polish spy in Moldavia to King Sigismund III it was mentioned that Prince Michael "has no other intention but to move against Poland."[25] Expressing the concern of contemporary rulers, Sigismund III told the Polish senators that Michael the Brave was like a haw on Moldavia. If he were to unite three rich and not at all small countries and rule them with absolute power, he would be a threat to Poland.

By assuming authority in Moldavia, Michael achieved the political unification of the Romanian Countries. With the pride and satisfaction of success, he added to his title of "Prince of Wallachia and Transylvania"[26] that of "Prince of Moldavia."[27] In the documents issued at Alba-Iulia, the center wherefrom he ruled the three Romanian Countries, Michael the Brave called himself: "Prince Michael, by Grace of God Prince of Wallachia and Transylvania and of the whole of Moldavia."[28] The establishment of a seal bearing the united arms of the three countries revealed his intention to establish a single political body; its component parts— Moldavia, Wallachia and Transylvania—would maintain their traditional forms of organization but would be subordinated to the supreme authority of Michael the Brave.

After trying without success to enthrone Ştefan, son of Petru Şchiopul, in Moldavia, Michael, at the instance of the Moldavian boyars who had joined his side, was inclined for a moment to place his son Nicolae Pătraşcu, whom he had left on the throne of Wallachia when crossing into Transylvania, on the throne of Moldavia. However, concern over the dangers that could face Nicolae Pătraşcu, especially from Ieremia Movilă, made Michael give up that idea. He set up a council of four Wallachia boyars and then entrusted the rule of Moldavia to Prince Marcu, son of Petru Cercel; Marcu's reign lasted only a few days.

In Moldavia, as in Transylvania, Michael tried to win the boyars to his side and, most of them did indeed take the oath of alliegance to him; at the same time, to prevent the flight of the population he decided—without implementing this measure—to exempt from taxes for a period of six years the inhabitants of the towns and villages that were destroyed in the war.

The union of the three Romanian Countries had to be consolidated. First, it was necessary to have it acknowledged by the House of Austria on whose behalf Michael had ostensibily acted. Therefore, negotiations with Emperor Rudolf were resumed. Michael renewed his previous demands and added new clauses concerning Moldavia. As a skillful diplomat, aware of the opposition of the Imperial authorities to his demands regarding Transylvania which, in essence, envisaged recognition of the hereditary character of his rule in that province, Michael sought the emperor's consent only for his rule in Transylvania as governor "during his lifetime and, after his death, to have his sons succeed him." As for Moldavia, "it should be inherited by sons and daughters just as Wallachia."[30] The renewal of other demands which he had made after the conquest of Transylvania: recognition of his right ot make awards, to be the supreme judicial authority, and to bear the title previously held by Sigismund Bathory, revealed Michael's determination to establish in the newly created political body an absolute hereditary monarchy.

The socio-economic structures of the Romanian Countries, as well as the rapid political changes that affected the durability of the union, deprived Michael of the forces on which the absolute monarchs of the period relied and of the time necessary for completing the work which had been so admirably started. Worried by the successes of Michael the Brave, whom he wanted as a faithful vassal, Emperor Rudolf tried to remove him from Transylvania by using experienced diplomats like Pezzen, by encouraging the ambitions of generals such as Georgious Basta or even by encouraging the dissatisfied Magyar nobility, an action which was to prove dangerous for the emperor himself.

In the summer of 1600, Basta and the imperial army he commanded joined the Magyar nobles who had risen against the Romanian prince while he was in Moldavia, and managed to defeat Michael the Brave in the battle of Mirăslău (September 18, 1600). Defeated, the Romanian prince had to cross the mountains into Wallachia, which was then threatened by Jan Zamoyski and his Polish army. Zamoyski had restored Ieremia Movilă on the throne of Moldavia and brought Simion Movilș with him to enthrone in Wallachia. An attempt to check the advance of the Polish army ended in Michael the Brave's defeat in the neighborhood of Buzău. In that desperate situation, Michael decided to address a memorandum to Emperor Rudolf, justifying his actions and offering to go in person to

Prague to convince the emperor of his loyalty or, at least, to prove to him that their basic interests coincided.[32] The fact that after Michael's withdrawal from Transylvania the Magyar nobility changed its position and showed hostility toward the emperor when it concluded an alliance with the Poles and recalled Sigismund Bathory to the throne, determined Rudolf II to order Michael and Basta to regain Transylvania for the Habsburgs. Suppressing for a moment the grudge they had for each other, the two commanders succeeded in conquering Transylvania in the battle of Guruslău (August 3, 1601). Shortly after the victory, on Basta's orders, Wallonian mercenaries assassinated, on Cîmpia Turzii, Michale the Brave who still hoped that he could salvage something of what he had achieved during the last few years.

The union of 1599-1600 of the Romanian Countries was related to the necessity to setting-up a powerful anti-Ottoman front. It was promoted by the economic, political and cultural links of the three states, by the consciousness of ethnic unity and of the fact that in ancient times the three countries formed a single ethnic-territorial unit under the name of Dacia. Animated by the idea, which had already given birth to some projects and which gradually grew in him, of reconstituting Dacia, Michael the Brave, by strengthening Wallachia's military capacity and by exploiting opportunities provided by a fluid international political situation, was able to transcend traditional forms of political and military alliances among the Romanian Countries by achieving their political union. He was, however, frustrated in his plans for integration of the three countries into a unitary state. Nevertheless, despite the temporary nature of his achievements, Michael became a symbol of the Romanian struggle for unity for later generations.

After the death of Michael the Brave, in Moldavia, the Movilă family were the executors of the will of the Polish noblemen and of the boyars. In Transylvania the fight between the Habsburgs and the local nobility on the one hand, and the pretenders to the throne on the other hand, led to anarchy. In Wallachia the real masters were the boyars of the Buzeşti family. The political instability was also due to the interference of the Ottoman Empire, the Habsburg Empire and the Polish Kingdom in the internal affairs of the three Romanian Countries. Under those unfavorable conditions the persevering efforts made by some of the ruling princes to maintain the state autonomy are noteworthy. Collaboration among the Romanian Countries increased because of the need to join in common diplomatic and military efforts.

The Wallachian voivode Radu Șerban and the prince of Transylvania, Stefan Bocsai, acting as equals, concluded an alliance at Tîrgoviște (1605) and Gabriel Bethlen ascended the throne of Transylvania with the help of Wallachian and Moldavian troops. Bethlen realized the significance of that act and planned to set up a kingdom of Dacia through the union of Transylvania, Wallachia and Moldavia. However, Ottoman and Habsburg opposition precluded implementation of such a project.

It is noteworthy that because of Bethlen's intervention in the Thirty Years' War, Transylvania became a major factor in European politics. In his anti-Habsburg campaigns, Bethlen received military help from Wallachia. "A thousand brave courtiers mounted on horses" led by Spatharus Mihu[33] took part in the battle fought in the vicinty of the river Tîrnava (1623).

The prince of Transylvania was also worried by the unrealistic anti-Ottoman attitude of Gaspar Grațiani, voivode of Moldavia, who joined the "Milice chretiene" of the Duke of Nevers. When, in August 1620, the Turks in Jassy were massacred on Grațiani's orders and the voivode joined the Polish side, Bethlen mobilized his forces to defend Transylvania's frontiers.[34]

After the death of Gabriel Bethlen, Gheorghe Rakoczi I, Matei Basarab and Vasile Lupu, rulers of the three countries, collaborated in a common effort to liberate Transylvania, Wallachia and Moldavia. Rakoczi, elected in 1630 as prince of Transylvania, sought to use Wallachian help also against the Habsburgs, who were trying to regain their lost hold on Transylvania. The close links and cooperation between the princes of Transylvania and Wallachia, which led to the treaty of 1635, aroused the suspicions of the Porte. The Ottomans rightly suspected Matei Basarab and Gheorghe Rakoczi I to be members of a Christian alliance directed against them. In the spring of 1636, Matei Basarab "declared himself to be ready to rise in the defence of the country"[35] were he to receive military assistance from Emperor Ferdinand II. The Ottomans dethroned Rakoczi in the autumn of 1636 but Rakoczi counteracted and on October 10/20, 1636, he defeated the armies of the Pasha at Buda and at Salonta. Matei Basarab, supported by Transylvanian troops, also, deployed his forces along the front lines of that battle. The Porte, more cautious than usual, reconfirmed Rakoczi as prince of Transylvania. Encouraged by this turn of events, Matei Basarabs' boyars engaged in negotiations with the Imperial representatives in Vienna and even sought to conclude an alliance with Venice also in 1639. Matei Basarab was to become the head of this alliance—"general of the entire Orient." The Austrian resident at the Porte considered him "a second Mihai Vodă"[36] (Michael the Brave). However, this plan failed to bear fruit as the Habsburgs and Rakoczi were involved in the Thirty Years' War and a war of liberation broke out in the Ukraine.

Rakoczi's diplomatic activities and military successes scored in the Thirty Years' War alarmed the Porte. To remind Rakoczi of his being only the prince of a vassal country, the Sultan increased the year tribute by 5,000 thalers, justifying his action by the territorial aggrandizement of Transylvania through the Treaty of Linz. Concurrently, Poland's king, Vladislav IV, sought Rakoczi's participation, alongside Poland, Wallachia and Moldavia in an anti-Ottoman coalition. Janusz Radziwill, the Grand Hetman of Lithuania, went to Transylvania and secured Rakoczi's adherence. To secure Moldavia to the alliance, the Poles promoted Radziwill's marriage to Maria, the daughter of the Moldavian ruler Vasile Lupu. The marriage took place in Jassy in 1645. In return, Vasile Lupu informed Alexei Mihailovici, the Tsar of Russia, of the alliance and shought his support also. But there was to be no military action against the Porte as the pro-Ottoman Polish Diet refused to approve the funds necessary to raise an army.

In 1656 Gheorghe Rakoczi II, the new prince of Transylvania, concluded a convention with Carol X, the king of Sweden, who was then engaged in a war against Poland. The campaign of Rakoczi II, supported by Wallachian and Moldavian troops, began in January 1657 and ended, after he had been abandoned by the Swedes and Cossacks, with the surrender of the allied armies to the Tatars. This defeat, reflective of Transylvania's diminishing military capacity persuaded Mehmed Kuprulu, the celebrated Grand Vizier of the Ottoman Empire since September 15, 1656, to react vigorously. The Grand Vizier, determined to set affairs in order decided to remove all vassal rulers who engaged in political and military activities without the consent of the Porte. Consequently, Gheorghe Rakoczi II, Constantin Serban and Gheorghe Serban were dethroned in October 1657.[35]

The Romanian voivodes, however, were just as determined to oppose that action. "Only with arms in hand" Constantin Serban told Rakoczi on December 15, 1657 "will you be acknowledged as prince by the Ottomans." On December 31, the same Constantin Serban assured him that he would support him in an anti-Ottoman war, with both soldiers and money. But all efforts were in vain given the military superiority of the Turks and their allies, the Tatars. In Transylvania, the nobility decided on August 1 (the Diet of Alba-Iulia) to surrender to "the humor of the Porte."

Mihnea III, the new voivode of Wallachia continued to entertain secret relations with Rakoczi and sought the support of the Wallachian boyars for war against the Porte. The boyars, however, were uncooperative. "Your Highness," they stated, "we are a small country... powerless and helpless. The Turks are strong, big and they can defeat the whole world."[37] Mihnea, nonetheless, continued his relations with Rakoczi and an alliance between the two was signed at Rucăr on October 4, 1659. The former voivodes Constantin Serban and Gheorghe Ştefan adhered to that treaty. Shortly thereafter, the allies sought to support Constantin Şerban efforts to become ruler of Moldavia.

Even before the meeting at Rucăr, Mihnea III as a worthy follower of Michael the Brave, first crushed the power of the boyars and tehn of the Turks in the country. He put to death the Turkish creditors and in the battle of Frăteşti and Călugăreni defeated the Ottoman troops. The *dorobantzi* groups, helped by Transylvanian detachments, seized Brăila and Giurgiu, moved into Moldavia and crossed the Danube to launch raids against Silistra, Rusciuc, Nicopolis and Hîrşova. Mihnea himself summarized his actions: "Many Christian princes who fought against the Ottomans did not do as many things as we did in such a short time." As a matter of fact the prince attained remarkable success but the Tatars and Ottomans attacked him from south and east, he was then compelled to flee to Transylvania.

At Turda, on December 18, 1659, aware of the help he could receive from the peasantry in his anti-Ottoman fight, Gheorghe Rakoczi II distributed leaflets whereby he promised exemption from tributes for one year to anyone who would come to his assistance. He also used emissaries who promised the serfs and free peasants they not only would receive liberty but even elevation to the ranks of the nobility if they were to side with him. About 600 outlaws, "gallant Romanians," led by the priest Gheorghe of Ciurila answered this call. The invasion of Transylvania by Tatar hordes and by a Turkish army thwarted other steps that might have been taken for the country's defense. The decisive battle, fatal for Gheorghe Rakoczi, took place on May 22, 1660 on the plain between Gilău and Florşti, during which the prince was killed.[38]

As a result of the lost battle, Transylvania could no longer resist Austrian expansion; the advisers of Transylvania's prince, Mihai Apaffy, signed a declaration dictated by the Austrian general, Caraffa, whereby "the protection" of Emperor Leopold was officially agreed to. In fact, by the Leopoldine Diploma of 1691 Transylvania was transformed into a province of the Habsburg Empire.[39]

In the last decades of the seventeenth century, Wallachia and Moldavia had to choose between an alliance with Poland, Austria or Russia to withstand the Ottoman pressure. Şerban Cantacuzino, Wallachia's ruling prince contacted Vienna as well as Poland's king, Jan Sobiecki, and sent a mission to Moscow. Although Şerban Contacuzino sympathized with the "Holy League" he was forced to participate in the seige of Vienna (1683) on the side of the Turks. He maintained secret relations with the besieged whom he provided with news about the Ottoman army and, following the Ottoman's defeat, Şerban initiated secret negotiations with a view toward removing the Ottoman yoke. Şerban, however, did not wish to replace Ottoman domination by Austrian domination he therefore established relations with Sobieski and with the Russian tsar. Belgrade's collapse in 1688 and the raid of the Austrian troops headed by General Veterani into Wallachia, however, compelled Şerban Cantacuzino to abandon these ingenious diplomatic maneuvers and to join the Austrian side.

After the sudden death of Şerban Contacuzino, Constantin Brîncoveanu was elected ruling prince in Wallachia at the very moment when a Wallachian delegation was on its way to Vienna to take an oath of loyalty to the Emperor and formally adhere to the "Holy League." In the main, Brîncoveanu agreed with the position of the delegation but he made implementation of the accord with the Habsburgs contingent upon securing substantial military aid because "the Tartar and the Turks are still in power."[40] Upset by Brîncoveanu's hesitation the emperor deployed his troops, headed by General Heisler, beyond the mountains in 1689. But the Austrians were chased back to Transylvania and defeated in the battle of

Zărneşti (August 21, 1690). This daring military operation revelaed Brîncoveanu's determination to defend the country's autonomy against both the Ottomans and the Austrians. During the ensuing years, the alert prince developed friendly relations with his enemies and/or allies both from the north and the south. His clever manipulations bore fruit. In 1695, Brîncoveanu was made "Prince of the Holy League" and secured concessions from the Porte as well.

In 1711, however, Constantin Brîncoveanu's position became vulnerable as a new war between the Ottomans and the Russians broke out. One of his principal advisers, Toma Cantacuzino crossed over with part of the Wallachian horsemen to the Russian side and helped them seize Brăila. In reply, the Turks seized Brîncoveanu and beheaded him and his family in Constantinople.

In Moldavia, after the defeat of the Ottoman army in front of Vienna, several boyars and the prince Stefan Petriceicu sought Sobieski's help for ridding the country of Turkish domination. Subsequently, Moldavia's Constantin Cantemir concluded a treaty with Austria, Poland's rival, at Sibiu, on February 15, 1690. Two decades later by the Treaty of Lusk, negociated by Dimitrie Cantemir and Peter the Great, Moldavia's autonomy was guaranteed within the frontiers established by Stephen the Great, but the provisions of that treaty could not be implemented as a result of the Ottoman victory over the Russians at Stanileşti (1711).

The struggle and the diplomacy in which Moldavia, Wallachia and Transylvania engaged over the years, served the fundamental imperiative of the sixteenth and seventeenth centuries, strengthening the union and defense of the state autonomy.

NOTES

1. *Tezaur de monumente istorice*, vol. III, p. 129.

2. P. Paruta, *Historia Vinetiana*, Veneţia, 1605, part I, pp. 681, 689.

3. O. Clemens, *Zum Turkenfeldzug des Kurfursten Joachim II. von Brandenburg*, in *Jahrbuch fur Brandenburgische Kirchengeschichte*, 1939, vol. 34, pp. 88-96.

4. F. Braudel, *La Mediterranee et le monde mediterraneen a l'epoque de Philippe II*, ed. a 2-a, Paris, 1966, vol. II, pp. 469, 428-429, 453-460.

5.   *Istoria României*, vol. II, p. 821.

6.   Sc. Callimachi, *Pagini despre Ion Vodă cel Cumplit scrise în secolul al XVI-lea de istoricul francez De la Popeliniere*, in "Studii-Revistă de istorie," 1952, an 5, no. 2, pp. 175-185.

7.   Al. Randa, *Pro republica christiana*, Munchen, 1964, pp. 62-63; an extensive bibliography concerning Michael the Brave is included in *Mihai Viteazul. Culegere de studii*, edited by P. Cernovodeanu, C. Rezachevici, Bucharest, 1975.

8.   Eudoxiu de Hurmuzaki, *Documente privitoare la istoria români-lor*, tom. III, supliment II, București, 1900, p. 532.

9.   Ibid., pp. 411-412; A. Veress, *Documente privitoare la istoria Ardealului, Moldovei și Țării Românesti*, vol. IV, București, 1931, pp. 247-248.

10.   A. Veress, op. cit., vol. V, p. 338.

11.   Tarih-i Selaniki Mustafa efendi, in *Cronici turești privind țările române*, vol. I, the 15th and the middle of the 16th centuries, by Mihail Guboglu and Mustafa Mehmed, Editura Academiei Republicii Socialiste România, București, 1966, p. 398.

12.   N. Iorga, *Scrisori de boieri. Scrisori de domni*, ediția a III-a, Văl-enii de Munte, 1932, p. 227.

13.   A. Veress, op. cit., vol. VI, p. 49.

14.   Ibid., pp. 76-77.

15.   *Documente privind istoria României. B. Țara Românească, vea-cul XVI*, vol. XI, Editura Academiei Republicii Populare Române, București, 1953, pp. 366, 372, 378.

16.   Ibid., pp. 370, 371, 373, 374 and 376.

17.   Ibid., p. 368.

18.   Ibid., *veacul XVII*, vol. II, p. 340.

19.   Eudoxiu de Hurmuzaki, op. cit., pp. 529-530.

20.   In the treaties concluded with the representatives of Wallachia on May 20, 1595 and Moldavia on June 3, 1596, Sigismund Bathory called himselfī *"Nos Sigismundus Dei gratia Regnorum Transilvaniae, Moldaviae, Valachiae, Transalpinae et Sacri Romani Imperii Princeps, Partium Regni Hungariae Dominus et Siculorum comes etc."* (Eudoxiu de Hurmuzaki, op. cit., pp. 309 and 477).

21.   N. Iorga, *Documente nouă în mare parte românesti relative la Petru Schiopul și Mihai Viteazul*, Bucharest, 1898, pp. 43-44.

22.   Ibid., p. 46.

23.   A. Veress, op. cit., vol. VI, p. 99.

24.   *Documenta Romaniae Historica, B. Ţara Românească*, vol. XI, Editura Academiei Republicii Socialiste Rom=nia, Bucharest, 1979, p. 529.

25.   Petre P. Panaitescu, *Documente privitoare la istoria lui Mihai Viteazul*, p. 120. About the rumors according to which Michael the Brave sought Poland's division or the Polish throne see *Predica iezuitului Petre Skarja despre înfrîngerea lui Mihai Viteazul* (Petre P. Panaitescu, op. cit., pp. 144-156).

26.   *Istoria României*, vol. II, Editura Academiei Republicii Populare Române, Bucharest, 1962, pp. 978-990.

27.   *Documente privind istoria României, B. Ţara Românească, veacul XVI*, vol. VI, p. 378.

28.   Ibid., p. 385.

29.   N. Iorga, op. cit., p. 49.

30.   Ibid.

31.   Ibid., p. 50.

32.   R. W. Seton-Watson, *Histoire des Roumains*, P. U. F., Paris, 1937, p. 78.

33.   *Monumente Comitialia Regni Transylvaniae*, vol. VIII, p. 165.

34.   C. Gollner, *La Milice Chretienne, un instrument de croisade au XVII siecle*, in *Melange de l'Ecole Roumaine en France*, vol. XIII, 1935-1936, Paris, pp. 59-118.

35.   *Istoria României*, vol. III, p. 166.

36.   C. Rezachevici, *Les relations politiques et militaires entre la Valachie et la Transylvanie au debut du XVIIe siecle*, in *Revue roumaine d'histoire*, an XI, nr. 5, 1972, pp. 761-772.

37.   *Istoria României*, vol. III, p. 190.

38.   M. Depner, *Das Furstentum Siebenburgen im Kampf gegen Habsburg*, Stuttgart, 1938.

39.   *Istoria României*, vol. III, p. 207.

40.   C. Giurescu, *Tratatul lui Constantin Cantemir cu austriecii*, in *Convorbiri literare*, t. XLIV, no. 2, Jassy, 1910, pp. 274-290.

ROMANIAN ARMED FORCES AND NATIONAL DEFENSE
IN THE EIGHTEENTH CENTURY

During the eighteenth century, Southeastern Europe was torn by numerous wars, brought about by the aspirations of the Great Powers to solve or benefit from the "Eastern Question." The great protagonists of the wars in Southeastern Europe during the eighteenth century were the Russian and the Habsburg Empires, after 1726 linked by an alliance with offensive goals, and the Ottoman Porte. The high frequency and growing length of the military clashes—1710-1711; 1716-1718; 1736-1739; 1768-1774; 1787-1792, carried out to a great extent on the territory of the Romanian Principalities, reveal the decisive impact of the "Eastern Question" had on the historical evolution of the Romanian people during the eighteenth century.

A overview of the issues shows that Romanian military participation in these conflicts was multilateral: engagement of heterogeneous forces alongside of the Moscow army in 1711 (Moldavia), cooperation with the Ottoman forces in 1737-1739 and 1787-1789 (Wallachia), anti-Ottoman insurrections, the little war 1716-1718 (Wallachia, Moldavia), 1769 (Wallachia), the actions of the volunteers coming from various social classes and categories 1736-1739 (Moldavia), 1769-1774 (Moldavia and Wallachia), 1788-1792 (Moldavia and Wallachia).

The Russian-Ottoman war of 1710-1711 is part of the second great northern conflict (1700-1721) unleashed by Tsar Peter I, Augustus II,

King of Poland, Great Elector of Saxony and Friedrich IV, King of Denmark, to divide the possessions of the Swedish Kingdom. The retreat of
Charles XII, King of Sweden, and of the remnants of his army defeated
at Poltava (June 27, 1709) in southeastern Moldavia, near the Tighina
(Bender) stronghold gave the Tsar and his councillors the opportunity to
embark upon a new offensive, an anti-Ottoman one this time, in the hope
of deriving advantages for the Russians from the Eastern Question. The
Russian command maps that had come into the hands of King Charles
XII, who was in Tighina, had shown as principal objectives of the Russian
policy the Crimea and Constantinople. The intensive Russian propaganda
in Southeastern Europe, founded on Orthodox solidarity, on the anti-
Ottoman liberating mission that Russia, the great co-religionary power of
the time, the would-be heir of Byzantium, was closely connnected to the
achievement of these plans. Taking into account this reality, a part of the
Romanian boyars favored an alliance with Russia. This policy was first
implemented during the negotiations with the Russian diplomats in Jawo-
row and Jaroslaw (Poland), by the plenipotentaries of some of the great
Moldavian boyars, and by those pf Prince Dimitrie Cantemir, (appointed
in Novembe 1710 by the Ottoman Porte). The diplomas of Peter I—the
most important one being issued in Luck on April 13/24, 1711, acknowledged the Principality of Moldavia with its old southern borders (the Lower Dniester and the Maritime Danube including also the Tighnia, Cetatea
Albă, Ismail strongholds, the Bugeac, which was annexed by the Ottomans during the last two centuries, the territory known as Bessarabia). In
turn, the Romanian Principality, being for the future in alliance with Russia, was to take part, with its army, in the campaign of the Russian troops
against the Ottoman Empire.

In accordance with the views of the Ottoman headquarters, the Romanian Principalities had to build up a floating bridge at Oblucitza to enable the Ottoman army to cross the Danube and secure its supplies. Dimitrie Cantemire, Prince of Moldavia, and Constantin Brîncoveanu, Prince of
Wallachia, mobilized part of their armies, a measure consented to by the
Grand Vizier and the Boyars' Council, concentrating the troops at the
Cetatzuia monastery near Jassy and at Albeshti near Urlatzi, respectively.

The Moldavian prince and his councillors informed the Russian headquarters about the military situation—the Islamic troops were believed to be
weak, amounting to about 95,000 soldiers, among which 30,000 Tatars—
and without underestimating the enemy they drew up a plan for preventing

the Ottomans from crossing the Danube through the rapid advancement of the Russian army to Oblucitza. On the Russian army's vanguard crossing the Dniester (May 27, 1711 [old style]) Dimitrie Cantemir's messenger informed Russian headquarters of the possibility of an iminent Tatar raid in Moldavia; he also pointed out the threats posed to the food supplies by a locusts' invasion which damaged the crops, the fear of considerable increase of the Ottoman troops not to mention the strength of the Turkish artillery. The Prince asked for a Russian detachment to defend the capital and his throne. Concimitantly with the arrival ofthe Russians (3,500 soldiers, of whom 500 were Romanians under Captain Postolachi Chigheciu) the Prince issued a manifesto calling for the taking up of arms by all able-bodied citizens against the Ottomans under the penalty of confiscation of their estates (June 11). The army of Moldavia of 10,000 soldiers (170 "banners" with captains and 17 colonels) would be battle fit with the support of funds provided by the Russian headquarters.

Because of Voltaire's classic work *Histoire de Charles XII* the old and new historiography of that war held to the opinion that the failure of Peter I's anti-Ottoman campaign was due to the bad advice and unfounded promises of Moldavia's prince. Actually, the strategy put forth by the Romanians originated in the experiences of the last campaigns waged against the Ottomans in Moldavia by Jan Sobieski, the king of Poland. The Russian headquarters, which initially had intended to assume the offensive along the Dniester and the Pruth, gave up the project because of the increase in Ottoman forces and, especially because the retreat of King Charles XII and of other Swedish, Polish, and Ukrainian refugees to Chilia. Hence, the plan of carrying on the offensive in the central-Moldavian direction of the river Pruth. However, compared with the Romanian strategic proposals, the new Russian plan did not take into account the principal provision of the former: rapid advancement toward the south to prevent the crossing of the Danube by the Ottomans. Instead of this march, the Russian troops, commanded by General B. P. Sheremetiev, remained near Jassy, the capital of Moldavia, until July 5, 1711, when Peter I, the delayed traveller through Poland arrived there.

Constantin Brîancoveanu, fully aware of the immediate danger of the Principalities becoming the theater of war, as the Ottoman army's concentration south of Oblucitza had been completed, made his participation in the anti-Ottoman war conditional on a rapid move designed to protect the

Danube or failing that, he offered himself as an intermediary in peace negotiations. The Russian headquarters rejected these proposals, and availing themselves of the betrayal of the Great Spathar of the Wallachian army, Toma Cantacuzino—who had run away from the camp of Albeshti to the Russian lines—decided on the displacement of a corps of 10,000 soldiers (Generals Ronne, Bawr, Toma Cantacuzino, Brigade Commander Kropotov) to conquer Brăila and provoke the general defection of the entire Wallachian army led by Prince Constantin Brîncoveanu in order to use it in the anti-Ottoman war.[1] The Grand Hetman of the Moldavian army, Ioan Neculce, unsuccessfully opposed the troops' dispersal.[2]

On July 9, 1711, the Ottoman forces (about 119,000 military, half of them being first-line combatants) led by the Great Vizier Baltagi-Mehmet Pasha crossed the Danube, the event being immediately announced in Jassy through Romanian messengers. The Russian headquarters, after a short period of confusion, favored a plan whereby the Russian forces would march down the Sereth Valley, nearer to Transylvania. The project left the eastern territories of Moldavia between the rivers Pruth and Dniester prey to Ottoman and Tatar invasions.

On July 11, 1711, Peter I decided to begin the march of his army (about 80,000 military, out of whom 54,000 combatants, the rest being merchants, coachmen, servants and women)[3] together with a Romanian expeditionary corps (about 6,000 soldiers) from the Moldavian army, under Dimitrie Cantemir and Ion Neculce's command, to the south. Two hundred twenty kilometers separated the two belligerents: the allied Russo-Romanian camp was set at Gura Jijiei, the Ottoman-Tatar one at Cartal. The strategic solving of the all-out campaign depended on the occupation of the Falciu ford, which allowed the control of both sides of the Pruth. The Russian vanguard (7,000 soldiers; General Janusch), although led by a Romanian detachment (500 men) sent by Dimitrie Cantemir, marched only 100 kilometers until July 18, being 25 kilometers north of the ford when it was confronted by the Ottoman troops. They had started from Cartal, covering 120 kilometers to the ford, and had already begun to cross the river on three bridges then built. A Tatar corps continued to move on to the north on the eastern bank of the river very soon leaving behind the line of the Russian army.

Under the circumstances, a Romanian messanger called the vanguard back at Gura Saratzii where the bulk of the army was set up. The movement was blocked by the Ottoman cavalry, which encircled General

Janusch's Corps (July 19). Prince Dimitrie Cantemir stepped in with 20 "banners" of the Moldavian army and attacked the Ottomans on the way between Gura Saratzii and Stănilești, right near the Vlădichii marsh, thus making possible the retreat of the Russian vanguard. He was the last to leave the battlefield after a three hours' fight. In the evening of July 19, the corps led by Generals Sheremetiev and Janusch and the Romanian prince retreated to Casele Banului, while the Russian rearguard (15,000 soldiers, General Reptain) was four kilometers north of Stanileshti, encircled by the Ottoman-Tatar troops. This difficult situation determined Peter I to ask confidentially the opinion of the Romanian Grand Hetman, Ioan Neculce, on his plan to flee together with his wife to Transylvania, escorted only by 300 Russian and Romanian soldiers; the army was to be led by General Sheremetiev and Prince Demetrie Cantemir. The high Romanian dignitary pointed out the insecurity of the roads controlled by the Tatars and refused to assume the responsibility for executing the Russian sovereign's plan. On July 20, 1711, the Sheremetiev-Janusch–Dimitrie Cantemir corps retreated, being nevertheless on a war footing and defended during their halts by *chevaux-de-frise*, till Stanileshti, where they formed the rearguard. Here, in a bend of the river, the allied camp was immediately encircled by the Ottoman-Tatar army. The terrain which had permitted the Janissaries' advancement to the neighborhood of the allied lines was cleared of the enemy through the intervention of the Moldavian army, including the abovementioned surrounding terrain in the Russo-Romanian camp.

Since the evening of July 20, 1711, Peter I ordered General Sheremetiev to write to the Ottoman headquarters about the Russians' readiness to enter peace negotiations; the proposal, however, was not accepted by the Grand Vizier. Confronted with the heavy bombardments of about 4,700 artillery pieces of various calibers, started by the Ottoman side, Dimitrie Cantemir suggested to the Russian headquarters a general attack by all available forces designed to conquer the positions of the Ottoman artillery. In this case the Romanian prince had in mind the battle of Zenta (1697), where the success of this type of maneuver was decisive in the Ottomans' defeat. Peter I, however, rejected the proposal considering that it was impossible to displace the enemy cavalry corps.

The Romanian prince's plan was nevertheless adopted on July 21 on General Wittman's insistence, who assumed responsibility for the attack. The Romanian troops and the Cossack detachments were set in the second defensive line of the camp, while the Russian infantry was in the first line of attack. The attack was arrested by the Ottomans after General Wittman's and General Bolkonski's deaths. A shocked Peter I left the command to General Sheremetiev, ordering him to set on fire almost all the luggage and to start the last general attack the next day. The Russian sovereign told his staffs: "I am at least in the same bad situation as my brother Charles (XII of Sweden) was at Poltava."[4]

However, the next day (July 22, 1711), at dawn, the Grand Vizier delivered an ultimatum to the Russian command which was accepted: the ensuing peace negotiations were concluded by noon the same day. The treaty comprised no provision regarding the Romanian Principalities, the Russians being satisfied with obtaining free passage for their army. The conquest of Brăila (July 25) by the army corps led by Generals Ronne and Toma Cantacuzino could no longer affect the general result of the campaign.

The allied troops, escorted by the Ottomans and Tatars and supplied on the Grand Vizier's orders, began to retreat toward the north, along the Pruth. Several times detachments of the Moldavian army, avoiding the escort, had to fight against the Tatars, who plundered and robbed the country, to the chagrin of the Russian command: "Then Sheremet(iev) ordered the Moldavians to let the Tatars be, and no longer fight against them as they had concluded peace and he would not support them; any one fighting the Tatars would be in for it. The Moldavians began to shout and curse him, how could it be that they were not to go on and fight, as they see their parents and women and sons enslaved by the Tatars, and even Sheremet(iev) heard them cursing with his own ears. And he told them that they should ignore the Tatars, as the Emperor would free them (Peter—o.n.) and given them estates in Moscow. Wasn't he ashamed to say what was not becoming, such a great man as he was."[5]

During the night of July 23-24, the Moldavian army corps left the Russain camp and, led by Dimitrie Cantemire, moved toward Jassy. At Movila Răbîiei it attacked the Tatar troops which were escorting convoys of slaves. The Moldavians dispersed the troops and freed the prisoners. After a short stay in Jassy (July 25-27), Dimitrie Cantemir disbanded his army while he, followed by several loyal subjects, took refuge in Poland with the Russian army.

Through negotiations conducted by the great boyars, by former Prince Nicholas Mavrocordat (1709-1710) and by his brother, Great Dragoman John, Moldavia regained her former international status and her relations with the Ottoman Porte. A few years later the stronghold and county of Hotin became an Ottoman pashalik as a safety measure taken by the Porte which was confronted with a new state of affairs in the Russian-dominated Polish Kingdom, following the loss of Camenitza and Podolia.

Only five years had elapsed since the Peace of Pruth and the Romanian Principalities became the theater of a new war between the Habsburg Empire and the Ottoman Porte. In April 1716, having concluded a defensive alliance with Venice—engaged in war with the Porte—the Court in Vienna intervened in the conflict. Both empires planned to derive advantages from an offensive on the Sava-Danube frontier stretching from Croatia to the Timish Banat. According to the belligerents' plans, the Romanian Principalities were to play but a minor part, corresponding to the strategic-logistical possibilities of the epoch, as the exclusion of their territory from the conflict was considered more useful. The Porte expected the Romanian princes, Michael Racoviță in Moldavia and Nicholas Mavrocordat in Wallachia, to pursue the same cautious policy as that of Constantin Brîncoveanu during the war of the Holy League (1684-1699). Nevertheless, it recommended a military build-up on the frontiers so that 3,000 men belonging to the Wallachian army were placed as an observation detachment at the Iron Gates. In a report submitted to the Count of Stainville, the Military Governor of Transylvania, Baron Tige, the Imperial Commander of the Brașov stronghold, had to admit that the same security measures were also taken against the possible encroachment on the territory of Wallachia by undisciplined Ottoman and Tatar troops (May 1716).[6]

What followed seems a sequel to the events which occurred in Wallachia during the war of the Holy League, during Șerban Cantacuzino's reign (1678-1688). This time, however, the Romanian military and diplomatic preparations were less developed. A part of the country's boyars, led by the Metropolitan Anthim of Iviria, encouraged by the entry of isolated imperial detachments—"the German soldiers"—into Mehedintzi,

Gorj and Dimbovitza, following the Ottoman defeat at Petrovaradin
(August 5, 1716) sought Habsburg suzerainty over the Principality. In
turn, Nicholas Mavrocordat (December 25, 1715-November 4, 1716) using
the Romanian troops at his disposal—forces commanded by Radu Popescu,
the Minister of the Interior, and a well-known chronicler (d. 1729)—managed to defeat the Tatars and recover the spoils secured by the Tatars
after the fall of the Timishoara stronghold (October 12, 1716). However,
on November 14, 1716 an imperial detachment (Captain Stephan Dettine
alias Pivoda) guided by the boyars, came from Oltenia and in agreement
with part of the Princely Council (High Spatharus Radu Golescu, Great
Chancellor Grigore Baleanu) and with the support of the guards, invaded
the princely court in Bucharest. Prince Mavrocordat was arrested and as
a "prisoner-of-war" was taken in confinement to Sibiu. The inadequate
contingent of imperial troops retreated to the hilly area of the country
having robbed the capital. They took shelter in fortified monasteries
such as Margineni (Prahova county) wherefrom they continued to fight
against the Ottoman-Tatar forces along the Danube. Meanwhile, by the setting up of a town guard militia in Bucharest, order was restored.[7] The boyars,
who had also retreated to the hilly area, tried to restore order elsewhere to
pursue the fulfillment of the provisions of the old agreements between Prince
Şerban Cantacuzino and the government of Emperor Leopold I of Habsburg (1688) by offering, in the name of the estates, the crown of Wallachia to the son of the former, George Cantacuzino. At the same time,
the Romanian boyars suggested to the Imperial Court a far-reaching plan
of military action designed to ensure the new status of the Romanian
Principality under Habsburg suzerainty. The plan was based on the postu-
late of the strategic unity of Wallachia and Transylvania, and the securing
of the border along the Danube through conquest of the Ottoman bridgeheads of Brăila, Giurgiu, Turnu (Măgurele) by Romanian and imperial
forces (5,000 German soldiers, 7,000 Hussars). Vienna answered only
with encouragements and vague promises.

The first reaction of the Ottoman Porte to the changes in Wallachia was
to order its troops on the Danube to overrun the Romanian Principality.
The resourceful Grand-Dragoman John Mavrocordat, who found the way
out from a similar situation in Moldavia in 1711, assumed the responsibility of restoring the prince's authority in Wallachia, and was invested by
the Porte (November 21, 1716). The Habsburgs' inability to secure the

defense of the Principality determined the people to rally to the new rule, which proved to be a genuine restoration of the former regime of Constantine Brîncoveanu.[9]

As new prince, John Mavrocordat, immediately undertook peace negotiations with the Military Command in Transylvania (General Stainville). On February 8, 1717 the Convention of non-aggression and good vecinity was concluded in Sibiu, whereby peace and commercial ties between Transylvania and Wallachia were established. A retreat line of the imperial garrisons was set-up (Cîmpulung, Rîmnicu-Vîlcea, Cozia-Tismana, and the rest of Oltenia), and a similar one, on the Danube, for the Ottoman ones. In a letter to Eugene of Savoy, Mavrocordat considered the uncommon state of affairs in his country. Inasmuch as it lacked strongholds, Wallachia, he stated, could not serve as a military basis for the imperial forces.

The day following the suppression of the Ottoman resistance at Belgrade, (September 18, 1717), part of the Tatar auxiliary troops of the Porte returned through Wallachia, plundering and robbing. Joined by a Turkish pasha who was then in Bucharest, Prince John Mavrocordat faced them at the bridge over the Mostiste, at Cornătel (today Mănăstirea, Călărași county) and rescued about 1700 captives.[10] In the aforementioned letter to Eugene of Savoy, Prince John Mavrocordat clearly stated his position: "I took care of this country, spared and saved it against all those who tried to tear it up cruelly, and from now on I shall also do it, so help me God."

In Moldavia, the actions of the imperial troops had an altogether different course. In this Romanian Principality too, part of the boyars and the petty-boyars, particularly those inhabiting the mountain area between the Carpathians and the Sireth, dissatisfied with Michael Racovită's rule (1715-1726) who had surrounded himself by favorites and relatives, attempted to adopt a similar course of action as that in Wallachia. Detachments led by Vasile Ceaurul, Gheorghe Velicico, alongside of few imperial troops (commanded by Captain Francois Ernaut) took over control west of the Sireth, setting up bases and supplies stores at the Neamț stronghold, at the fortified monasteries Cașin (Bacău) and Mira (Vrancea). The rebels and Captain Ernaut's attempt to seize Prince Racovită during an unexpected expedition directed against the princely court of Jassy (over January 9-12, 1717) failed. Benefitting by the support of five or six thousand Tatars, "banners" of the Romanian prince repulsed the attack and later destroyed the military bases at Neamţ (January, 1717), and at the Caşin and Mira monasteries (May, 1717). The victories scored in Moldavia gave the Porte the opportunity to seek achievement of the plan to restore its suzerainty over Transylvania and recustate Francis Rakoczi II as ruler. The Tatar troops and the Moldavian army led by Prince M. Racovitză were to force the passes in the Eastern Carpathians, opening the way to the Rakoczian restoration. The expeditionary force crossed the mountains by surprise on unguarded paths, and assumed the offensive in the north-eastern part of the Transylvanian Plain, cutting off the logistic lines of the Bistritza stronghold and beseiging it (August-September 1717). The Ottoman defeat at Belgrade forced the retreat as the prince of Moldavia being concerned over the Tatars' reactions.[11] In fact, many Tatars went on a rampage against the Romanian population their incursion through the area of Chioar and Maramuresh. On their return from Maramuresh, however, the Romanian local forces blocked the Tatars access to the Prislop pass and crushed them.

The peace treaty of Passarowitz (July 21, 1718), concluding the war, was based on the principle *uti possidetis*, which led to the annexation by the Holy Roman-German Empire, of Oltenia, a territory of about 27,000 square kilometers wrested from Wallachia.

After less than two decades of peace, elapsing from the war of 1716-1718 to the new Russian-Austrian Ottoman conflict unleashed in 1735/ 1737, the Romanian Principalities of Moldavia and Wallachia were once again engaged in a military operation to reestablish order in the Bugeac, where the Tatars, had rebelled (1727). The headquarters of the invasions, was temporarily annihilated by the concentric military pressure exerted by the expeditionary forces of Moldavia (3,000 infantrymen, 4,000 cavalry men, and 12 guns) those of Wallachia, led by the princes Grigore Matei Ghica (1726-1733) and Nicholas Alexander Mavrocordat (1719-1730), and those of the Ottoman ones (winter 1728-1729).

The evolution of the Russian-Austrian-Ottoman war of 1735-1739 on Romanian territory was altogether different. Connected through the anti-Ottoman offensive treaty (1726), the two great empires undertook for the first time a joint political-military operation on the Danubian front. The occupation of Moldavia and Wallachia was agreed upon by both the Russian Fieldmarshal Cristof Burckhardt Munich, and by the Court War Council in Vienna.

In turn, the Prince of Moldavia, Gheorghe Ghica (1735-1741) and his brother, the Great Dragoman of the Porte, Alexander Matei Ghica, both participants in the military councils and negotiations of the Ottoman Empire in the area of military actions, worked for a political settlement of the conflict, or in any case, for the transfer of troops to the battlefield on the east of the Dniester. Fractions of the Romanian boyars, entertaining relations with the Cantemir family which had taken refuge in Russia, considered the possibility of Moldavia and Wallachia breaking relations with the Ottoman Porte. Should a contemplated agreement with the Russian Empire be reached, Oltenia was to be recovered from the Austrians, and the unification of Wallachia would thus be achieved.

During 1737-1738, the Romanian Principalities were confronted only with the imperial offensive along the border from the Olt and the Carpathians, as the Russian government refused to cooperate with Vienna. On July 1/12, 1737, isolated imperial detachments crossed the frontier trying to establish military bases in the hilly area, in the fortified monasteries in the Principalities. Urged by General and Count of Bonneval, the Grand Vizier decided to send troops (3,000-5,000 soldiers) to support the Romanian princes in the face of the imperial military pressure. The army of Wallachia (comprising about 10,000 men) backed by the Ottoman troops cleared the territory of Wallachia of Habsburg forces (October, 1737). After negotiations with the Porte, against the background of the Austrian successes on the Danube, the Prince of Wallachia, Constantin Nicholas Mavrocordat (1735-1741) and the princely council appealed to the Romanian estates of Oltenia to reunite with the Principality (October 28-30, 1737).[12] At that time the imperial military administration in Oltenia was rapidly disintegrating, the population seeking refuge in the hilly and wooded areas, while Turkish and Tatar bands plundered the left bank of the Danube unhindered. Under the circumstances, on November 7/18, 1737 the princely Romanian army under Grand Spathar John Mavrocordat) supported by Ottoman troops moved toward Oltenia: around Rimnicu Vilcea, the resistance of the last imperial effectives (about 10,000 soldiers, led by Major Baron Hagenback) was overcome. On November 13/24, in the name of the population of Oltenia, Archbishop Clement of Rimnic officially accepted Prince Constantin Mavrocordat as ruler, an act marking the reunification of Wallachia. In spite of Seraskier Pasha of Vidin's involvement and of anarchy brought about by his troops, the

Romanian prince set up his administration of the country west of the Olt, under the leadership of the Grand Ban and Caimacan Matei Bălăcescu (December, 1737).

It was almost simultaneously (September) that the Austrian military presence in Moldavia was annihilated, too: a Romanian army corps under the command of Grand Spather Teodor Paladi and of the Grand Hetman Constantin Psiolu (Ypsilanti), of about 2,000 people, eliminated the last imperial resistance (vice-Colonel Countr Orsetti) on the Uz valley (Bacău).

In the summer of 1739 the Principalities were again confronted with numerous military operations, concurrently with the offensive of the army of Fieldmarshal Munich through Poland toward Moldavia.

After defeating the main Ottoman forces at Stăuceni (Hotin) on August 28, 1739, the Russian army using a detachment of about 1,000 Romanian volunteers, led by Colonel Constantin Antioh Cantemir, occupied upper Moldavia. Prince Grigore Ghica, surrounded by an exclusively Romanian Princely Council retreated to lower Moldavia (Galatzi). However, the Russian victory in Moldavia had no consequences, due to the concluding of the Peace of Belgrade (September 18, 1739), an event which marked the last successful undertaking of French diplomacy of the old regime in Near Eastern affairs. The peace reestablished, with minor modifications, the northern Pontic Ottoman-Russian frontiers.

At the news of the conclusion of the peace, Fieldmarshal Munich, the Russian Commander, ordered an offensive raid toward Bucharest with an army corps (about 10,000 soldiers under Generals Kapnitza and Frolov) guided by the Brigade Commander C. Cantemir and Major Dumitraşcu and A. Cantemir with their volunteers and recruits. After a clash around Focshani with the troops of the Moldavian prince, the Russian corps was divided up: part of it plundered the Vrancea region and returned; over a half of it (General Frolov, Colonel Stoian, Major Cantemir) moved on Buzău. Upon the violation of the territory of Wallachia, Prince Constantin Mavrocordat and the Princely Council organized the defense of Bucharest, enlarging the army with new militia troops recruited from all strata and hastily trained according to western methods.[13] After the plunder of Buzău, Frolov's army corps, fearing a Romanian counterattack from Wallachia combined with an Ottoman one from Brăila, sought refuge in Transylvania through the Buzău pass.

The Peace of Belgrade sanctioned the reunion of Oltenia in the Wallachian Principality. Concomitantly, after the retreat of Munich's army from

Moldavia, the Porte consented to the return and the reunion, albeit temporary, of the Hotin area and stronghold to the Principality of Moldavia.

During the second half of the eighteenth century, the Russian Empire, led by the most important political leader after Peter I, Catherine II, sought a rapid military solution to the Eastern Question. The neutralization of the French influence, after the alliance concluded by the Versailles government with the Holy Roman-German Empire (1756) seemed to greatly facilitate the realization of Russian plans against a greatly weakened Ottoman Empire.

The Romanian military factor was present in both Russian-Ottoman wars, 1768-1774 and 1787-1792, the latter with the participation of the Habsburg Empire.

Favored by the entrance of Russian troops into Moldavia, on November 1769, the members of the Princely Council led by the Grand Spatharus Pîrvu Cantacuzino and in agreement with Prince Grigore Alexander Ghica (October 1768-November 1769) organized an insurrection designed to liquidate the Ottoman military presence in Wallachia. Supported by a detachment of Romanian volunteers (700 men, Colonel Ilie Lăpușneanu), called from Moldavia, the princely troops led by the Grand Spathar and the population of Bucharest crushed the resistance of the Ottoman forces (about 5,000 fighters) and drove them from the capital (November 16-17, 1769). Immediately afterwards, under the leadership of a military council dominated by Pîrvu Cantacuzino, the recruitment in the counties and the setting up of an armed force was initiated which defended Wallachia against the Ottomans for forty days, until the arrival of the first Russian troops.

The Grand Spatharus Pîrvu Cantacuzino fell at the head of a detachment in the battle of Grădiștea (December 11, 1769), on his way to the Comana monastery, where the imprudently advancing Russian vanguard (Colonel Karazin) had been isolated and encircled by the Ottomans.

In the subsequent fights against the Ottomans on the Romanian territories the volunteers enlisted in both principalities and even in Transylvania distinguished themselves. On the occasion of the siege of Silistra (June 1773), the regiment of Romanian Hussars, led by Colonel Răducanu Cantacuzino, distinguished itself through spreading the Russian flank (General Kakavinski) and seizing an Ottoman battery of twelve guns.

Actually, during the campaign of 1773 the Romanian regiment was twice cited in orders of the day by the Russian commander-in-chief, Marshal Rumiantzev.

The Russian victories in the anti-Ottoman war worsened the relations between the Petersburg government and the imperials, opening the prospect of a general European conflagration. Given the circumstances, the Russian and the Prussian courts resorted to a formula which vitiated the traditional system of balance of power through alliances, in favor of one calling for mutually equivalent annexations (1769-1772). The system of compensatory partitions, whose first victim was Poland (1772, 1793, 1795), established "intimate" relations between the Russian and the Austrian courts; it affected the relations of the Romanian Principalities with the Ottoman Porte, relations subsequently specified by *hatti-sherifs* of the Sultan.

After a short period of armed peace, marked by the annexation by Russia of the Tatar Khanate of Crimea, formerly an independent state (1774-1783), a new Russian-Austrian-Ottoman war broke out (August 1787). In Moldavia the outbreak of the conflict occasioned the reoccurance of the events of 1769. During November 23-25, 1787, under the leadership of the Metropolitan Leon Gheuca the population of Jassy, at the sound of bells tolling, took up arms and chased away the undisciplined and troublesome Ottoman troops. According to the Prussian General Consul Konig "upon hearing the bells toll the Moldavians are able to defeat 60,000 Turks."[14] The Porte was thus forced to transfer its troops to the Polish-Russian frontier without allowing them to be stationed in Moldavia. Subsequently, by agreement between Prince Alexander Ypsilanti (1786-1788) and the Princely Council, a detachment of the Romanian army (Răducanu Rosetti) allowed the Habsburg troops to move onto the capital. Together with the Princely Guard, the Habsburg forces repulsed the Ottoman troops (April 19, 1788). However, in Wallachia, Prince Nicolae Mavrogheni (1786-1790) who had reorganized an army of about 11,000 fighters[15] decided despite the opinion of several boyars, to prevent the occupation of the province by the allies. The active defense of the passes in the Carpathians was crowned by several incursions into the Sibiu and Brașov area (July-August 1788) a fact which brought about, according to the report of the English ambassador at the Porte, Sir Robert Ainslie, "a spirit of disaffection appears among the lower classes of people in Transylvania, some of whom have voluntarily joined the Prince of Wallachia."[16] Encouraged by these successes and by the fact that the prince had succeeded in controlling southern Moldavia, the Porte appointed Nicholas Mavrogheni as Prince of that Romanian principality as well (March 1789). Only the victory of the Turks at Plăineşti Mărtineşti (Rîmnicu Sărat) by the allied troops led by General Suvorov and the Prince of Saxa-Coburg (September 1789)—a battle during which only Nicholas Mavrogheni's expeditionary corps managed to retreat with its cannons—was to pave the way for the Habsburg occupation of Wallachia (November 1789).

The outbreak of the French Revolution and a new partition of Poland led to the conclusion of the war through the treaties of Sistov and Jassy. The treaties had no notable consequences over the statutes of the Romanian Principalities.

To the uninitiated, a close look at the eighteenth century Romanian military establishment may reveal many disparities. In fact, however, confronted with wars among the "superpowers" of the time, the Romanian political and military decision-makers promoted a policy of emancipation, in an attempt to prevent the Principalities from becoming theaters of conflict. Throughout the century of hard wars, the rulers of the Romanian Principalities prevented the disappearance from the map of Europe Moldavia and Wallachia. In the development of their relations with the Ottoman Porte, the Principalities never lost the right to keep their own military forces and to defend their frontiers. An act sent to the Sultan explicitly stipulated this for the Romanian principality between the Dniester and the Carpathians: "the defense of the abovementioned land is incumbent on the princes of Moldavia and it is not necessary to name and use soldiers from the Porte for its defense."[17] During the last decades of the eighteenth century the "Treaties of Geography and Statistics," of priest Hugas Ingigian, recorded in each of the Romanian Principalities armed forces numbering 6,000 infantrymen and cavalrymen plus the Princely Guards.

The impossibility of finding a formula accpetable to all the European Great Powers involved in the Eastern Question, as well as the logistics characteristic of the Southeastern European theater of war, prevented the solving of the problem of succession of the Ottoman Empire in the eighteenth century along the lines sought by the governments in Vienna or in St. Petersburg. This allowed the Romanian decision-makers, through their realistic utilization of the military forces at their disposal, to defend, and preserve the existence of the Principalities of Moldavia and Wallachia.

NOTES

1.   Ion Neculce, *Letopisețul Țării Moldovei*, (The Chronicle of the Land of Moldavia), Iorgu Iordan edition, Bucharest, 1975, p. 197.
2.   Ibid., p. 204.
3.   Nicolae Costin, *Opere* (Works), vol. I, Jassy, 1976, p. 334.
4.   Voltaire, *Histoire de Charles XII*, ed. A. Waddington, Paris, 1890, p. 183.
5.   Ion Neculce, op. cit., p. 221.
6.   C. Giurescu, *Oltenia sub austriaci, Documente* (The Oltenia under the Austrians. Documents), vol. I, Bucharest, 1909, p. 13.
7.   Mitrofan Gregoras, *Cronica*, (Chronicle), in D. Russo, *Studii istorice greco-române* (Greek-Romanian Historical Studies), vol. II, Bucharest, 1939, p. 446.
8.   Banul Mihai Cantacuzino, *Genealogia Cantacuzinilor* (The Genealogy of the Cantacuzino Family), N. Iorga edition, Bucharest, 1902, pp. 214-249.
9.   N. Iorga, *Istoria românilor* (The History of the Romanians), vol. VII, Bucharest, 1938, p. 38.
10.   Hurmuzaki, VII, pp. 190-191.
11.   Nocolae Chiparissa, *Cronica* (Chronicle), in *Cronicarii greci cari au scris despre români* (Greek Chroniclers Writing About the Romanians), Constantin Erbiceanu edition, Bucharest, 1888, p. 82.
12.   N. Iorga, *Studii și documente* (Studies and Documents), XVI, pp. 3-6; C. Giurescu, *Material pentru istoria Olteniei supt austriaci* (Documents Concerning the History of Oltenia under the Austrians), vol. III, Bucharest, 1944, pp. 282-285.
13.   Constantin Dapontes, *Ephemerides daces*, ed. E. Legrand, vol. II, Paris, 1888, pp. 176-177.
14.   Hurmuzaki, X, p. 35; Hurmuzaki, Supliment I/II, p. 49.
15.   Florin Constantiniu, *Premisele formării armatei române moderne (secolul XVIII-începutul secolului XIX)* (The Premises of the Making of the Romanian Modern Army [18th-early 19th centuries]), in "File din istoria militară a poporului român," 7, 1980, p. 15.

16. The Library of the Romanian Academy, Msse, English documents, I, f. 46.

17. *Documente turceşti privind ţările române* (Turkish Documents Concerning the Romanian Principalities), vol. I, 1455-1774, edited by Mustafa A. Mehmed, Bucureşti, 1976, p. 210.

Mihail E. Ionescu and Ioan Talpeş

MILITARY FACTORS IN THE DEVELOPMENT OF ROMANIAN NATIONAL CONSCIOUSNESS IN THE EIGHTEENTH AND NINETEENTH CENTURIES

During the eighteenth and nineteenth centuries Southeastern Europe was swayed by fierce military vying to inherit an empire—the Ottoman— in decline. The main protagonists of the affair were the Tsarist and the Habsburg empires, their "march" toward the Mediterranean Sea being aimed at taking possession of the Balkan territories, ruled by the Ottomans. Throughout more than sixteen decades—from the Russian-Romanian-Ottoman conflict of 1711 to the Russian-Romanian-Turkish War of 1877-1878—the "Eastern Question" implied over thirty years of wars, the majority being waged on the old Dacian territory. Entailing extensive deployment of military forces—Russian, Ottoman, Austrian—the conflicts had devastating consequences for the entire socioeconomic and political life in the three Romanian principalities.

However, the so-called "Eastern Question"—although exerting a powerful influence on the continental balance of power—was not only a confrontation between the great powers for assuming domination over vast southeastern European territories. A component of a differenty type, which would ever more distinctly and successfully claim its pre-eminence, was also included. The emergence and then the rapid development of the oppressed peoples' national movements on the territories in litigation became an autonomous factor in the two-centuries old development of the Eastern crisis, as they succeeded in compelling their recognition as legitimate "successors" of a rule that had been justified by nothing.

The concomitent expansions toward the Dacian territories of both Russia (1711) and the Habsburg Empire (which annexed Transylvania in 1699) meant *de facto* that the Romanian territory became involved in the "Eastern Question."[1] Almost at the same time we record the assertion of the autochthonous factor—propelled by the emergence, development and strengthening of the national consciousness—claiming ever more forcefully its natural right to assume the responsibility in the area of its own interests. This demand was the outcome of a laborious, long-lasting and multifarious process, objectively brought about by economic transformations and mainly by the obvious disintegration of the feudal order and the simultaneous emergence and development of capitalist relations and their social concomitants, the bourgeoisie and the proletariat.

Which were the "levers" for the assertion of the Romanian factor in the Eastern Question as a whole? The answer to this question must take into account the far-reaching issue of the development of national consciousness, and the ascertaining of the reasons thereof. From among the impelling stimuli of the national consciousness we should point out the vast cultural activity—initiated by great seventeenth century chroniclers which was continued, at a level of outstanding learning, by Dimitrie Cantemir and taken over by the first generation of *Şcoala ardeleană* (The Transylvanian School)—and the political-ideological factor—on the basis of which unity and independence of Romania was claimed—both being firmly substantiated by the structural transformations which occurred within the Romanian society. The collective consciousness of the Romanian people was imbued with the idea of its unity as a people, the peasant masses in the three Romanian Principalities being the true nurturers of the deep awareness of the common origin, language and territory. In our area of interest particular attention should be given to institutions as stimuli in the development of the national consciousness. In the absence of vigorous capitalist means of production on the Romanian territory, an important role in promoting the renovating efforts was incumbent on the above-mentioned institutions. In the absence of a strong bourgeoise, its role in impelling the national consciousness was and had to be strengthened through the activity of the existing institutions, among which the school, the church and the army played their part.

In both Wallachia and Moldavia the ruler was the initiator of designs and plans, which once carried through, would contribute to the acceleration of the development of the capitalist production relations and the assertion of the autonomy of the Romanian principalities; due to its conservative nature, the church would become a reliable factor in arresting either the Tsarist or Habsburg denationalization attempts; the school would educate generations of youths to take pride in belonging to a distinct people having a glorious past. The apparatus in the service of these institutions—the administrative-fiscal one, in the case of the ruler, the clerical one, in the case of the church and the didactic one, as regards the school—achieved its thorough affiliation to a distinct national community to its highest interests.

Among the institutions stimulating the national consciousness the army, through its actions in keeping with the highest interests of the Romanian collectivity, the cadres it provided for the national liberation movement and extensively disseminating in the ranks of the people's masses the self-awareness of being Romanians has an outstanding importance.

The army—and by extension of the sense, the military factor—played a characteristic part in the national shaping of the Romanian society. The Romanian military factor with its specific characteristics, harmoniously integrated in the unanimous strife of the Romanian nation to attain unity and independence. Given the great powers' vying for the Romanian territory, it acquired an altogether outstanding value, becoming the instrument for achieving the vital national desiderata.

The development of the Romanian armed forces during the eighteenth-nineteenth centuries can be historiographically categorized in the triad: the Romanian army during the pre-revolutionary period; the army of the revolutions of 1821 and 1848-49; the army of the Union and of the war for attaining Romania's complete independence. This division, entailed by both the structure of the military body as such and the goals of the Romanian national struggle, has precise chronological limits. The evolution of the armed forces during this historical period can be fully grasped only in close connection with the progress of the national liberation movement, as both of them blended making up an original dialectical unity.

The Romanian Army During The Pre-Revolutionary Period

The eighteenth century witnessed a last great show of the masss rising of the entire people in defense of the homeland—the characteristic feature of the Romanian military effort throughout the Middle Ages—on the eve of the establishment of the Phanariote regime. The chronicler Ion Neculce pointed out the wide popular support that the fight of Dimitrie Cantemir, the Prince of Moldavia, against the Ottoman Empire enjoyed in 1711: "Therefore, the boyars had already started coming from treck to join the army. Very few were those who did not come. . . . Likewise, the hirelings, if they heard of it, directly came from everywhere to enlist under the colors. . . and not only the hirelings did come, but also the shoemakers, tailors, furriers and tavern-keepers. The boyars' servants left their masters to join the army."[3]

The failure of Cantemir's attempt to win Moldavia's full independence and voivode Constantin Brîncoveanu's, Prince of Wallachia, tragic end, also as a result of his attempt to regain the independence, meant the establishment of the Phanariote regime in the Romanian Principalities.

As regards the national military force, the Phanariote regime deliberately promoted a policy of cutting down the military forces. In this respect, it pursued a predatory fiscal policy, designed to incorporate the social categories traditionally considered to be the military reserve into the mass of taxpayers.[4] In describing the Moldavian army of 1759, Nicolae Iorga, relying on the account of a Polish chronicler contemporary with the events, relates the outcome of that policy: "one hundred Russians with the captain of *darabani*, one hundred *seimeni* led by *bas-ceauşul*, one hundred of *ulani* led by *baş-bulucbaşa*, one hundred *chasseurs* with their captain, one hundred gunners, one hundred *arnauts*. With flags in their hands, and Aga as chief, two hundred town guards soldiers, with two captains beside the militia proper (terms denoting various military categories).[5] However, despite the hardening of the Porte's policies, in keeping with the fiercer vying among the Ottoman, Tsarist and Habsburg empires for the Dacian area, we record the maintenance of some autochthonous military establishments, which, taken as a whole, reveal the existence of an embryonic military body. Unfortunately, it became an instrument for maintaining internal order and public security exclusively, as the external security was incumbent, according to Constantinople, on the Ottoman army.[6] From among these old military institutions, as they were recorded by the documents of the time, there were preserved: "the old guards of the mountain passes with the local captains, the *călăraşi*, *dărăbani*, the hirelings, (the mercenaries' former name) *hotnogii*, *ceauşii*, *vătafii*, all under the command of a *vel-căpitan* who was the commander-in-chief of these people."[7]

Despite the Porte's attempts to liquidate the national military force, old military forms of organization thus continued to function. Moreover, the socio-political forces guided by the idea of national liberation assiduously designed and sometimes succeeded in setting up military means capable of ensuring the independence of the Romanian Principalities.[8]

The first great occasion to outright claim the chrystallization of a national military organism with its natural internal and external functions occurred half a century after the establishment of the Phanariot regime, and afterwards the desideratum was ever more frequently present in the memoranda addressed to foreign courts. In 1769 the establishment in Wallachia of a native army, made up of a corps of 20,000 soldiers, with cavalry and artillery units and of an army of 12,000 soldiers in Moldavia. Similar memoranda and petitions were submitted in 1772 or during 1788-1791.[9] These demands reflect awareness of the fact that in the conditions of permanent interference and encroachment by the great neighboring empires, only an independent military force that could ensure an independent national life.

Running parallel to these demands—asking the addressees' approval—the establishment of the autochthonous army corps tended to become an independent factor in the so-called "Eastern Question." Such was the case of the well-known "volunteer corps" which fought side by side of the armies that engaged the Ottoman armed forces and of the military category of the *pandours*. The setting up and use of the volunteer corps stemmed from diverse initiatives—princely, boyar or even external—but it could only materialize on the fertile ground of that "trend toward the army"—to use Nicolae Iorga's expression—which "could not do otherwise but stir a people in which life had not been stopped."[10]

The phenomenon of the voluntariat, opening wide perspectives in the subsequent developments, is well-known in Romanian history. In 1739, at the height of the Russian-Turkish war, 3,000 Moldavian volunteers[11] were present in the ranks of the opponents of the Ottoman army, whereas during the next conflict between the two empires a corps of about 4,000 Romanian volunteers fought against the Ottoman army, their number gradually increasing as the war went on to 12,000 in Moldavia alone.[12]

In the ensuring war which broke out in 1787, these nuclei of the national army became a subject of dispute among the three empires—the Ottoman, the Tsarist and the Habsburg. Each wanted to become the exclusive beneficiary of the growing "trend toward the army" to subject the Dacian area to its domination. To stimulate the Romanian military endeavors, the imperial governments involved, resorted to both promises and threats, and even sudden and brutal dissolution of the military organization when their actions exceeded the intentions or ran counter to the will of the respective governments.

Three phenomena, within this "trend toward the army" conspicuously point out the role played by the military factor in the development of the Romanian national consciousness.

The first is outlined by the attempts of some Romanian boyars to set up army corps, that, in the context of the clashes among the great powers in the area, would fight for the elimination of Ottoman rule. Pîrvu Cantacuzino's army, made up of about 6,000 soldiers, including about "4,000 volunteers" and 2,000 arnauts, which liberated Bucharest in 1769 from the Ottomans,[13] was the protagonist in the most important Romanain-Ottoman confrontation during the Phanariote epoch, at Comana, during that very same year.

The second is the establishment of exclusively Romanian military units at the Transylvanian border of the Habsburg empire, enacted by the Court in Vienna in 1762. Two regiments were set up in Transylvania—at Năsăud and Orlat—and a Romanian batallion was organized in the Banat (1768). In 1773, given the two Romanian infantry regiments in Transylvania, the Romanian regiment of Dragoons and the Romanians of the Hussar regiment (including Romanians and Szeklers), the number of Romanian military personnel in Transylvania amounted to 9,000 men.[14]

As a genuine "military stratum," the nomenclature used in the memorandum submitted to Vienna in 1791, the *Supplex Libellus Valachorum*, this nucleus of the Romanian army was a powerful component of the national emancipation movement in Transylvania.[15]

The third was a corps of Romanian military commanders, set up during the military operations, within the pre-revolutionary army. Fully aware of the army's national mission, they were "due to Tudor, the sone of the peasant from Vladimiri Gorj . . . the first army commanders we had,"[16] in the century of the Romanians' self-assertion.

This part of our study leads to the following conclusions:

(1)   During the eighteenth century, the dynamic assertion of the national consciousness was accompanied by a strong resurrection of the military spirit, or, in other words, the intensification of the "trend toward the army." At the same time we record the sometimes successful attempts to reorganize some autochthonous armies;

(2)   the actions of the nuclei of the "revolutionary army" objectively tend to individualize the Romanian factor as part of the "Eastern Question";

(3)   throughout the century, the phenomenon of the voluntariat and implicitly, the existence and activity of the *pandours* paved the way for the structures of the future national modern army, providing it with part of the command corps.

The Army During the Revolutions of 1821 and 1848-1849

The crucial moments of the Romanians' national emancipation during the nineteenth century—Tudor Vladimirescu's revolution in 1821 and the general Romanian revolution of 1848—gave birth to an army of a new type. This new army, we called it revolutionary, was on the one hand an outcome of the stage attained by the national emancipation struggle and on the other hand its forceful stimulus. An analysis of the rank-and-file and command cadres of the Romanian revolutionary army enables us to comprehend the way it acted as a stimulus of the national emancipation movement and the development of the national consciousness. In both Tudor Vladimirescu's army and the revolutionary armies of 1848 the popular element was overwhelmingly present.

On January 23, 1821 Tudor Vladimirescu isused in Tismana his first proclamation to the inhabitants of Wallachia, calling on them to make up "the assembly organized for the welfare and benefit of the entire country," to take up arms or "iron pitchforks or spears."[17] The proclamation drew an immediate and far-reaching response. A contemporary noted that the Romanians "by the thousands ran to join under his banner," and that Tudor "as supported by the entire Romanian peasantry."[18]

From the very beginning, Tudor's revolution had as one of its major goals the attainment of the internal independence of the country and the expulsion of the Ottomans from the bridgeheads they held north of the Danube.[19] The ties between Tudor and the "loyal" boyars were also aimed at Wallachia's liberation from Ottoman rule. The proclamation comprised also a reason for the revolution, asserting the inalienable right of the nation to replace by force an authority which was not its own. The military uprising of the entire people in 1821, strongly asserted the national consciousness of the people.[21]

The Revolution of 1848 proclaimed that the people's participation in the revolutionary army was indispensable for the achievement of the national ideals. Thus, in the manifesto issued in 1848, the revolutionary leader of the Banat, Eftimie Murgu, stated: "in keeping with our interests, if we want to remain free, we shall all take up arms and be able to defend our rights in case of need. Therefore, consider the army, or the national guard as a guarantee of these rights, of our national liberation."[22]

The validity of these positions was proven in the war waged by Avram Iancu (1848-1849) in the Apuseni Mountains, which were turned into a "true Romanian Republic."[23] General Magheru's proclamation, on September 28, 1848, announcing the dissolution of the Rîureni camp, where tens of thousands of defenders of the Revolution in Wallachia were concentrated reiterated: "Cherish in your Romanian hearts the feelings of patriotism and nationality animating you, and never forget that whenever your Homeland needs you, you are in duty bound to respond and die for the attainment of our sacred rights."[24]

As affirmed by our historiography, the experience of the 1848 revolutionary army paved the way for the establishment of the national army. "Answering the crucial requirements of the destinies of the country and supporting a just and noble cause, the military system, worked out theoretically and partially put into practice by the 1848 revolution, will be considered in the ensuing decades also as most realistic and suitable to the Romanian traditional spirit."[25]

The command officers of the revolutionary army were taken over by the representatives of the classes and social categories mostly interested in attaining the aims of the epoch: the crushing of the feudal system and the unhindered development of the capitalist relations; the making of the Romanian unitary state, on the ancient Dacian territory; the attaining of

the coountry's complete independence; the radical modernization of the
sociopolitical structures. The fact that the representatives of the classes
and social categories, supporting the national emancipation movement,
held the key-offices of the revolutionary armies was not only the guarantee of their commitment to the national cause but also the source of
powerful influences on the largest strata of the society.[26] As for "statutes
armies," which are to be discussed later, the officers and junkers were
in fact the leading representatives of the rising national spirit. Such officers include Vasile Cîrlova, Grigore Alexandrescu and Nicolae Bălcescu.
Many of the leaders of the national party came from the ranks of the
officers' corps: Ioan Cîmpineanu, I. C. Brătianu, Nicolae Golescu, Cezar-
Bolliac and others. In addition, other officers would make themselves
conspicuous as leaders of the revolution, such as the Voinescu brothers,
Christian Tell, Mikhail Kogălniceanu, Scarlat Crețulescu, Gheorghe Magheru
and others.

The events of 1848 were to bring about the promotion to the command
offices of the Romanian army of a revolutionary generation of leaders,
who asserted themselves through military capacity and unswerving belief
in the justness of the national ideals and their achievements. Nicolae Bălcescu characterized this new generation of military leaders as follows:
"the generals of this peasant army were priests and young men who had
just graduated from schools of theology, philosophy and law; they had
never laid their hands on arms until that time, but in the face of necessity,
they had to act as generals and win battles. Lacking military knowledge
and ignorant of the principles of military art, they came to learn them at
the height of battles."[27] Such were the tribunes of Avram Iancu's revolutionary army, who turned the natural fortress of the Apuseni Mountains
into a genuine bulwark of the revolution. Compelling recognition during
the national emancipation movement, the army, in its turn, continuously
provided important contigents of cadres to the national emancipation
movement and finally to the Romanian modern state. The national bourgeoisie, called on to be the leading class of the Romanian national movement consisted largely of dynamic and energetic elements provided by the
military organizations of the country.

The Romanian military body established by the Organic Statutes
deserves special attention. The initiative for setting up the Moldavaian
and the Wallachian armies was external, as it was the direct outcome of

the treaty between the two competing empires in the area, the Tsarist and the Ottoman. However, the establishment of the autochthonous armies—the so-called "statute armies"—was an objective necessity. The national military factor had become so conspicuous during the development of the Eastern Question that the rival empires could hardly ignore it. Indeed, in the context of the Russian-Ottoman war of 1828-1829, the establishment of autochthonous armies was insistently demanded both in Jassy and Bucharest by the most diverse social and political sources; in early 1830, special committees were organized in the two capitals of the Principalities to work out the organizational basis of the new military institutions.[28] The expectations of the initiators, as well as those of the previsions of the foreign consuls accredited in Bucharest and Jassy, proved to be groundless. The Tsarist government was not inclined to set up national armies as it was only concerned with the securing of effective police and frontier guard operations. The matter was handled, as expressed in the 380th Article of the Organic Statutes, when the "militia" was set up "to ensure security and good order, as well as obedience to the laws."[29]

In spite of the limitations imposed on the development of the army, of huge obstacles stemming from the Statutes of the two Romanian Principalities, the action undertaken in 1830 was enthusiastically welcomed. In referring to those moments, *Curierul Românesc* (The Romanian Messenger) in Bucharest described the following state of mind: "The Romanian uniform and the setting up of the army have caused great excitement and joy all over the Capital. Every Romanian sees his nation reviving from the drowsiness and decay foreign intrigues brought about, he is transfigured with joy, hopping and embracing his brothers to whom he talks, weeping, laughing not knowing what to do."[30] Undoubtedly, such enthusiasm sprang from the belief in the future of these "militias," for with the expansion of the framework of state autonomy, there arose the possibility of establishing an army, "linked to the oldest, best and most lasting traditions of the country itself."[31]

In September 1834, the Turkish *firman* recorded the setting-up of the much debated "militia," which in Wallachia comprised "32 Staff-officers, 164 oberofficers, 501 unterofficers, 81 musicians and six physicians, 3,541 soldiers and 685 horses;" in Moldavia, in 1843 "the militia" included "a Staff of 8 Staff officers, 30 oberofficers, 182 unterofficers (!), 892 soldiers, a squadron of cavalry (204), a ship (22 mariners)."[32]

As the national emancipation struggle gained in intensity, the statutes armeis were to become instruments for the dissemination of national ideas, through the educating of its contigents. In some instances, such as during the battle of Dealul Spirii waged in September 1848 by the soldiers of the Bucharest garrison against the invading Ottoman army, they assumed the functions of a national army.

From the standpoint of the relationship "military factor-national consciousness," the historiographic reconstitution of the revolutionary armies (premises, structure, operations) leads us to the following conclusions:

(1)   In the field of the national emancipation movement the "revolutionary army" represented the explosive stage of the "trend toward the army." On the one hand, it represented the independent assertion of the Romanian military factor on the territory of its competence, during the clash of the great powers vying for it, and on the other hand, it was the incarnation of the concept of the revolutionary army;

(2)   "The revolutionary army" made itself more and more conspicuous as the instrument for carrying out the national political desiderata—unity and independence;

(3)   The armies of the Romanian revolutions proved to be an inexhaustible reserve of cadres for the national emancipation movement, functioning, as powerful stimuli in the modernization of the national state, just as the national emancipation movement provided, in turn, a great number of cadres for the national army.

The Army of the Union and of the War for Winning Romania's Complete Independence

This formulation designates the military body's achieving the Union and fighting during the war of independence. The abolition of the military structures entailed by the Revolution, the result of the foreign intervention that supressed the Revolution of 1848 in the Romanian Principalities, opened a new stage in the evolution of the military factor with the Romanians. Aware of the fact that despite limitations imposed on Romanian military bodies and because of the Romanians' seeking autonomy from the protective powers, the governments of the bordering empires tried, by all means available to hinder the development of the Romanian armed forces. It was for that purpose that the measure of abolishing the Romanian regiments of frontier guards in Transylvania, in 1851, was enacted by the Court in Vienna which realized, after the events of 1848-1849, that the guards could easily become the nucleus of the national army of the Romanians in Transylvania.

The contradictory purposes of the European Great Powers, that were interested in maintaining or changing the political and military balance in the Romanian zone, favored the development of the Romanian autochthonous army albeit for their own advantage. Thus, through the Peace Treaty of Paris, concluded on March 30, 1856, among other provisions concerning the future statutes of the Principalities the Great Powers acknowledged the Principalities' right to "have a national army, organized in order to maintain safety at home and secure the borders; no obstacles can be put in the way of extraordinary defensive measures, the Principalities and the Sublime Porte would find themselves obliged to take to reject and repel a foreign attack."[33] From the modest beginnings mention before, immediately after the Treaty of Paris in 1857, Wallachia came to have at its disposal effectives amounting to 19,252 soldiers and officers (6,459-standing troops and 13,893-irregular troops), whereas Moldavia had 5,696 men in regular troops.[34]

On August 19, 1858, the Convention of Paris was concluded, establishing a new framework of international law for the Romanian Principalities. The main point imposed and obtained on this occasion was the stipulation included in Article 42 of the Convention, which assumed great significance later: "The standing armies of the two Principalities will have an identical organization, so that in case of need they could unite and make up a single army."[35] The making of a powerful national army was the major goal of the policy promoted by Al. Ioan Cuza, the prince elected in January 1859 by both Romanian Principalities. The main goals pursued were the ensuring by the "armed force," destined to guarantee the rights stipulated through the "moral power" of the treaties, of "the borders and the autonomy at home"—as Mikhail Kogălniceanu, the well-known patriot and statesmen said.[36] After ardent debates at home and political and diplomatic actions on the international arena, meant to annihilate external opposition, on November 27, 1864, the Law for the Organization of the Army was passed.[37]

In accordance with the provisions of the new law, the effectives of the standing army amounted to 19,345 men and, in case of need, the army was to be brought up to full strength by 24,548 men included in the territorial army.[38] As soon as it had been acknowledged by the suzerain and the guaranteeing powers, the law was subjected to subtler measures which, contributing to implementation of the concept of the "armed nation," were aimed at building up the country's military force at a level compatible with the great national goals confronting our people." A first act of the times that were to come took place during the spring of 1866, when in answer to the concentration of Ottoman forces at Rustchuk, aimed at interfering with the preparations for Romanian independence, the Romanian government informed the consuls of the Great Powers that Romania "is determined to oppose energetically any violation of its territory or rights, sand if such were the case, it would take the defensive measures dictated by circumstances."[39] Thus, the modern national Romanian state proved that it had acceded to the indispensable means to assert itself freely in the community of the other European peoples. Mirroring this reality, King Carol I, the army's commander and chief, characterized in 1866 the military factor throughout the existence and progress of the Romanian people as follows: "Due to the army, Romania was able to go over long historical periods, in which nations once powerful withered away. Our old military institutions are re-established today and their solid organization would secure the future of our beloved Homeland."[40]

In keeping with the Romanian public opinion's firm belief that the achievement of the next goal of the national program—the regaining of the state independence—called for a powerful military body, no efforts were spared for its development. The outcome of all endeavors was "the national army of independence" which, facing the army of the Ottoman Empire on the south of the Danube, gained international recognition for the sovereign state of Romania. During 1877-1878, at Plevna, Rahova and Vidin, the army contributed decisively to the achievement of the unanimous Romanian desire for independence.

It is therefore obvious that the post-1848 decade was not a hiatus in the development of the Romanian military factor, in spite of the abolition of the revolutionary armies by foreign intervention. It clearly results that the 1848 generation was able to make the best use of the historical experience and to ensure the growing development of the national military power, skillfully maneuvering among the contradictory interests of the Great Powers concerned with Southeastern Europe.

The Prince of the Union—Alexander John Cuza—and his successor—
Carol I—shaped the military body in accordance with the next aim of the
national liberation program: the attainment of complete state independence. The army of independence was the outcome of a long process of
organizing the autochthonous military structures, shaped by the growing
self-awareness of the Romanians, in the chronological period we referred
to.

Set in a strategically unstable area during the eighteenth and nineteenth
centuries, coping with extremely complex internal and external circumstances, the Romanian political and military factor forcefully asserted
itself, as the only one legitimately entitled to assume responsibility on the
territory of old Dacia. It had become an important force in the "Eastern
Question," succeeding in making itself conspicuous on its territory of competence; over the entire chronological period under study, the military
factor developed in accordance with the dynamics of the development of
the national consciousness of the Romanian liberation struggle.

During a first stage, it successfully resisted external attempts to annihilate it and in spite of limitations affecting it, compelled recognition in
the military operations of the "Eastern Question"; the volunteers and the
armies set up in 1830—which had an exclusively internal role—were manifestations of the "trend toward the army," a fundamental component of
the national consciousness.

Concomitantly with the "explosive" assertion of the national consciousness—the revolution of Tudor Vladimirescu and the Revolution of
1848—"the trend toward the army" became general. It was the manifestation of the frame of mind of the people, who were fully aware that the
national and social claims can be attained only by the use of force against
the competing great powers in the area. The setting up of a strong army
to guarantee the achievement of the goals of the Romanian revolution—
union and independence—became a main programmatic objective of the
national liberation movement.

The bordering empires tried to "control" the Romanian military factor
and, implicitly, to check the Romanians' emancipation struggle. The case
of the statutes armies, which lay at the foundation of the future national
army of united Romania, is a persuasive example of thwarting such at-
temps.

Many leaders of the national liberation movement—military commanders and statesmen, ideologists and promoters of culture—carried out their activity in the ranks of the army, a phenomenon indicative of the close relationship between the military factor and the development of the national consciousness.

Throughout the entire period, within this framework of the Romanian socio-political life, the army did not function autonomously. It harmoniously blended with the national liberation struggle, consistently militating for the implementation of its desiderata. The impetuous progress of the Romanian fight for union and independence found valuable and indispensable support in the national military establishment.

NOTES

1. Andrei Oțetea, *Scrieri istorice alese* (Selected Historical Writings), Dacia Publishing House, Cluj-Napoca, 1980, pp. 107, 126.

2. Cf. Major-General Dr. Ilie Ceaușescu, *Războiul întegului popor pentru apărarea patriei la români. Dire cele mai vechi timpuri pînă în zilele noastre* (The Entire People's War for the Homeland's Defense. From Remotest Times to Our Days), Military Publishing House, Bucharest, 1980, pp. 85-101.

3. Ion Neculce, *Letoposețul Țării Moldovei* (The Chronicle of the Land of Moldavia), I. Iordan edition, Minerva Publishing House, Bucharest, 1975, p. 197.

4. Dr. Florin Constantiniu, *Premisele formării armatei române moderne—secolul XVIII—începutul secolului XIX* (The Premises of the Making of the Romanian Modern Army—the 18th-early 19th centuries), in *File din istoria militarâ a poporului român* (Pages from the Military History of the Romanian People), Bucharest, Military Publishing House, 1980, pp. 13-14.

5. N. Iorga, *Istoria armatei românesti* (The History of the Romanian Army), 2nd volume (From 1500 to Our Days), 2nd edition, Publishing House of the Ministry of War, Bucharest, 1930, p. 223.

6. Apostol Stan, *Renașterea armatei naționale* (The Rebirth of the National Army), Craiova, Romanian Writing Publishing House, 1979, pp. 12-13.

7. N. Iorga, op. cit., p. 224.

8. Dr. Fl. Constantiniu, op. cit., p. 14.

9. *Arhiva românească* (The Romanian Archives), volume 1, pp. 209-210, 213-216.

10. N. Iorga, op. cit., p. 238.

11. Apostol Stan, op. cit., p. 26.

12. Ibid., p. 44.

13. Cf. (Mihai Cantacuzino), *Genealogia Contacuzinilor* (The Genealogy of the Cantacuzinos), N. Iorga edition, Bucharest, 1902, p. 179.

14. Carol Gollner, *Regimentele grănicereşti din Transilvania 1764-1851* (The Frontier Guard Regiments in Transylvania 1774-1851), Military Publishing House, Bucharest, 1973, p. 57.

15. Op. cit., p. 131.

16. N. Iorga, op. cit., p. 238.

17. *Documente privind istoria României. Răscoala din 1821* (Documents concerning the History of Romania. The 1821 Uprising), volume I, Bucharest, 1962, p. 208.

18. N. Iorga, *Un cugetător politic moldovean de la jumătatea secolului al XIX-lea: Ştefan Scarlat Dăscălescu* (A Moldavian Political Thinker of the Mid-19th Century: Stefan Scarlat Dăscălescu), in "Academia Română, Memoriile Secţiunii Istorice," 3rd series, volume XIII, 1932, pp. 52, 54.

19. Apostol Stan, op. cit., p. 187.

20. Academician Andrei Otetea, *Tudor Vladimirescu şi revoluţia din 1821* (Tudor Vladimirescu and the 1821 Revolution), The Scientific Publishing House, Bucharest, 1971, p. 204.

21. Apostol Stan, op. cit., pp. 210-213.

22. Eftimie Murgu, *Scrieri* (Writings), the Publishing House for Literature, Bucharest, 1969.

23. Nicolae Ceauşescu, *România pe drumul construirii societăţii socialiste multilateral dezvoltate* (Romania on the Way to Building up the Multilaterally Developed Socialist Society), volume 8, the Polish Publishing House, Bucharest, 1973, p. 173.

24. *Anul 1848 în Principatele Române. Acte şi documente* (The Year 1848 in the Romanian Principalities. Acts and Documents), volume 14, pp. 426-427.

25. Major-General Dr. Ilie Ceauşescu, op. cit., p. 123; see also Major-General Dr. Constantin Olteanu, *Contribuţii la cercetarea conceptului*

de putere armată la români, (Contributions to the Investigation of the Concept of the Armed Forces with the Romanians), Military Publishing House, Bucharest, 1979, pp. 154-156.

26. Apostol Stan, op. cit., p. 187.

27. N. Bălcescu, *Corespondentă* (Correspondence), volume 4, Bucharest, 1962, p. 17.

28. Apostol Stan, op. cit., p. 252.

29. Apud N. Iorga, op. cit., p. 249.

30. Apud Lt.-Colonel V. Nădejde, *Centenarul renașterii armatei române 1830-1930* (The Centenary of the Rebirth of the Romanian Army 1830-1930), The Romanian Culture Printing House, Jassy, 1930, p. 29.

31. N. Iorga, op. cit., p. 248.

32. Ibid., p. 249.

33. D. A. Sturdza a.s.o., *Acte și documente relative la istoria renașterii României* (Acts and Documents concerning the History of Romania's Rebirth), volume II, Bucharest, 1889, p. 1068.

34. Lt.-Colonel V. Nădejde, op. cit., p. 95.

35. Ibid., p. 99.

36. Apud Major-General Dr. Ilie Ceaușescu, op. cit., p. 129.

37. Ibid., p. 130.

38. Major General Dr. Constantin Olteanu, op. cit., pp. 185-186.

39. Ulyse de Marsillac, *Histoire de l'armee roumaine,* Bucharest, 1871, p. 145.

40. Lt.-Colonel V. Nădejde, op. cit., p. 165.

THE UPRISING OF HOREA' CLOŞCA AND CRIŞAN, 1784

The extensive documentation, the torrent of facts, reveal conclusively the peasant character of the 1784 uprising led by Horea. Neither by its causes, nor by its evolution, neither by its organization nor by its aims and its mentality did the uprising go beyond what is termed as peasant. The miners among the rebels were also peasants, as were the priests. There was, indeed, nothing "non-peasant" about the uprising.

Naturally, the encouraging reflections of the Enlightenment, of imperial reformism were evident as were the echoes of the Romanian political struggle. But they were moulded into peasant patterns, translated into peasant language. The objectives set forth in the ultimatum sent to the nobility when victory was recorded, that capital act of the uprising, was strictly within the peasant mentality although the form was intellectual. It was not at all the outcome of the socio-political precepts of the intellectuals, rather it expressed the aspirations of peasants in revolt. Better than any other act it stated the ultimate goal of the uprising: the total abolition of the nobility and of its property. However, that goal was enunciated in victory. The uprising was less programatic, previously-planned action; it was, above all, a *dies irae* of the peasant masses who started to avenge the sufferings, to free themselves, to destry an unjust world. Its final target, the abolition of feudal relations acquired with the rebels a simplier form, more radical and destructive, in a vision characteristic of peasant mentality: nobility and serfdom should no longer exist!

Salis and Popescu, who were supposed to have a role in the uprising, were at the same time supposed to have played other parts too: to entice

117

the people to emigrate to Russia, and respectively, to join the Russian army. But there is no solid proof of this. Useless to say that throughout the uprising there was not among the peasants even the slightest allusion to emigration to Russian or to enrolling in the Russian army and the names of Salis and Popescu were unknown to them.

Salis could not be discovered anywhere, although his name circulated in a spectacular manner. In imagination he appears here or there, even in several places at the same time, or everywhere because in fact, he in person or his emissaries were to be found nowhere. And, as he was not to be found, his identity was related to a homonym, Count Salius, a former officer of the Szekler frontier guard regiment. That person was absent from the country for at least ten years, living in Moscow as an inspector in a commercial intitute. While there, he read in a Hamburg newspaper that he was supposed to be the leader of the uprising and, on December 22, he wrote a letter to the Austrian ambassador in St. Petersburg, Cobenzl, in which he related the adventures of his life.[1] The story of his life was also published in the newspaper.

The travels of Mihail Popescu are well known. He left Vienna, through Pest, being followed step by step by the army, up to the frontiers. He had to avoid the theater of the uprising and changed his route to the north passing through Bukovina to reach Bucharest. Although the Emperor himself, interested as he was in the problem of the outside interference, insisted on the investigation of such interference. The commission could not implicate either Salis or Popescu. In fact, the commission, after extensive inquiries and in possession of impressive documentation, reached the conclusion that there was no interference, either from outside or from within.

The possibility of a tactical maneuver of the Court, in its conflict with the nobility with regard to the land property, is also to be ruled out. In the existing intricate external circumstances the Emperor could not even take advantage of the uprising for his reforms, under the pretext of saving the noblemen. The suppression was too urgent a necessity to allow temporization or political maneuvers. If the revolt would have been suppressed promptly, the estate problem would have had to be postponed once more. There is no question of direct encouragement from the Emperor. He was a reformer and an enlightened monarch but he could never encourage directly an uprising of the lower strata. And there is no hint that

he could have done it out of political expediency. The direct encouragement mentioned by both sides is merely figments of the imagination. The
Emperor gave only indirect encouragement by his attitude toward the
peasantry and its problems. The "kind emperor" image consciously projected by the imperial regime, was only a stimulus to action.

Suggestions about the Romanian intellectuals' link with the uprising,
under the sign of freemasonry, namely of a "Crucian Fraternity," made
later on the basis of a manuscript of a Viennese freemason, of 1786. The
implausible informer, whose name is not given, said that he himself had
seen the act by which Aulic Councillor Beer, chief of Vienna's police,
informed the Emperor about the arrest of the "brothers." The whole
scheme is fictitious and anachronistic. A fanatic Romanian secret society
in Vienna, with branches in several towns, encourages the uprisings, and
keeps secret meetings on a freemasonry pattern. The society is mainly
composed of "older and wiser" men! To stir up the uprising members
collected great sums of money from fellow members while younger members, of those still in power, went to Transylvania and joined the rebels.
The scenario is also relevant: meetings were held in the house of a rich
merchant, the anteroom of the meeting place was decorated with full-size
busts of three "martyrs for the right cause of the people," of "the holy
Romanian trinity." Horea, Cloşca and Crişan, on an alter covered with
purple cloth. Horea with a crown of thorns on his head and with the
legend *"Hora rex Dacia."* As a distinctive sign the members had a thin
cord wrapped thrice around the naked body, like the one Crişan used to
hang himself in prison, and which they wore in memory of the "three
great patriots" swearing eternal revenge against the "killers." A spectacular and gloryfying production.

It is an obviously late production, at a revolutionary level, when a cult
of the revolutionary trinity could be imagined or when the Romanians
could be accused of such a cult. Everything was woven around the traditional association of the "sworn brothers," an association common among
the Romanians in the Banat and especially in Transylvania. The entire
production was, in fact, ceremoniously described by a Viennese newspaper
Provinzialnachrichten in 1786.[2] There are, however, significant aspects
in that production as far as the echo, imporance and later interpretations
of the uprising are concerned.

The supposed connection with the "Rose Crucians" is of importance.
Freemasonry was active, especially at certain social levels. Freemasons

were princes, courtiers, high officials, great noblemen, outstanding representatives of the intellectuals or of the bourgeoisie, civil servants. Among
the freemasons were Count Gheorghe Banffy, vice-chancellor of Transylvania, Gheorghe Aranka, a well-known man of letters, J. C. Eder, Joseph
Franz Sulzer, Mihail Brukenthal, Martin Bochmeister, Dr. Ioan Piuariu-
Molnar, Dr. Burutz, Ştefan Koszta, the governmental secretary, and so
forth. It is said that the lodge of the Rose Order, for instance, included
under German names, even Gherasim Adamovici, the future Orthodox
bishop of Transylvania, Petru Petrovici, the Orthodox Bishop of Timişoara, Iosif Ioanovici Şacabent, the Orthodox Bishop of Vîrşet, and the
Canon of Cenad, who was descendant of Romanian ruling princes.[3] Governor Samuil Brukenthal was a freemason too. Freemasonry in the Empire,
however, was humanitarian, enlightened, reformist but not revolutionary
and did not go beyond love for mankind.

Incidental participants in the uprising, of men such as Alexandru
Chendi should be explained by the mere fact that the peasants did not
know how to read and write. Other Romanian names which did not belong
to the peasants, such as those of Ioan Piuariu Molnar, the doctor, Dimitrie
Eustatevici and Dimitrie Iercovici, secretaries of the Bishopric, Popa Sava
of Răşinari, Vicar Ioan Popovici of Hondol, Archpriest Iosif Adamovici
of Abrud, Ştefan Koszta of the Government, Ladislau Pap, vice-count of
Zarand, Lieutenant Caliani, which appear in the records of the uprising
were not related to the rebels but acted for the official side. Their role
was not to influence the uprising but to appease it. Iosif Mehesi too, might
have been an advisor or a guide of the peasants at the Chancellery, and
there may have been others too, even from Vienna, but they were not
involved in the uprising as such. This is not to say that there was no hid-
den compassion for the uprising; in fact the names of numerous priests
who took part in the uprising were lost in the mass of peasants.

The "mysterious" captain with a red shako, who accompanied Horea
at Bucium and who was depicted in the historiographic literature as a
military or political mentor was none other than Niculae Tulea of Rîu
Mare, a peasant captain in Romanian clothes. The documents merely
mentioned a man with a soldier's red shako and sword and not an officer.
The various other names which were included in documents, chronicles
and newspapers were only the products of confusion or imagination. "Unknown" captains in uniforms who were seen here and there by the peasants
were but peasants dressed in different clothes, taken from captives, in

order to emphasize in this way, or by other distinctive signs, their position as leaders. The supposed political relations of Horea are either circumstantial or imaginary.

With the knowledge we have today we can say that there was no foreign or non-peasant inmixture in the uprising. Even if there were such interference they would have been only peripheral and non-essential.

The uprising was entirely of the peasants both in its causes and its actions. Nothing occult, nothing which was forced, nothing staged, nothing improper, nothing which was not of a peasant character is seen or felt. By its spontaneity, but its full and authentic peasant veracity it is in the line of peasant uprisings in Russia, in Bohemia and in other parts of Europe. It belongs within the scope of the antifeudal struggle of the time, within general history.

Like all peasant uprisings in general, it affected the entire social structure, everything which belonged to the ruling system, everything which belonged to the oppressive authority, everything which meant wealth, nobility, dignitaries, rich townsfold. It generally avoided, however, by virture of its slogans, everything that was imperial or connected with the serfs or the poor.

The wholly peasant character of the uprising is personified by Horea himself. Throughly peasant, he did not transgress the bounds of the peasantry either by position, by dress, by education or by mentality. To this day we are not certain whether he knew how to read and write. His school life, his own experience as a travelled man, his own work, his travels to Vienna were substitutes for education. Socially he was no more than a serf or a free landless peasant. His material condition placed him in the poor strata of the peasantry; after his death nothing was left but the small cottage on the top of the hills. His traveling helped him to know better, more directly, the life of his fellows and generalize the discontent he himself felt as an oppressed peasant. His actions also fully testify to the clear-cut peasant character of the uprising. All his actions are at a peasant level, all his orders are in agreement with the simple slogans propagated in various forms, even simpler, by the peasants in revolt, they express the same mentality in the same language. He is thoroughly peasant both during the uprising and before he judges.

It is precisely this identity that makes his personality important and representative. Horea's personality is important not by being above the masses but by perfect identification with them. It is greater not through

singularity but through multiplication. Only thus could he play, and he
did play, the role of undisputed head of the uprising, only thus could he
become its mobilizing symbol. What made him different from his fellows
were his natural features, personal psychology, a deeper sense of justice
and injustice, a more ardent passion, greater courage which transcended
the bounds of reason, a spirit of self-sacrifice for the benefit of all. In the
heat of the uprising there was no sign of his being tempted by higher
positions or wealth; he was peniless, waiting for money from the villages
to go to Vienna. He not only personified the people's anger but he also
propagated it, activiated it, unleashed it at the risk of his own life. Horea
was the soul of the people, not the superior man above them. And there
is something more: the indefinable which moulds the popular hero, the
touch of secrecy which helps him accumulate virtues which are denied
to the common people, the secrecy which spellbinds the crowd, stirs up
its imagination, creates the legend and makes the hero immortal.

During the uprising, the most active was Crişan, but he acted as Horea's
representative. Cloşca too, always faithfully carried out Horea's orders.
Crişan showed independence of action; he ralled the serfs on the noble-
mens' estates. The uprising unfolded on two planes, corresponding to
its dual aspects—cameral and nobiliary—of serfdom but it was unitary.
Crişan obeyed the imperial orders transmitted by Horea. Actually or
symbolically Horea embodied the ultimate goal of the uprising: not only
the cameral but also the nobiliary serfdom, i.e., serfdom itself, had to be
destroyed.

A thorough analysis of the uprising reveals the true scope of Horea's
role. He was the soul of the agitation preceding the uprising, he is the
name which started the uprising, his name polarized the revolutionary
action, he was the man who had the courage, for the benefit of the cause,
to construe an "Emperor's order" which mobilized the peasantry—the
most meaningful order for the common people. And they believed it as
they believed that the Emperor wished them well and only noblemen
were against them. From there it was only a step to the order to start
the revolution and he was the one who gave that order.

Horea's instinct for leadership was substitute for the art of leading.
He did not leave, even for only a moment the citadel of the mountains,
he did not come in person to negotiate with the authorities or the army
except in the mountains, he could not be lured and he successfully avoided

the traps. Permanently followed, he could not be discovered and arrested either before or during the uprising. When he was caught for a moment by enemy peasants at Bucium, he was quickly liberated by his faithful peasants.

Once it started, the uprising spread quickly covering large areas beyond Horea's control. As he disposed only of rudimentary means of communication, Horea soon lost control of events as the scope of the uprising expanded. As the uprising spread rapidly from village to village, more and more peasants became involved, new leaders emerged, orders and slogans were adapted to local needs and conditions as the villages took revenge against their own landlords. The uprising acquired local forms because unhampered by programatic orders, it assumed a spontaneous, empirical, peasant character.

Horea's name however, continued to be important. The rebelling peasants, in their need for a leader, attributed to him all the features and all the virtues of a leader. Everything took place in his name and ostensibly on his orders. In his absence the uprising created his imaginary leadership.

After all, Horea was the man who travelled to Vienna, in whom the Emperor confided, the man who kept the Emperor's secrets and transmitted his orders and therefore, in the minds of the peasants, he was no longer a common man like them. They visualized him dressed in rich, princely clothes, wearing a golden star and gold crosses on his chest. He could be neither caught, nor arrested and tried like any other peasant. Even before his death he became a legend. He was the "prince," the "emperor" called up to save the peasants from slavery. Horea, the person was surpassed by the imaginary Horea, blown up to the proportions of the uprising itself, to the limits of the popular imagination in full effervesence.

In the minds of the contemporaries, internal or external, of the noblemen, or of the press, the head of the uprising could not be a common man. They either superimposed him on another or endowed him with superior qualities, with a political consciousness greater than that of the masses. Consequently, he was either a priest or archpriest, a bishop's brother, or captain in the imperial army . . . a highly educated man who spoke German and read German literature. As they did not know him, the contemporaries could confine various physical or moral images or the man, could freely imagine faults or virtues. "Horea seemed to have been born to be a ruler and indeed as long as he played that role he was up to it" wrote *Politiches Journal* of Hamburg and the well-known German booklet *Horja und Klotska*. The imagination could carry still further the concoctions of the adversaries to enhance his guilt, the title of *Rex Daciae*; it could elevate the "prince" and "emperor" created by the popular imagination to the sphere of a great political objective and it could raise the popular struggle onto an all-comprehensive national political struggle.

Real or imaginary, Horea played a primordial role in the uprising to such a degree that the event remained in the mind of the contemporaries and in history as "Horea's uprising." Detractors and admirers saw him in various ways, but not even the detractors could deny his capital role in the uprising. Nor could they deny his sacrifice and his courage in facing death. Likewise, hostile historians could not deny a legitimate intention: the emancipation of the people. A quotation from Francis Szilagyi, author of a scientific monograph on the uprising: "The impartial historian must also admit that this great malefactor had at heart the fate of his oppressed people and its liberation although he used the most blamable means for the attainment of this noble goal, he never betrayed the cause to which he devoted his entire activity and life, and sacrificed his life and to which he was faithful to the end even on the scaffold, facing the most horrible death."[4]

The essence of the uprising was obviously social. It falls within the great peasant uprisings of the past and of this century in Romania and in other countries. The difference is that those of the past took place at the time of the establishment of servitude and usually resulted in its strengthening, while the others led towards its abolition. Horea's uprising did not look back, to the past but to the future. It did not aim at improving but at destroying the feudal relations. The program stipulated: noblemen should no longer exist, they should leave their estates forever and their land should be divided among the common people, namely those who till it. A simple but radical vision, definitely revolutionary. A vision aiming farther than the agrarian programs of the revolution in the subsequent century, which it foretold. However, it was not the radicalism of the democratic-bourgeois revolution, but a peasant radicalism indigenous to the peasantry which envisioned only its ultimate aim. This radicalism affected especially Western revolutionaries, Brissot in particular.

However, at this level and in the specific conditions of Transylvania, the uprising was much more complex, corresponding to the problems of the time. It had deep and inseparable national implications and delved into the problems of the Romanian people in Transylvania and everywhere.

The uprising wought to free all serfs, but in general, only the Romanian serfs participated in it. First of all the serfs themselves considered it an uprising of the Romanians: i.e., the uprising of the Romanians was directed against the noblemen and the Hungarians. The two notions are merged even when they appear in isolated slogans. The uprising was regarded even more definitely Romanian by those affected but it: the noblemen and townsfolk. The documents also recorded, among the accusations directed against the rebels, its anti-Hungarian character. The noblemen in particular, eager to deny that they were in any way responsible for the outbreak of the uprising, classified it as purely national and denied its social character: to them, it was the toutcome of national and religous hatred, of the hostile nature of the Romanians, of their inborn hatred toward noblemen and Hungarians, toward their religions.

Such a generalization could easily be reached by either side. In Transylvania, against the background of the overwhelming number of Romanians among the serfs and especially within the area of the uprising, Romanian was almost synonymous with serf, and master—including the apparatus at his service, the domanial or county official—was synonymous with Hungarian. The distinction was exacerbated by religion. The Romanians were exclusively Eastern Orthodox while the Hungarians belonged to the reformed Catholic, Calvinist or Unitarian religion. Romanian, Orthodox, serf are superimposed and become synonymous. In its essence, the struggle alos included the Hungarian serfs, as it aimed at freeing the entire peasantry; in practice, however, it included them only to a very small extent. First of all because the uprising encompassed only very few areas inhabited by Hungarian serfs. Secondly, because the slogans and targets of the Romanian people would naturally create feelings of doubt among the Hungarian serfs. The solidarity of the serfs, on which the struggle was grounded, cannot be denied. Whenever possible, the uprising also drew to its side Hungarian serfs and the unrest outside the scope of the uprising, especially the movement for military conscription before the uprising, definitely involved Hungarian and Saxon serfs too. The capital act of the uprising, the ultimatum, covered without doubt, all the serfs. In spite of the slogans, the rebels did not attack and did not harm Hungarian serfs, except accidentally; it happened indeed to those who placed themselves at the service of the masters, committed abuses in such capacities or tried to defend their masters. Sometimes they fell victims to the devastation of the landlord courts, where they lived. Equally severe punishments were meted out to their Romanian fellow-serfs who were guilty of the same infractions. However, the slogans calling for exterminations resulted in rather few human victims—at most 150 people were killed because the majority of those threatened saved themselves. There were cruelties but they were few. The number of peasants who fell victim in the wave of reprisals was much larger. And the reprisals would have been more cruel—the sentences met out in the beginning bear evident to this —had the Emperor not checked the fury of the nobility. In fact, it was not the slogans for the extermination of the nobility and of the Hungarians that mattered, but their implementation according to specific conditions. But ultimately, what mattered was the abolition of serfdom itself. The Romanian serfs were at the head of the struggle because they constituted the overwhelming majority, and also because they were subject to the most onerous forms of serfdom, to the greatest oppression not only as serfs but also as people.

Moreover, the problem of the Romanian people itself, repudiated by the "political nations" both with respect to its existence and to its religion was becoming more acute in the eighteenth century. It reflected a fundamental, primary atavic and centuries-old enmity; a natural adversity, an empiric, silent struggle. A struggle stimulated, directly or indirectly, by the national political struggle in progress, by its essence made known to the serfs primarily by priests who participated both in the political struggle and in the uprising.

Previous religious hostilities among Romanians, the confrontations between the Uniates and non-Uniates almost disappeared, they were hardly discernible in the heat of the uprising. They showed solidarity against the religions of the enemies, and the common Orthodox "law," with its full popular fanaticism merged into a common socio-national course, into a common struggle. The cross carried as a banner in front of the peasant groups suggests a Romanian Crusade. The country itself was, and had to be, a Romanian country. The Orthodox faith was the Romanian faith, the other faiths were those of the rulers, of the Hungarians. The conversion of the Hungarians to the Orthodox faith meant their conversion to the Romanian faith, their merging with the Romanian people. In the peasants' mentality noblemen-Hungarian-ruler-papist-Calvinist-Unitarian overlap, are inseparable. All notions are adapted to the narrow range of personal experience, of local conditions, they are variants of a common general vision. Hence, the inconsistency, the difference in the language of the slogans. As viewed by the peasants, the Romanian question was simplified, it was to be solved either by destruction or by conversion. That was the simple peasant solution to the national problem.

Historically, the question of the Romanian people in Transylvania and of Transylvania itself, was one and same. However, the emancipation struggle was henceforth to be from two directions: one, that of the intellectuals, starting from the top, from the national aspect and the other, that of the peasantry, starting from the bottom, from the social aspect, both, however, rising above religious differences. The essence of the struggle carried out by the intellectuals was the elevating of the Romanians to the status of a political nation. The peasant struggle focused on the abolition of serfdom. The two overlaped, but each addressed the problem of the nation itself, one in a scientific, theoretical manner, the other in a revolutionary way. They were the two facets of the same problem, supplemented each other and then merged into the single, all-comprehensive, revolutionary program of the nation in 1848. In the historical perspective, the uprising made the program of the nation complete by adding to it the social dimension, merging the reformist methods of struggle with the revolutionary ones. The peasantry had the merit of having started, by itself, the revolutionary process of the emancipation of the nation.

Moreover, the idea of Romanian solidarity, the solidarity of the three Romanian Countries, was gaining ground both inside Transylvania and abroad. A solidarity which was virtually imaginary, like a desire, a normal expectation on the part of the Romanians, like a possibility, a fear, on the part of opposing sides and even on the part of the imperial regime itself. Interest in the uprising must undoubtedly have been great in the Romanian Countries also. Rumors about actual or possible support were circulating among the rebels as well as among the nobles. The imperial regime was also vigilant. Assistance did not materialize; however, contemplation of that possibility was significant. Horea himself, credited with a high degree of political consciousness, was presumed to have had links with the Romanian Countries. And so, it was imagined that a deputation was

sent by Horea to the Prince of Moldavia, to secure through him the protection and support of the Porte. Horea was credited with the intention
of seeking common action by the three Romanian Countries to restore
Dacia and even the Roman Empire! And, significantly, these alleged intentions were given credence in Europe. Indeed, the idea of a Romanian
kingdom of Dacia awakened European interest in the fate of the entire
Romanian people, and thus attributed to the uprising a European significance. As part of the general anti-feudal struggle of the times, the uprising brought to the attention of the West the question of the Romanian people, and, as any event of this type, stimulated revolutionary consciousness. In the historical framework of the Romanian people, it was
the first social revolutionary action, i.e., for eliminating the feudal relations, while on the national plane, it sharpened Romanian consciousness,
it stimulated and exacerbated the national struggle of the Romanians
and their opponents alike.

The uprising was ultimately suppressed by force of arms. It could not
succeed because the conditions were not ripe for the overthrow of the
feudal world and the peasantry alone could not have done it by itself.
But it could not and it did not remain without consequences. It had assumed proportions too large and it had aroused hopes and dangers too
powerful not to have had consequences, first and foremost in imperial
policy.

The abolition of serfdom in Hungary and Transylvania was a direct
outcome of the uprising. It is true that the imperial decree by which it
was abolished did not satisfy the demands of the rebel peasants and it
did not meet the objectives of their struggle. It made no difference to
their social slogans and even less to the national-religious ones. And, in
comparison to the decree issued in the hereditary lands of the Empire,
it had a major drawback. It was not accompanied by a second text granting the subject the ownership of the land.. The statutes of the land remained unchanged, as providedfor in the *Tripartitum*, which also restricted the liberties that were granted. The right to move was to be limited by the obligation of the serf to find another serf to replace him. Moreover, under the prevailing socio-economic conditions, the emancipated
peasant could at best change one master for another. The peasants had
not rebelled to obtain the right to move nor to change the name of serf
to that of *colon*, but, simply, to destroy serfdom itself. And even less did

they rebel for the land system sanctioned by the *Tripartitum*, what they asked for was ownership of the land. The serfs' struggle began under the sign of reformism, in the name of the Emperor. Encouraged by his struggle against the nobles and identifying it with their own struggle against the nobility, the peasants soon concluded that his reformism was insufficient and resorted to revolution. However, institutionally, the abolition of serfdom was a remarkable step forward. It removed the personal servitude which marked the harshest stage in the history of serfdom in Transylvania.

The serfs' understanding of the abolition of servitude was limited. He could not understand many of the subtleties of the Decree. It was difficult to understand and even to explain the sinuous text that set his right to dispose of his possessions in the superimposed right to property of his master. He could not see clearly what were the changes, the difference between serf and *colon*. But of course, he retained the expressions: "liberation, free movement to be free without the permission of his master, to learn trades, cannot be forced to serve the court, he is free to receive work in accordance with the understanding reached with the master, cannot be dispossessed or driven off his inherited land without legal grounds, cannot be forced to move from one place to another." Obviously he understood them in the spirit of his aspirations. He was tempted to think that serfdom itself was abolished. In his mind "people free to move" easily equated with "free people." For instance, the serfs of the Ghurghiu estate when asked if they were serfs or not, answered: "to our knowledge we are serf on the estate but a few weeks ago, His Imperial Highness made us free men." And this is how the Decree was understood in many places throughout Transylvania. The Decree raised hopes of liberty in the minds of the serfs which had to be contained by force, however, not without leaving their imprint on the peasants' minds.

The subsequent reforms did not overlook the specter of uprisings. Such outbreaks had to be prevented in the future and that could not be expected, unless the abuses that had generated the uprising of 1784 were to be corrected. On the other hand, the specter of the uprising facilitated the Emperor's reforming work, adoption of his policy of curtailing the privileges of the nobility and of limiting its power. Relations between master and serf, elevated by the enlightened regime to the level of a major state problem, assumed a sense of urgency after the uprising and the issue of the abolition of serfdom became paramount despite obvious difficulties. The abolition could be annuled even by the Diet which reversed the reforms of Joseph II after his death. Although even during Joseph's reign the agrarian problem could not be solved and relations between nobles and peasants were, even after Joseph's death, to be controlled by the state and had to conform to legal norms.

The uprising shook for a moment the entire feudal, nobiliary or cameral edifice, the entire social edifice of the country, from top to bottom, but, in fact, it was a confrontation between its two basic blocs: the serfs and the nobles. It was on that basis that the socio-national complexity of the struggle developed. The physical confrontation between the two adversaries covered but a part of the country, but the nobility everywhere would live in fear of a possible revolt of the serfs. It continued to think of revenge and to oppose imperial reforms. The waves of opposition raised by the nobility against the imperial reforms of Joseph II toward the end of his reign and even the elimination of the reforms after his death, could not restore the old relations as they were before the uprising. The great uprising and the specter of new ones made for resignation and reconciliation with the imperial regime.

Likewise, the peasants would not forget their temporary success, the tremors they produced, the fears they aroused. A deep change took place in their mentality, they became aware of the righteousness of their cause and conscious of their power. They knew that the uprising had not been in vain, that Horea's banner had a lasting meaning. Even the cruel death, which they witnessed convinced them that Horea did not survive his calvary. For a long time the belief persisted that he was not dead, that another person had been executed in Alba Iulia. For many, Horea was in Vienna, holding a high office, doing all jobs; the orders favoring the masses were issued by him. The opposite camp sullied his memory with all kinds of horrors. However, the popular tradition kept the unsullied image, and carried it on through legend, verses, and beliefs; it modified in his favor verses which initially were unfavorable to him, such as those of the long "Song of Horea and Cloșca." It even associated and confused him with Avram Iancu. It branded his betrayers forever: in the bread made out of the wheat bought with the betrayal money they found blood, the blood of Horea!

NOTES

1. M. Auner, *Zur Geschichte der rumanischen Bauernauf-standes im Siebenburgen*, 1784, Sibiu, 1935, pp. 17-18.

2. Brabbee, Gusztav, *Fratres de cruce*, in "Hazank," VIII (1888), pp. 391-393.

3. Abafi Lajos, *A rasza-rend* in "Hazank," V (1886), pp. 12-13.

4. Szilagyi Ferencz, *A mora-vilag Erdelyben*, Pest, 1871, p. 234.

Constantin Antip

THE REVOLUTION OF TUDOR VLADIMIRESCU

"The year 1821 commences the modern history of Romania, the year 1821 ends our Middle Ages..., the year 1821 awakens the national awareness from its painful lethargy...."[1] wrote Bogdan Petriceicu-Haşdeu, an outstanding personality of the nienteenth century in history, linguistics and literature. Nicolae Iorga, the greatest Romanian historian of all times, considered that 1821 was "a great and bold revolution" which, viewed not only in the national but also in the international context meant "a great step forward in the political conception on the national and people's liberties in these Eastern areas."[2] Andrei Oţetea who devoted his entire life to research on the Revolution led by Tudor Vladimirescu said that it was a nationwide revolution "directed both against the feudal order and the Ottoman domination."[3] The Programme of the Romanian Communist Party, adopted in 1974, stresses: "The 1821 revolution led by Tudor Vladimirescu marked the beginning of the modern history of Romania, a cornerstone in the fight for liberty and social justice for shaking off the yoke of foreign domination and the affirmation of the Romanian people's national rights. Although defeated, it strongly shook the old system heralding the future revolutionary transformations."[4]

These considerations which specify the importance and the role of the 1821 Revolution and of its leader in history are based on the objective, scientific appraisal of the internal causes and international circumstances, of the movement and of the immediate and long-range consequences.

133

The 1821 Revolution had its causes in the conditions prevailing in the Romanian society which required changes in the economic, social and political fields. As compared to other European countries, especially those in Central and Western Europe, the development of the Romanian Principalities had been, for a long time, obstructed by numerous factors. Here, the feudal order lasted longer and hindered the emergence and development of capitalist relations. This obsolete system was further aggravated by the political regime in Wallachia and Moldavia, that was known under the name of the Phanariot regime, which had the role of ensuring the Ottoman domination over Moldavia and Wallachia at a time when the national emancipation movement was gaining in strength. The Phanariot regime restricted the autonomy of the two Romanian lands, but could not abolish it.

The aggravation of the obligations toward the Porte, the intensified exploitation by feudal boyars, the extreme fiscal extortion imposed by the Phanariots, the unnumerable abuses of the administration, the Ottoman monopoly on trade, made the social and economic oppression more onerous for the rank and file of Romanian society. "The complaints which were sent to me, those which I myself read, as well as the investigation made by reliable men have convinced me that the people, who bear on their shoulders the entire burden, are completely ruined.... "[5] wrote the Russian General Bagration, who was stationed on Romanian soil during the Russo-Turkish war of 1806-1812. In a book published in 1820, the British Consul Wilkinson wrote in this connection: "There is no other people in the world more oppressed by a despotic government and more overwhelmed by taxes and duties than the peasants in Moldavia and Wallachia."[6] Against this background the tension within the Romanian society grew in intensity. Conflicts between peasantry and boyars sharpened and the opposition of the townsfolk—the middle strata and the emerging bourgeoisie—toward the ruling class became more manifest. The acts of disobedience and revolt in the villages as well as the movements in towns directed against the great boyars, the administration and even against the princes demonstrated that the old relations of production came more and more into conflict with the new productive forces promoted by the bourgeoisie, that the economic feudal structure in the Romanian lands and the Ottoman-Phanariot regime which maintained it were in acute crisis.

While the irreconcilable social-antagonisms opposed the peasantry, the middle strata and the emerging bourgeoisie to the boyars, the former wishing to abolish the feudal system and the latter to maintain it, on the national plane the interests were converging. All Romanian social forces, except for a minority of the boyars faithful to the Phanariot regime, joined their efforts for national emancipation pursuing the transformation of Wallachia and Moldavia from autonomous states, under the suzerainty of the Porte, into fully independent and sovereign states. This solidarity was grounded on the development of social consciousness, on the assertion of the Romanians' right to a life of their own. The process of building the national consciousness was strongly reflected in the movement of the intelligentsia of Transylvania at the close of the eighteenth century. Known by the name of the "Transylvanian School" it struggled for the equality of the Romanians with other co-inhabitants, their recognition as a political nation. The ideas of the School also spread into Wallachia and Moldavia where they became weapons in the struggle for freedom, independence and national unity.

Greatly inbued with conceptions of the Enlightenment which dominated the spiritual background of the progressive forces in most European countries and undermined the philosophical, moral, political and institutional systems of the feudal order, the Romanians' ideals of emancipation were favored by the strong echo of the great modern revolutions of the last quarter of the eighteenth century: the Independence War of North America in 1775-1783 which proclaimed as sacred the principle of liberty and independence, and the French Revolution of 1789 with its famous slogan: liberty, equality, fraternity! Referring to the echo the ideas of the French Revolution had among the Romanians, a letter of 1793 by a Frenchmen living in Bucharest stressed that some people knew by heart the Romanian translation of the Declaration of the Rights of man.[7] In 1794 the Governor of Transylvania requested the Court of Vienna to reject the petition which asked permission for the publication of a Romanian newspaper "because, nowadays, when the situation is aggravated with every passing day, the dissemination of newspapers is more unacceptable than ever before, because the dangerous ideas of liberty of the French are quickly propagated and everything published in the paper can be easily misinterpreted and opinions can produce disturbance of the public order."[8] In this respect, illustrative is also an order issued in 1804 by Moldavia's ruling price which asked that investigations be conducted to find out the name of the person who had sent "a sort of written complaint, without signature, which reveals the spirit of French disobedience and dared to address terrible words to the ruler."[9]

In the second half of the second decade of the nineteenth century, against this background, all classes of Romanian society were sensitive to the idea of rising against foreign domination. Grasping this agitated frame of mind, the French Consul in Bucharest wrote in 1816 that "the Romanian people expect the greatest benefits to result from a revolution which is for them desirable and near."[10]

The Romanians' revolutionary tendency reflected the board movement of the peoples in Central and Western Europe against "the quiet slavery" imposed, after Napoleon's fall, by the reactionary coalition of the Holy Alliance as well as the revolutionary effervescence of the peoples in South-Eastern Europe which aimed at removing Ottoman domination. This explains the adherence of the Moldavian and Walachian boyars, prelates, merchants and artisans to the *Hetairia*, a secret society, whose aim was to liberate Greece and other Christian peoples from the Ottoman yoke. Tudor Vladimirescu himself, who was to lead the 1821 Revolution in Walachia, cooperated with *Hetairia* given the similarity of goals.

Tudor Vladimirescu was born in 1780 into a family of free peasants in the village of Vladimir in the Gorj county. Through education, trade, and administrative experience, he rose above peasant status and became a typical exponent of the middle strata whose ranks included well-off peasants, tradesmen, artisans, petty boyars and whose aspirations were bourgeois, hence progressive in character. His varied activities allowed him to become acquainted with movements prevailing among various social categories, which proved useful in setting the goals of the revolution. His military knowledge and experience acquired in the 1806-1812 War, when he was the commander of a corps of Romanian *pandours*,[11] also held him in good stead. Tudor commanded important forces, of more than 6,000 *pandours* at a time, and he distinguished himself through his military skill, talent and galantry in many confrontations with Ottoman troops. He was subsequently promoted to the rank of lieutenant and was awarded the Russian Order of St. Vladimir.

His sharp mind, strong character, skillfulness as a commander, perserverence, knowledge of the people and their aspirations, and his many other qualities made Tudor Vladimirescu a natural organizer and leader of the general insurrection.

The right moment came by the middle of January 1821 when the ruling prince died and a successor had not yet been appointed by the Porte. Three of the highest boyars of the country affiliated with the Hetairia immediately contacted Tudor and concluded an agreement with him under which the latter assumed the obligation of calling the people to arms while the boyars would secure the necessary material support.

During the night of January 18-19 Tudor, accompanied by a group of soldiers of the princely guard left for Oltenia where he took up quarters at the fortified Tismana Monastery. On January 23, he issued a famous proclamation, the so-called *Tismana Proclamation*, in which the aims of his action were set forth. The essence of that program was incorporated in the slogan *Justice and Liberty* which meant the abolition of privileges and equality before the law. To this end it called the people to struggle, to join the revolutionary army called the Assembly of the People. "Brothers living in Wallachia, whatever your nationality," the Proclamation read, "no law prevents a man to meet evil with evil. . . . How long shall we suffer the dragons that swallow us alive, those above us, both clergy and politicians, to suck our blood? How long shall we be enslaved? . . . . Therefore, brothers, come all of you and deal out evil to bring evil to an end, that we might fare well. . . . And you should come to wheresoever you will hear that the Assembly convned for the good and the benefit of the country and whatsoever the leaders of the Assembly advise you to do, do it faithfully and wheresoever they will summon you to come, there you should come!"[12] The Proclamation can be considered a genuine declaration of war against the boyars,[13] the feudal system and the Phanariot regime. The abolition of the boyars' privileges and the overthrow of the Phanariot regime implied *sine qua non* the idea of liberation from Ottoman domination.

All historical sources point to the far-reaching echo of the Proclamation. Hundreds and thousands of people answered Tudor's ardent call. "Day by day armed men are adding to his strength and he fascinates the souls of the common people, captivating them with words about freedom. . . . "[14] wrote the great boyars in a complaint sent to the Porte against Tudor Vladimirescu. In a report sent to Chancellor Metternich, the Austrian agent in Bucharest, Fleischackl von Hakenau, compared the rising of the *pandours* to the rolling snowball which would soon become an "avalanche" because all over the country recruitment was taking place increasing the army of that "brave man. . . deeply appreciated and loved by the pandours."[15]

In a short period of time Tudor Vladimirescu succeeded in raising all of Oltenia and to organize an army which could not be opposed by any local force.[16] The recruitment was not spontaneous but organized and methodical. To this end, skilled and experienced captains were used and assembling centers were set up. The army was recruited from all strata of the population and its basis consisted of pandours who, as former fighers in the latest Russo-Turkish war, had good training in the use of weapons and in fighting. The fighters were organized into infantry, cavalry and artillery troops. Wishing to give to its infantry the pattern of a regular army, Tudor Vladimirescu organized it into regiments of one thousand people each which, in turn, were subdivided into companies while the cavalry was divided only into companies (50-200 people); weapons consisted of rifles, pistols, swords, spears, axes, etc. and the artillery was also equipped with two cannons. It was a new form of organization—the tactical unit now was the regiment whose combat capacity was twice that of the battalion—the tactical unit of the volunteer pandours on the 1806-1812 campaign.[17]

The revolutionary army was settled in a military camp at Țînțăreni, a place that had a central position and was located at the confluence of five valleys which offered easy access and communication in all directions. Tudor's army was there for three weeks—February 4-28—passing through a thorough process of organizing and disciplining the units and subunits, of military and moral-political training. Concomitantly, according to a judicious general plan, all of Oltenia which was under Tudor's political control was turned into a revolutionary basis of the People's Assembly: the main monasteries were fortified in order to resist the fire arms of that time; they were to be indeed genuine strongholds, able to put up prolonged resistence against an enemy better equipped with effectives and weapons. "The monasteries beyond the Olt," said Tudor, "are filled with provisions and occupied by pandours; there I can resist two or three years fighting for the rights of this country until I win. . . ."[18] Subsequent developments confirmed Tudor Vladimirescu's clear-sightedness.

At the beginning of March, the revolutionary army left for Bucharest to assume control over the political center of the state, and therefore, over the entire territory of Wallachia. At Slatina, a town on the Olt, he stopped to meet other revolutionary or adhering groups. On this occasion Tudor stated, in addition to the social targets which had already been indicated, the national aims of the movment. He tried to strengthen, in the minds of the People's Assembly which amounted to eight thousand people, the idea that its struggle could be successful because it was joined not only by the Romanian people, including leading patriotic boyars who had pledged their support, but also by foreign allies. According to historical sources, Tudor Vladimirescu told the pandours that Alexander Ypsilanti, the chief of the *Hetairia*, "had entered the territory of Wallachia with a large army" and "he was followed by the great Russian power." Clarifying his intentions, he added "We shall only help Prince Ypsilanti to cross the Danube so that he can fight for the liberation of his country; the Russians shall help us to take back the strongholds on our land and then they shall leave us to live free, according to our laws. . . ."[19] In fact Tudor had always in mind the external background against which the Romanian revolution was to take place. A testimony to this is his correspondence with Alexander Ypsilanti before the latter crossed the river Prut, the understandings with the Serbians, the information concerning the causes of his movement he sent to the Emperors of Russia and Austria at the Laibach Congress of the Holy Alliance to secure the support of at least one great European power, in that case Russia, and the benevolence or, at least, neutrality of Austria. To the same effect, Tudor tried to negociate with the Porte: in a petition sent to the Sultan and in several other letters he described the miserable condition of the people and of the country as a result of boyar oppression and abuses committed by the Phanariots.

A war council, held in Slatina, drew up the plan of the march of the People's Assembly toward the capital city which sought urgent measures to secure the bases in Oltenia against possible Ottoman attacks, to guarantee the orderly and disciplined movement of the main forces toward Bucharest, to ensure the flank of the army against the Ottoman garrisons on the Danube and to maintain the connection with the base in Oltenia; to establish contacts with Alexander Ypsilanti and to coordinate the actions of the two forces.[20]

The pandours started the march on March 10 and, at a speed of twenty-five kilometers a day—a performance equal to that of a regular army of the time—reached Cotroceni (about two miles from Bucharest) and on

March 21, at the head of the pandours and numerous people, Tudor Vladimirescu triumphantly entered the capital. When he arrived in Bucharest he received an unpleasant piece of news. Tsar Alexander I had condemned the revolution in Wallachia which he compared to revolutionary developments in Western Europe. The Tsar declared that Tudor Vladimirescu had forfeited the title of Knight of the Order of St. Vladimir and his position as a Russian protege. He treated the Hetairia in the same manner. After having entered Iaşi, Moldavia's capital, at the beginning of March, Ypsilanti hinted that powerful Russian armies would come to support him. Due to this "fatal act of rashness" by which it was disclosed that Russian supported the Hetaria, Tsar Alexander I repudiated Ypsilanti, who had been his aide-de-camp, and dismissed him from his service.[21]

Russia's repudiation had serious implications for the Romanian revolution, for the Hetaria movement, and to a certain extent, for relations between the leaders of the two movements. A large number of boyars, frightened by the Tsar's disavowal, tried to leave Bucharest. In the meantime the Hetaria army, abandoned the previous plan of crossing the Danube and settled on Wallachian territory still nourishing hopes of a Russian intervention. Therefore, Tudor had to adapt to new circumstances. He arrested the members of the Divan who intended to go to Tîrgovişte, a town near the Transylvanian border, where Alexander Ypsilanti had set up his camp. For more than a month the People's Assembly exercised its power in the capital and the greatest part of Wallachia and Tudor was proclaimed prince on the eve of his departure from Bucharest. In cooperation with the boyars and the clergy who remained in Bucharest, he tried to negotiate an agreement with the Ottomans. The attempt failed because the Ottoman representatives who he contacted (the pashas of Vidin, Silistra and Brăila) demanded that he should lay down his arms and, more than that, cooperate with them in the suppression of the Hetairia movement. Tudor could not accept laying down his arms and also rejected the idea of any action against the Hetairia, despite growing dissension between the two movements as the Hetairia army usurped the power of local administrative bodies in the areas where it had settled, tried to entice the troops of the People's Assembly, and committed other abuses.

Faced with the Porte's offensive against the Romanian Principalities (at the beginning of May, the Ottoman army entered Moldavia with some

18,000 men and Wallachia with some 15,000) Tudor reached the only possible conclusion: the time had come for armed resistance against the invaders. He thought it would be a long resistance. Which place would be best? Bucharest? The balance of forces showed that an armed confrontation with the Ottoman army in the capital would have been unwise and would have destroyed the city. Tudor therefore decided that the resistance could be successful only if it was organized beyond the river Olt, namely in the zone which had been prepared as a base of the revolution. Thus, on May 15 the popular army left for Oltenia. On the way, exploiting the feelings of discontent and irritation among pandours as well as the dissatisfaction of a number of captains with Tudor for having put to death nine pandours who were guilty of robbery, a group of conspirators isolated Tudor from his army and turned him over to Alexander Ypsilanti. Given the prevailing intrigues, Ypsilanti considered the pandours' march to Oltenia as a hostile action, the more so as the Hetairia intended to occupy the very positions which had been fortified by the Romanian revolutionaries. He ordered the assassination of Tudor Vladimirescu. After having been tortured, the fearless leader of the Romanian revolution was secretly shot during the night of May 27-28, 1821 and his body, hacked with swords, was thrown into a pond. "So Tudor's life was ended by treason, without investigation, without trial,"[22] wrote the Russian Colonel Liprandi, a contemporary of the tragic events.

The murder of Tudor Vladimirescu deprived the Revolution in Wallachia of the single, firm and daring leadership he had established both politically and militarily. Left without their commander, the pandours resisted Ottoman attacks until the end of July. Illustrative in this respect are the battles of May 28 and 29 at Zăvideni and Drăgășani. When they reached the Olt, the pandours learned that there were 3,000 Ottoman soldiers in Drăgășani and they decided to fight against them. To cross the river by surprise in the Drăgășani zone, they thought of a stratgem— to send a small detachment to perform a demonstrative action meant to deceive the enemy and engage it a few kilometers farther than the place where the main pandour forces had decided to force the river. Out of 2,000 volunteers 300 were chosen to cross the river in the dark; they occupied several houses. Informed about the presence of pandours, the Ottomans arrived on the morning of May 28 and a day-long battle started; although the ratio of Romanian to Ottoman forces was 1 to 10, the

Ottoman attacks were repelled. In the meantime the bulk of pandour units crossed the river and on May 29 they launched a strong offensive against the enemy who was camped in a monastery and two big manor houses. The galantry of the pandours was revealed by the results of the battle: the enemy lost 1,000 people (500 dead and 500 wounded) while the Romanians only 229 men (156 dead and 75 wounded). That was a telling confirmation of the fact that they army of the people, of the 1821 Revolution, could face superior enemy forces.[23]

The Revolution in Wallachia elicted a strong response from the other Romanian provinces, Moldavia and especially Transylvania. Referring to Moldavia, the Austrian agent in Iaşi, Iosif von Raab, stated in a letter addressed to Chancellor Metternich that the principles upheld by Tudor Vladimirescu with regard to the abolition of the Phanariot regime, restoration of the former privileges of the Romanian Principalities, limitation of the boyars' powers, fairness in justice, were received with satisfaction and "openly commended" by the tradesmen, petty boyars and peasants.[24] In turn, Fleischackl von Hakenau, the Austrian agent in Bucharest, informed the Chancellor that "the spirit of freedom and disobedience imprinted by Tudor" will spread "like a contagious disease" to the Romanians in Transylvania who were also not property treated "by the feudal masters of the domains."[25] Tudor's revolutionary movement stirred up the hopes imprinted in the conscience of the Romanians of Transylvania by Horea, the leader of the 1784 peasants' uprising.

Transylvania's governor, Banffy, grasped this state of mind and ordered the border districts to take special measures because "this great Principality, neighboring with Wallachia, has close economic and trade relations, as well as religious and national links and for good reasons we can be afraid that the disorder and the dangerous principles, similar to those of the so-called movement of Horea, could penetrate by secret means our country and the lower people who are already inclined toward such ideas."[26]

The steps taken to this effect, however, could not stop the spreading of the news about events in Wallachia beyond the Carpathians and their influencing the oppressed Romanians. The news were not only received but were discussed by Transylvanian Romanians. Numerous Romanian peasants were arrested, interrogated and tried for disseminating propaganda. Illustrative in this respect is the case of three inhabitants of Sulighete village in the county of Hunedoara: Bedea Adam, Ungur Ignat and

Kiş Toma. They were arrested following denunciations by local noblemen. Bedea Adam was accused of reading to the villagers a paper which ran: "It is announced that in the East a prince by the name of Todoraş has risen, in the beginning with a small army which grows day by day; several hundreds and thousands have gathered until now. God helps them because they want to bring justice; now they are in Wallachia where they settle scores with the boyars and if everything goes well until Easter they will come here, because a prince will come from below to make justice here too."[27] The second accused peasant, Ungur Ignat, had already established the date of Tudor's arrival—the day of Saint Teodor which that year fell on the Tuesday before Easter.[28] The third, Kiş Toma, told villagers that "even if they take the arms from us, they cannot take all the axes, so that at every tenth or twentieth house he will find one and he knows to make a big bludgeon out of them with which he will hit the landlord so hard that he will kill him and throw him to the dogs. . . ."[29] The attorney accused them of instigation and disturbanc of the public order and asked for the death penalty. But although they were not put to death the sentences were very harsh.[30] The severe sentences given to those who spread the ideas of the Wallachia Revolution were meant to frighten the Romanian peasants, to eradicate the influence of such ideas because, as Alexe Noptsa, the Count of Hunedoara, wrote "All circumstances point out that the Romanian peasants here are in sympathy with the events in Wallachia and in case there is an incursion from that part they will undoubtedly join them."[31]

Although the 1821 Revolution could not fulfill its social and national goals its aftermath was important. The main immediate consequence was the abolition of the Phanariot regime and the restoration of the rule of native princes. As Andrei Oțetea rightly points out, the replacement of the Phanariot princes with native princes was not a mere change of figureheads but a genuine revolution which relieved Wallachia and Moldavia of the heavy financial duties toward the Phanar—set up by the Phanariot cartel in 1819—and of the indirect duties toward the Porte (the sums now remained in the Principalities), and created more favorable conditions for the stability and development of the economic, social and cultural life.

Showing that the revolution led by Tudor Vladimirescu freed the Romanians from the Phanariots and restored to the country its fromer

right, Nicolae Bălscescu, the great historian, political and revolutionary
militant of 1848, wrote that in 1821 "the people demanded that the
power should be taken" from the hands of the boyars, "that all Romanians be free and equal in their country; in brief, they demanded that the
state should be a Romanian one, they demanded the rule of democracy."[32]
The above quotations emphasizes the bourgeois-democratic character
of the 1821 Revolution. The exercising—through the People's Assembly—
of real power, the setting up of forces for armed action and defense, the
people's revolutionary army—which represented the revival of the Romanian army institution—which was to serve the interests of the people
and of the country, the administrative changes and the checking of abuses,
the tax-relief measures, the attempt to give the country a constitution
through the document elaborated in April—namely *The Demands of the
Romanian People*—and other measures initiated by Tudor Vladimirescu
demonstrate that the 1821 Revolution was different from previous social
movements, to wit, the peasant uprisings of the Middle Ages, that it had
a bourgeois orientation, naturally commemsurate to the maturity of the
emerging bourgeoisie and middle classes of Romanian society of that
time. A most valuable element of the political program of the 1821 Revolution was the idea of national unity which was clearly expressed in Tudor
Vladimirescu's letter, dated April 5, 1821, whereby mentioning that they
were "of the same nation" he urged the Divan of Bucharest to cooperate
with that of Iaşi "so that being the same in thoughts and deeds with
Moldavia we could both win the rights of these Principalities, helping
each other."[33]

The program of the 1821 Revolution set the direction of historical
progress in the Romanian Principalities for the next three decades. The
1821 Revolution made possible achievements in economic, social and
administrative fields, freedom of trade and abolition of the guild monopoly, which favored the development of industrial manufacturing, of the
home market, and access to the world market; it also led to the organization of the state on the principle of separate powers—executive, legislative, judicial—a fact which helped the modernization of public institutions; to the re-establishment of the national army and the flourishing of
culture. All these achievements led to the growth and strengthening of
capitalist elements during 1822-1848, to the Romanian society's access
to the road of modern development.

The 1821 Revolution created a climate that was propitious for the promotion of progressive ideas which took shape in a number of reform projects, in the establishment of an anti-feudal national opposition, of secret societies among which the most advanced advocated radical social and political changes for the abolition of old rules and the establishment of a constitutional-democratic regime. For instance, a secret society in Wallachia, in 1840, contemplated the overthrowing of the existing social order and the instauration of a new one, the liberation of peasants and a land reform, the abolition of all feudal privileges, the freedom and equality of citizens before the law, the creation of a national army, republican government and the independence of the country.[34]

The 1821 Revolution had a powerful impact on the development of the national consciousness of the Romanian people. The work carried out by advanced elements for the development of education, literature, arts, theater and the press was meant to raise the consciousness of the people, to assert the Romanians' right to freedom, independence and unity. These positions were made clear in leading Romanian publications of that period: *Curierul Românesc* (The Romanian Courier) and *Albina Românească* (The Romanian Bee) both issued in 1829 in Bucharest and Iaşi respectively, the daily *România* brought out in Bucharest in 1838, and *Gazeta Transilvaniei* (Transylvanian Gazette), published in Braşov in 1838. Romania was the old Dacia and that equation was explicitly expressed in the very titles of such major publications as *Dacia Literară* (Literary Dacia), Iaşi, 1840 and *Magazin istoric pentru Dacia* (Historical Review for Dacia), Bucharest, 1845. Wherever it was published, either in Wallachia, Moldavia or Transylvania, the press was an active weapon in the struggle for the general cause of the Romanians, strong, many-sided, national solidarity. On November 29, 1838, Ion Eliade Rădulescu, the editor of *Curierul Românesc* wrote George Bariţ, the editor of *Gazeta Transilvaniei:* "Dear Sir, I dar to express my opinion that from now on we should make our publications the mouthpieces of love and brotherhood among all Romanians, as this is our salvation."[35]

The ideal of the Romanians' independence and national unity was at that time a well-formed and consolidated ideology which, as everybody knows, always and everywhere constitutes the best expression of the effervescence of a social and national community. This ideology was to underlay political programs such as that formulated in the "Act for Union

and Independence" advanced in 1838 by a revolutionary group in Wallachia. It expressed the will and determination "to win Romanian sovereignty, to give [to the Romanians] a free and independent homeland for
all of the same nation."³⁶

This brief survey of the 1821 Revolution led by Tudor Vladimirescu
clearly points out—as in fact the entire Romanian historiography does—
that through its program and organization, through the wide response
it elicited from other parts and the impact it had on the subsequent
epoch, it confronted the Romanian society with all the great questions
related to the passing from Middle Ages to the modern age. Its ideas
were taken over and developed by the 1848 Revolution which, occurring
almost simultaneously in all Romanian territories on both sides of the
Carpathians, focused its program on the abolition of feudal privileges,
the liberation of dependent peasants, the promotion of bourgeois-democratic rights and liberties, the removal of foreign domination and the
achievement of national unity.

NOTES

1. B. P. Haşdeu, *Oltenescele (Discursul de deschidere la serbarea pe
Cîmpia Cotrocenii în memoria lui Tudor Vladimirescu)* (Opening Speech
at the Festivities on the Cotrocenii Field in Memory of Tudor Vladimirescu), Editura Librăriei S. Samitca, Craiova, 1884, p. 22.

2. N. Iorga, *Izvoarele contemporane asupra mişcării lui Tudor
Vladimirescu* (Contemporary Sources on Tudor Vladimirescu's Movement), Librăriile "Cartea Românească" şi Pavel Suru, Bucharest, 1921,
p. III, XII.

3. Acad. Andrei Oţetea, *Tudor Vladimirescu şi revoluţia din 1821*
(Tudor Vladimirescu and the 1821 Revolution), Editura Ştiinţifică,
Bucharest, 1971, p. 15.

4. *Programul Partidului Comunist Român de făurire a societăţii
socialiste multilateral dezvoltate şi înaintare a României spre comunism*
(Program of the Romanian Communist Party for the Building of the Multilaterally Developed Socialist Society and Romania's Advance toward Communism), Meridiane Publishing House, Bucharest, 1975, p. 31.

5. S. I. Samailov, *Răscoala de eliberare naţională din anul 1821 în
Ţara Românească* (The 1821 National Liberation Uprising in Wallachia),

in "Analele româno-sovietice-seria Istorie," no. 2, 1956, p. 97.

6. W. Wilkinson, *An Account of the Principalities of Wallachia and Moldavia*, London, 1820, p. 155.

7. Constantin C. Giurescu, *Contribuțiuni la studiul originilor și dezvoltării burgheziei române pînă la 1848* (Contribution to the Study of the Origins and Development of the Romanian Bourgeoisie to 1848), Editura Științifică, Bucharest, 1972, p. 72.

8. Constantin Antip, *Istoria presei române* (History of the Romanian Press), Academia "Ștefan Gheorghiu," Facultatea de Ziaristică, Bucharest, 1979, pp. 58-59.

9. Constantin C. Giurescu, op. cit., p. 72.

10. *Documente privind istoria României. Răscoala din 1821* (Documents on the History of Romania. The 1821 Uprising), vol. I, Editura Academiei, Bucharest, 1959, p. 82.

11. The *pandours* were recruited from among the free peasantry of Oltenia, a province in Western Wallachia1 they enjoyed special rights and were exempt from taxation as a reward for services connected with border guard duties, maintenance of public order, and militiary duties. In the first decades of the nineteenth century they were organized as a separate army coprs divided into battalions and companies, and were trained in military camps for a period of six months. The participation of pandour units and of other detachments of Romanian volunteers in the Russo-Turkish and Russo-Austrian-Turkish wars, during 1768-1812, was one of the forms of the struggle for liberation from Ottoman domination. (See General-Major Dr. Constantin Olteanu, *Contribuții la cercetarea conceptului de putere armată la români* (Contributions to Research on the Concept of Romanian Armed Forces), Editura Militară, București, 1980, p. 117).

12. Emil Vîrtosu, *Tudor Vladimirescu. Pagini de revoltă* (Tudor Vladimirescu. Pages of Revolt), colecția "Gînd și faptă," Bucharest, 1944, pp. 106-108.

13. Although the Proclamation asked that only "the ill-gotten property and wealth of the tyrant boyars were to be destroyed" and the boyars who supported or joined the movement were to be excepted, "as promised," the peasants did not understand this distinction; for the robbed and oppressed peasants all boyars were tyrants, their wealth was ill-gotten and therefore all boyar and monastery property was to be destroyed. (See

148   War, Revolution, and Society in Romania

Istoria poporului român The History of the Romanian People), edited by Andrei Oțetea, Editura științifică, București, 1970, p. 225.)

14.   *Documente privind istoria României. Răscoala din 1821* (Documents on the History of Romania. The 1821 Uprising), vol. I, Editura Academie, Bucharest, 1952, p. 222.

15.   *Revoluția din 1821 cendusă de Tudor Vladimirescu. Documente externe* (The 1821 Revolution Led by Tudor Vladimirescu. Foreign Documents), Editura Academiei, Bucharest, 1980, p. 73.

16.   Andrei Oțetea, op. cit., p. 222.

17.   Dan Berindei, Traian Mutașcu, *Aspecte militare ale mișcării revoluționare din 1821* (Military Aspects of the 1821 Revolutionary Movement), Ediția II-a revăzută, Editura militară, Bucharest, 1973, pp. 67-68.

18.   Dan Berindei, Traian Mutașcu, op. cit., p. 71.

19.   Ilie Fotino, *Tudor Vladimirescu și Alexandru Ipsilanti în revoluțiunea din anul 1821 supranumită Zavera* (Tudor Vladimirescu and Alexander Ypsilanti in the 1821 Revolution), Bucharest, 1874, p. 57.

20.   Dan Berindei, Traian Mutașcu, op. cit., pp. 82-83.

21.   In this capacity as head of the Holy Alliance the Tsar could not support a revolutionary movement. He could only be a supporter of order as it was conceived at the Vienna Congress of 1815. From his point of view, Russia had to appear a total stranger to the developments in Moldavia and Wallachia. The mission of the Hetairia was to create instability among the Christian peoples in the Ottoman Empire. That would enable Russia to consider the Ottoman government unable to ensure a state of affairs compatible with the maintenance of order and peace and would legitimize Russian intervention in the Ottoman Empire, with the consent of the other members of the Holy Alliance to reestablish order.

22.   Andrei Oțetea, op. cit., p. 427.

23.   Major-General Constantin Antip, *Războiul popular în istoria universală* (The People's War in World History), Editura Militară, Bucharest, 1976, pp. 99-100.

24.   *Revoluția din 1821 condusă de Tudor Vladimirescu. Documente externe.* (The 1821 Revolution Led by Tudor Vladimirescu. Foreign Documents), Editura Academiei, Bucharest, 1980, p. 91.

25.   Ibid., p. 83.

26.   M. Andrițoiu, M. Cerghedean, *S-a ridicat un crăiuț cu numele*

Toderaş. . . . (A Prince Called Toderaş), in "Magazin Istoric," no. 3, 1976, p. 3.

27. Loc., cit., p. 4.

28. Loc. cit.

29. Loc. cit.

30. Bedea Adam was sentenced to ten years at hard labor, two days a week only with bread and water; Ungur Ignat to ten years at hard labor and 1,000 blows, 25 once every three months; Kiş Toma to five years at hard labor and 500 blows.

31. Andrei Oţetea, op. cit., pp. 280-281.

32. N. Bălcescu, *Opere* (Works), vol. I, partea II-a, ediţia G. Zane, Bucharest, 1940, pp. 101-102.

33. Miron Constantinescu, Constantin Daicoviciu, Ştefan Pascu, *Istoria României, compendiu* (History of Romania, Compendium), Editura didactică şi pedagogică, Bucharest, 1969, p. 277.

34. Ibid., p. 289.

35. Constantin Antip, op. cit., p. 68.

36. Ştefan Ştefănescu, *Tudor Vladimirescu înainte-mergătorul renaşterii naţionale* (Tudor Vladimirescu the Forerunner of National Revival), "Scînteia," June 13, 1980.

37. G. Zane, *Prefaţă* (Foreword) *N. Bălcescu, Opere I, Scrieri istorice, politice şi economice 1844-1847* (Works I, Historical, Political and Economic Writings 1844-1847), Editura Academiei, Bucharest, 1974, p. 11.

THE REVOLUTION OF 1848-1849

The Romanian Revolution of 1848,[1] an event of exceptional significance in the history of Romania, was an expression of the centuries-old
aspirations of the Romanian people for freedom, national liberation and
social progress. Those aspirations were rooted in the determination of the
masses to abolish the feudal system, to free themselves from dependence
of the dominating neighboring empires. "The bourgeois-democratic
Revolution of 1848 was a crucial moment in Romania's transition from
feudalism to capitalism"—said President Nicolae Ceauşescu—"it gave a
powerful impetus to the growth of the Romanian people's self awareness,
expressed the determination of Moldavians, Wallachians and Transylvanians to break up the old feudal relations, to clear the way for the new
social system, to achieve national unity within the frontiers of a single
State, to unflinchingly advance on the road of progress and democracy."[2]
The Revolution was generated by the economic and socio-political contradictions of the period of transition from feudalism to capitalism. The
1848 revolutionary fighters, particularly the great revolutionary demo-
crat Nicolae Bălcescu (1819-1852), were the first to underline the historical link between the 1821 Revolution, led by Tudor Vladimirescu,
in Wallachia and the 1848 Revolution and spotlighted the continuity of
the effort for renewal of the structures and organization of Romanian
society. The Romanian Revolution, Bălcescu said, was no "ephemeral
phenomenon, without a past and a future, and without other causes than
the fortuitous wish of a minority, and the general European movement.

151

The general revolution was the occasion and not the cause of the Romanian Revolution. It originated in the past centuries and was hatched by
eighteen centuries of toil, suffering and communion of the Romanian
people with themselves."[3] Separated by an interval of almost three decades, the events of 1821 and of 1848 are in fact two phases of the same
revolutionary process, two expressions—identical in essence but different
in scope—determined by the changed historical conditions of the crisis
of the feudal society. At Tismana, in 1821, as well as at Iași (Moldavia),
Blaj (Transylvania) or Islaz (Wallachia) in 1848, the places where the demands of the Romanian people were enunciated, the unjust and anachroni-
cal medieval system was condemned by the rebellious masses; the programs of Tismana, Iași, Blaj and Islaz were in fact declarations of war by
innovating forces on the representatives of a decaying society condemned
by its very historical development.

"Justice and freedom," "Justice and brotherhood," the slogans which
were written on the banners of the revolutions of 1821 and 1848 synthetized in fact both the common and the distinctive features of the two
historic events. In 1821 the Romanian revolutionary forces were part of
the great effort of the peoples in Southeast Europe to free themselves
from the authority of the Ottoman Porte. The understood that to ensure
the unhampered development of the productive forces and to achieve
meaningful changes in the political superstructure it was necessary to remove the Ottoman domination which was the crutch and the guarantee
of the feudal system. Tudor's struggle had therefore the twofold significance of a national and social revolution which, because of historical
conditions, assigned priority to emancipation from foreign domination.[4]

The rule of native princes (Ioniță Sandu Sturdza in Iași and Grigore IV
Ghica in Bucharest), the abolition of the Ottoman monopoly and the
achievement of administrative autonomy through the Treaty of Adrianople of 1829, the process of state modernization which was accelerated
during the period of the *Reglement Organique*, created new conditions
for development in Moldavia and Wallachia. Under those changed condition the new class—the bourgeoisie—asserted itself ever more vigorosly
in both the economic and the political life. The retention of the privileges of the big landowners still prevented assumption of key positions
by the bourgeoisie, whose interests were identical, up to a point, with
those of the masses, and which was actively engaged, especially within

the framework of secret political societies (The "Carbonari" Movement, The Constitution, the Patriotic Association, Brotherhood, to name a few) in the struggle for power.[5] In 1821, the reputidation by the Tsar of the *Hetairia* and of Tudor's Revolution had allowed the cruel suppression of the two movements by the Porte. The memory of foreign occupation and its painful consequences was still too recent and the generation of 1848 understood that under those political circumstances the relationship between the national and social shcaracter, such as it was in 1821, had to be changed. The 1848 revolutionaries understood that, to avert the brutal intervention of the reactionary empires and the repetition of the tragic end of 1821, they had—at least officially—to direct their struggle first toward achievement of political and social changes and, after that, the attainment of the national ideal—unity and independence.

The identity of the essential claims ofthe programs of 1821 and 1848 as well as the perfect continutiy between the two movements is another proof of the fact that the 1848 Revolution was neither "the Romanian edition" of the events in Paris in February, nor the outcome of some generous minds, out of touch with the reality and guided only by intense reading of foreign literature. The 1848 Romanian Revolution was deeply rooted in the Romanian society and it was the expression of a great effort made by the progressive forces to solve, through revolution, the crisis of the feudal society.

The development of the productive forces, the emergence of the first forms of mechanized industry, the increase in marketable agricultural production of the big cereal growing estates could no longer exist within the ever more rigid patterns of feudal relations. The conflict between the new productive forces and the obsolete relations of production materialized socially and politically in the conflict between the burgeoning bourgeoisie, which included in its programs demands of the masses whose support they thus gained, and the big landowners who had the state apparatus under their control.

In Transylvania, national contradictions added to the contradictions generated by the emergence of capitalist relations. The movement for national and social emancipation of the Romanian people in Transylvania was every stronger in spite of the suppressing of Horea's uprising (1784) and the rejection of the *Supplex Libellus Valachorum* (1791). The Romanians in Transylvania, considered as tolerated and deprived of political rights, formed the majority of the population and covered, therefore, with their contributions the greatest part of the fiscal duties; they demanded fully equal rights with the other nationalities, and the solving of the problems generated by the maintenance *de facto* of the peasants' bondage. On both sides of the Carpathians the revolutionary changes were a topical question and the problems which the Revolution was called to solve were basically alike. In the three Romanian Countries the social and economic changes revealed the necessity of removing the feudal system which had become the main obstacle for the progress of Romanian society. At the same time, ever more vigorous was the Romanian people's will to put an end to foreign domination, the shield of the old system, which kept the rate of development of the Romanian nation behind that of other European nations.

Against this background, and also stimulated by the great tremor which shook the foundations of the obsolete or reactionary structures from the Atlantic to the Black Sea, a broad social and national movement emerged and developed in the Romanian Countries; their programs expressed the demands of all social categories whose aspirations could not be fulfilled within the feudal system.

The program of the 1848 Revolution focused on the agrarian issue which had to be solved. The abolition of personal servitude by the reforms of 1746-1749 of the Wallachian Prince Constantin Mavrocordat and the decree for the abolition of adscription promulgated by Joseph II in 1785 only replaced the personal bondage of the peasant with a real one resulting from the lack of ownership of the land tilled by him. The continuous aggravation of the regime of duties—especially of labor service—of the peasants to the landowners was the characteristic feature of the period antedating to outbreak of the Revolution. The emancipation of the peasants and the abolition of feudal servitude were laid down in *Our Principles for Reforming the Homeland*, a document of the Moldavian revolutionaries, in the Islaz Proclamation and in the program of Blaj as they were considered fundamental prerequisites for the rapid development of the new capitalist relations of production in agriculture and thus weaken the economic base of the big landowners, the social force which opposed the transformations envisaged by the Revolution. Granting land to the peasants, which had to secure an economic foundation for their freedom, was included in the 1848 program as the second stage of solving the peasant problem. The 1848 revolutionaries realized that the personal freedom of the peasant could be meaningful only if it were accompanied by redistribution of the land. To make the peasant the owner of a plot of land was also, according to the views of the revolutionary fighters, the most effective means for winning the peasant over to the cause of the revolution.

The correct understanding of the indissoluble link between the granting of land to the peasants and the consolidation of the Romanian nation made the radical leaders of the revolution militate for a democratic solution of the agrarian problem. "To have a homeland which we could defend," wrote Nicolae Bălcescu, "it is imperative to make the peasants owners."[6] A similar stand was taken by Mihail Kogălniceanu, the leader of the Moldavian revolution, who said "only a peasant who is an owner by loving this land will love his homeland too."[7]

As far as the foreign threat was concerned, the Romanian revolutionareis could not forget that it was the French peasants, who had become owners of the land, that defended the revolution in 1789 against foreign intervention. The dialectics of historical conditions made, however, that the very foreign immixture be the cause of narrowing the dialogue between the leaders of the Revolution and the peasantry and check the solving of the agrarian question. To avoid dissensions and to ensure a massive rally around the banner of the Revolution, the radical revolutionaries relegated the agrarian question to a lesser place. Nevertheless, the solutions envisaged by the Moldavians, the debates of the Bucharest commission for land reform, the talks at Blaj emphasized the urgency of the agrarian question and outlined ways for its future solution within the framework of the national state.

Although essential, the agrarian question was not the only issue of concern to the 1848 revolutionaries. An entire program of political and economic measures had to ensure the development of capitalist relations and enable ever broader categories to have access to public life. Political and civic equality, individual liberty, freedom of the press, of religion, the abolition of gypsies serfdom, equal and free education for the entire people had to guarantee the establishment of what Nicolae Bălcescu called "the rule of the people by the people." Concomitantly, the creation of conditions for the free development of industry and trade, the establishment of credit institutions—national banks, discount houses, or saving banks—the building of roads and canals, the abolition of export tariffs and of custom duties, the "return" to the state of the properties of the monasteries, the setting up of vocational schools, all these—envisaged by the revolutionaries—were meant to provide a solid economic foundation to the modern Romanian society.

The aggregate of economic, social and political measures of the revolutionary programs sought to achieve the primary objective—the social one— of the 1848 Romanian Revolution. Parallel to that objective was the other one—the national. The national idea was of lasting concern to the revolutionaries and an undercurrent of the revolution. It focussed on unity and independence. For the revolutionaries of 1848 the achievement of the two objectives was a unitary purpose and progress. Social progress could not be attained if foreign domination and control were maintained; independence would be a mere illusion if the feudal system was not abolished.

Undoubtedly, in 1848 the idea of national unity[8] was rooted in advanced minds and was manifest in numerous revolutionary actions. Although it could not be spelled out in the official programs, because of prevailing external circumstances, the ideal was present in the programs drawn up by the Moldavian revolutionaries who fled from Iași, after the suppression of the movement in March 1848, and it was extensively debated by the revolutionary press of the time in Wallachia and Transylvania. It was equally mirrored in the close links between the revolutionaries of the three Romanian countries. The participation of the Transylvanians in the Wallachian Revolution, especially as propaganda spokesmen of the Wallachians in the revolutionary struggle of the Romanians in Transylvania in the Apuseni Mountains, of the Moldavians and Wallachians in the great national assembly of May 13/15, 1848 when, on the plan of Blaj 40,000 people—mostly peasants—gathered, was the highest form of expression of Romanian brotherhood in the struggle for national political unity.

In July 1848, Al. G. Golescu, one of the leaders of the movement in Wallachia even proposed the setting up of a revolutionary action center in Bucharest which was to encourage the struggle of all Romanians for national unity. In the opinion of the 1848 revolutionaries that vital aspiration could be fulfilled wither all at once or, more likely, in stages; first the union of Moldavia and Wallachia and then, after the consolidation of the partly united state, the completion of that unity through the establishment of "Daco-Romania."

Of equal concern was the finding of the means and particularly of the proper moment for securing independence, preferably concurrently with the union. In the Brașov program of the Moldavian reovlutionaries called *Our Principles of Reforming the Homeland*—which was not for release but whose provisions were viewed as a solemn agreement among all signatories—this ideal was clearly expressed. Point xis of the program stipulated "the union of Moldavia and Wallachia in a single independent state." In a letter of March 1850 (from Nicolae Bălcescu to A. G. Golescu) the Romanians' union and independence were singled out as immediate targets of decisive importance for the fate of the Romanian nation. After this revolution, "we still have two more to fight: a revolution for national unity and, later, one for national independence so that the nation may fully enjoy its natural rights." And further on: "The question of unity has made great strides and is much simplier now. The union of Wallachia and Moldavia is a fact for everybody . . . and it cannot but be immediately achieved. The Romanians in Austria, by virtue of the Constitution of March and of promises made to them are all most insistently demanding the formation of a single nation of three and a half million people, and they will ultimately be successful. Therefore, when the two big groups of four million and of three and a half million are together who will be able to stop their union? Therefore, our Romania will exist. I have this inner conviction. He who does not see it is blind."[10]

In Transylvania, where the inability of Lajos Kossuth and his supporters to understand the essence of the national problem in the Habsburg Empire and to grasp the relationship between the revolutionary and the national struggle caused the forcible incorporation of Transylvania into Hungary and the resultant Romanians' determination to defend their national being by force of arms. The course of events convinced the 1848 revolutionaries that it was the establishment of a national state that could provide the Romanian people with a propitious framework for development and a protective shield against the expansionist or domineering tendencies of the great neighboring empires.

The interventions of Tsarist Russia, of the Habsburg Empire and of the Ottoman Empire put an end to the Romanian Revolution and temporarily prevented the attainment of its fundamental goals. The revolutionary struggle, however, was carried on in exile and its leaders were to return to their native land when the decline of Tsarist Russia began, because of the internal social crisis and defeat in the Crimean War. However,

just as the goals of the revolutionaries of 1821 were achieved, in part and
gradually, during the reigns of native princes and in the period of the
Reglement Organique, so the main aspirations of the "Forty-eighters"
were fulfilled in the period that followed the suppression of the Revolution of 1848. The Union of the Principalities in 1859, the land reform
of 1864 and the winning of state independence in 1877—principal goals
of the revolutionary program—were achieved in the course of three decades after the revolution.

1848 brought onto the stage of Romanian political life a tema of remarkable personalities—Nicolae Bălcescu, Mihail Kogălniceanu, Avram
Iancu, Eftimie Murgu, E. Hurmuzaki, C. A. Rosetti, Vasile Alecsandri,
Simion Bărnuțiu, Brothers Golescu, Costache Negri, George Barițiu,
Gheorghe Magheru, Al. Papiu-Ilarian, Dumitru and Ion Brătianu, Alexandru Ioan Cuza, Timotei Cipariu, Ion Heliade Rădulescu, Vasile Racliș,
etc.—who were ardent patriots, educated men with a deep understanding
of the realities and needs of Romanian society. All those revolutionaries
and politicians, devoted to the Revolution and the people to whom they
belonged, never faltered in their struggle for progress and independence.
It is indeed significant that the generation of 1848 provided the political
cadres of modern Romania.

However exceptional the leaders of the 1848 Revolution might have
been, they could not have made such a memorable imprint on Romania's
history had their actions not enjoyed the strong support of the people.
Indeed "the masses, determined to fight for a better, free and independent life, to ensure the country's development on the path of economic
and social progress, were the mainstay of the 1848 revolution in all Romanian Principalities."[11] In Moldavia, Wallachia and Transylvania, animated by the ideals of social and national liberation, the people played
a decisive role in the unfolding and consolidation of the revolutionary
movement. It was the masses that caused the inclusion of their demands
for economic and social progress in the revolutionary programs; it was the
people who fought the enemies of the Revolution, who defended the
Revolution against the foreign forces who wanted to crush it. The decisive role of the people in the Revolution was also emphasized, among
others, by Ion Ghica, a Wallachian supporter of the Romanian nation's
progress, who wrote in 1866: "I have seen and heard people who did assume the entire merit of the 1848 Revolution and I often thought: it's

a pity that Nicu Bălcescu is not alive for he would tell them, in his quick and deep style, that the awakening of 1848 was not the work of a man alone, or of a group or a party . . . he would tell them that nobody could have stopped that great Revolution and it would have taken place even in the absence of each of those who have dared to claim its paternity. The nation concurred and organized the Revolution . . . ."[12] History has proved that in all revolutions the use of the combat force of the people was a factor of success. The people, in arms, was therefore considered as the most reliable source of support of the 1848 Revolution. This concept materialized in the setting up of national guards which had to defend the revolutionary gains. In the view of the organizers, the establishment of the national guards had to offer the premises for the creation of a single military force of the three Romanian Countries with the main purpose of defending the Revolution, especially against its internal enemies.

The military aspects of the Romanian Revolution point to its autochtonous origin and unity character. The military programs drawn up in Moldavia, Wallachia and Transylvania were similar, sometimes even identical, revealing the same economic, social and political realities that caused the Revolution in all three Romanian Countries. Similar solutions were found for similar historical conditions. The objective requirements of the emerging capitalist Romanian society, as well as the close cooperation between the leaders of the Revolution on both sides of the Carpathians provided a genuine "military doctrine" of the Romanian Revolution which integrated specific plans of the bourgeois-democratic revolution with elements derived from the traditional military organization of the Romanians. Four fundamental elements can be traced out in this doctrine.

First, the "recovery" of the organizational system of the regular army whose ranks had been joined by revolutionaries. Second, the establishment of the national guard which was included in the plans of all bourgeois revolutions. The third component of the future army was the voluntary units of *dorobantzi* and *pandours*, irregular forces which constituted large reserve units suited to the demographic and economic conditions prevailing in the Romanian Countries. Lastly, the military doctrine of the 1848 Revolution was based on the concept of the entire people's army and of people's war which, having withstood the test of centuries of struggle against Ottoman aggression, could readily be adapted to the conditions prevailing in 1848 for the struggle against the enemies of the Revolution.

The fighters of 1848 viewed the implementation of the social program as the first stage of the revolution and the achievement of unity and the winning of independence as subsequent stages. In this broad historical perspective, the new military establishment had to be able to carry out missions specific to successful achievement of each stage of the struggle for social and national liberation of the Romanian people.

By envisaging identical army structures in the three Romanian Countries, the 1848 revolutionaries contributed to the foundation of the modern Romanian army. The transformation of the regular army from one committed exclusively to guard duties into an instrument of the revolution, the transition from an army built on the narrow foundations of class privileges to an army open to all social categories, and finally, the formulation of the conept of the popular war as a means of defending the Revolution—that was the legacy of the 1848 Revolution in the field of military organization and theory.

Even if the heroic efforts of the masses to liberate themselves from the yoke of feudal and foreign exploitation were not successful in 1848-1849, they were not inconsequential. The Revolution sharpened the combative spirit of the masses, increased their confidence in their own forces, and proved to be a school for future battles. As in all crucial moments of history, in the 1848 Revolution too the people proved to be a most resolute force that played a decisive role. The confidence in the people, and the people's support of the actions of the 1848 revolutionary forces were responsible for only the temporary suppression of the goals of the revolution. The continuing readiness of the people to pursue the struggle for the triumph of the cause of the "Forty-eighters," the triumph of the great national ideals, was to overcome the opposition of the coalesced forces of internal and international reaction to the Revolution.

The Romanian Revolution, deeply rooted in the autochtonous reality, forms part of the great revolutionary tide that engulfed the European continent in 1848. The parallelism between 1821 and 1848 is clear in this respect too. In 1821 the movement of the Balkan people was part of the broad revolutionary struggle that shook the continent from Spain to the Ottoman Empire, necessitating the intervention of the Holy Alliance. In 1848, the revolutionary action had an increased intensity and covered a larger area from Paris to Bucharest. Bucharest and Iași constituted the most advanced ports of the European Revolution. Stimulated but not determined by the events that occurred in othe European Countries, the Romanian Revolution, while sharing some of the elements of the other revolutions, had specific characteristics corresponding to the specific development of the Romanian society. To the bourgeoisie's struggle for power, which constituted the essence of the European revolutions of 1848, the Romanian Revolution added the agrarian and national issues. The role of the rural masses, the Ottoman domination, the Habsburg rule and the Tsarist protectorate also created conditions specific to the Romanian Revolution and left their imprint on the Revolution.

In 1849, when Hungary was the only country in Europe in which the revolutionary struggle continued, Nicolae Bălcescu militated for collaboration between the Romanian and Magyar forces, collaboration in which he saw the guarantee of success for the Romanian Revolution. At the same time, the 1848 revolutionaries of Moldavia, Wallachia and Transylvania displayed a true internationalist spirit as revealed in their close ties with revolutionary circles in other European countries and in the promotion of the ideals of equality and mutual respect among peoples. The same spirit of collaboration was manifest among the masses. Romanians and other co-inhabiting nationalities—Magyars, Saxons, etc.— fought together, on the same barricades, in the struggle against depotism and exploitation. The successes of the revolution in the Romanian Countries were enthusiastically welcomed by revolutionaries from abroad. Even if the necessity of joining the revolutionary effort was not always understood, the success of the struggle against internal and external despotism were considered to be part of a common revolutionary patrimony. After the suppression of the Revolution, a true "International" of the 1848 movement was constituted, which allowed revolutionaries from all countries to draft plans for renewed action. The 1848 movement revealed not only the great revolutionary potential of the Romanian people, but also its receptivity to the innovating, progressive ideas of that epoch. The Romanian 1848 Revolution was thus not only an episode in Romania's national history but also in the history of Europe, because the Romanian Revolution was a historic and organic part of the European revolution.

The revolutionary phenomenon in Romania was the result of the historic evolution of society in the Carpathian-Danubian area. As on the rest of the continent, the Romanian bourgeoisie was faced with the resistance of the large landowners who, protected by the provisions of the *Reglement*

Organique, held political power. As in the rest of Europe too, the masses played a decisive role in the revolution; in the Romanian Countries, just as in Germany or Italy, the social struggle also blended with the struggle for independence and national unity. The Revolution was so powerful a force that it took the combined military efforts of the Ottoman, Habsburg and Tsarist Empires to defeat it. The armed intervention of the Tsarist troops in the three Romanian Countries was to consolidate the Russian influence in Southeast Europe and thus sharpen the contradictions among the Great Powers concerned with the Eastern Question. The Crimean War, which in 1853, was caused by Russia's attempt to strengthen the position she had secured through the suppression of the 1848 Revolution to the detriment of the Porte.

At the start of the hostilities, the Romanian revolutionaries believed that they could but serve the ideals of 1848 through military action against the Tsarist forces. However, when the settlement of the problems that had caused the Crimean War shifted from the battlefield to the negotiating table, the Romanian revolutionaries engaged in an offensive designed to explain and defend Romanian interests to influential foreign governments. The question of the Romanian Principalities, which became an European problem, found its solution largely through the indefatigable work of the leaders of 1848 who greatly influenced both European governments and public opinion. If it is clear that without the struggle of the masses the 1859 Union would not have taken place, it is equally clear that without the actions of the 1848 revolutionaries in the main capital cities of Europe, the Congress of Paris would not have opened the way to the Union of the Principalities.

The historic importance of the 1848 Revolution consists therefore in the effort to resolve the fundamental problems of the Romanian society, at a decisive moment of its evolution. The entire modern history of Romania—from 1848 to 1918—is in fact, nothing else than the realization in successive stages, of the main goals of the 1848 movement: land reform, unitary state, national independence. The basis on which modern Romanian society developed are in fact the basis envisaged by the 1848 revolutionary program: the historic evolution of modern Romania was based on the blueprint presented at Iaşi, Blaj and Islaz. The principal reforms and measures adpted after 1859 did not however represent the total realization, in letter and spirit of the goals of the "Forty-eighters."

The bourgeoisie did not pursue its innovative goals with the same intensity during the period 1848-1918. Hesitations, vacillations and compromises were to limit the progress of Romanian society within the new framework created by the development of the capitalist relations. If the inconsistency of the bourgeoisie occasionally altered the contents of the reforms, the struggle of the masses provided much of the impetus for the achievement of the social and national goals enunciated in 1848. The land reform of 1864 cannot be understood without understanding the debates of the Commission established by the 1848 Provisional Government; the Romanian soldiers who through the bravery displayed at Grivița, Rahova and Smîrdan secured Romania's Independence are the successors of the soldiers who distinguished themselves in the heroic struggle of Dealul Spirii on September 13, 1848; and lastly, the masses who on December 1, 1918 confirmed at the meeting of Alba Iulia the completion of national unity through the union of Transylvania with Romania, were merely realizing the aspirations expressed seventy years earlier on the field of Blaj as tens of thousands of Transylvanian peasants and representatives of Romanians from other provinces shouted: "We want to unite with the Country!"

Toward the end of the nineteenth century, after the emergence and development of socialist and workers' organizations, the traditions of 1848 were assumed by the Romanian proletariat and interpreted in the spirit of its aspirations.[13] It is worthy to note that the spread of Marxist philosophy in Romania was facilitated by the favorable climate created by the democratic conceptions of leaders of the Romanian 1848 movement such as Nicolae Bălcescu, C. A. Rosetti, Mihail Kogălniceanu or Cezar Bolliac. To the "Justice and Brotherhood" envisaged by the 1848 revoluionaries, concept which in practice was still hazy in 1848, the proletariat, guided by scientific socialism, substituted the ideal of socialist society, in whose program the defense of liberty, of union and of national independence became fundamental points.

Thus, the 1848 Revolution appears as an event of crucial importance for the destiny of modern Romania, which would guide for a century the struggle of the Romanian people against internal conservative forces and against domination or interference by any foreign power, for social progress, welfare, unity, independence and sovereignty.

NOTES

1. For details see: Constantin Căzănişteanu, Dan Berindei, Gheorghe Florescu, Vasile Nicolae, *Revoluţia română de la 1848* (The 1848 Romanian Revolution), Editura politică, Bucharest, 1968, and *Revoluţia de la 1848 în ţările române* (The 1848 Revolution in the Romanian Countries), culegere de studii, Editura Academiei, Bucureşti, 1974.

2. *Istoria patriei şi a Partidului Comunist Român în opera preşedintelui Nicolae Ceauşescu* (The History of the Homeland and of the Romanian Communist Party in the Work of President Nicolae Ceauşescu), Editura militară, Bucharest, 1979, p. 202.

3. N. Bălcescu, *Opere* (Works), tom I, partea II, ediţia G. Zane, Bucharest, 1940, p. 99.

4. See Andrei Oţetea, *Tudor Vladimirescu şi revoluţia de la 1821* (Tudor Vladimirescu and the 1821 Revolution), Editura ştiinţifică, Bucharest, 1971.

5. D. Berindei, *Preludes de la revolution roumaine de 1848*, in "Revue Roumaine d'Histoire," t. XVII, nr. 3, 1978, pp. 427-446.

6. N. Bălcescu, op. cit., p. 198.

7. M. Kogălniceanu, *Texte social-politice alese* (Social-Political Excerpts), Editura politică, Bucharest, 1967, p. 386.

8. V. Netea, *L'unite nationale du peuple roumain dans les programmes et les manifestations de la revolution de 1848*, in "Revue Roumaine d' Histoire," t. XVII, nr. 3, 1978, pp. 409-426.

9. Val. Popovici, *Dezvoltarea mişcării revoluţionare din Moldova după evenimentele din martie 1848* (The Development of the Revolutionary Movement in Moldavia after the Events of March 1848), in "Studii şi cercetări ştiinţifice," Iaşi, Ştiinţe sociale, 1954, p. 448.

10. N. Bălcescu, *Opere* (Works), vol. IV. Corespondenţă, Bucharest, 1964, pp. 277-278.

11. *Programme of the Romanian Communist Party for the Building of the Multilaterally Developed Socialist Society and Romania's Advance toward Communism*, Meridiane Publishing House, Bucharest, 1975, p. 35.

12. Ion Ghica, *Scrisori către V. Alecsandri* (Letters to V. Alecsandri), Editura pentru literatură, Bucharest, 1967, pp. 364-365.

13. Al. Porţeanu, *La significance de la revolution de 1848 pour le mouvement ouvrier et socialiste de Roumanie*, in "Revue Roumaine d' Histoire," t. XVII, nr. 3, 1978, pp. 457-478.

Dan Berindei

THE MILITARY REFORMS OF ALEXANDRU IOAN CUZA
AND THE MODERNIZATION OF THE ROMANIAN ARMY

The establishment of the national state boldy raised the question of strengthening the army. The Union of 1859 was only a stage which had to be necessarily followed by others before *independence and completion of unification* of the nation within the borders of all Romanian territories was to be achieved. Because independence and completion of the state unity had to be won and the newly-created state had to be defended, reorganization of the military power became a matter of primary concern for the national state; this, as the newspaper *Românul* pointed out on January 8/20, 1864 was "a question of life and death."[1] Alexandru Ioan Cuza considered the establishment of a strong military force as an expression of the nation's will.

In August 1859 in a letter to Napoleon III, the ruling prince pointed out, inter alia, his intention of paying a great deal of attention to the "military organization."[2]

A few months later he made his plans even more clear to Victor Place. "I wish," wrote Cuza, "that the army, limited for the time being to our needs of public order, would be trained for every contingency . . . . " (se prepare a tout).[3]

Despite the difficulties caused by the establishment of the modern state, the atmosphere was clearly in favor of the accomplishment of this important task. "This double election," wrote an officer of those times, "assured the setting up of the national army and spurred on the general desire to bring the army up to the level of the best armies in Europe."[4]

165

The strengthening of the army represented a complex process which had to be dealt with from the very beginning of the double election of January 5 and 24, 1859. The army had to prove, as Cuza himself said on January 1/13, 1864 that "Romania exists."[5] But its attaining the level reached by Europe's modern armies met with serious internal and external obstacles. The state's precarious resources in a period of extensive reorganization, coupled with the apprehension of the masses with respect to the intentions of the politically conservative and moderate circles represented, of course, one obstacle. The Porte's suzerainty and uncertainties regarding the position of the Great Powers, especially of the large neighboring empires, also limited the possibilities for military development. Essential for strengthening the army—as described by Cezar Bolliac[6] —related, first and foremost to the integral unification of the two armies and their "reorganization on the basis of a new system."[7] Then a unitary army had to be set up endowed with the characteristic features of a modern army in matters of organization, equipment, financing and training. Strengthening of the army was not designed for the pursuit of aggressive actions but, rather to demonstrate the viability of the Romanian state; ". . . we do not arm ourselves for conquest," pointed out a radical organ, "we arm ourselves like the Serbians, like the Montenegrians, like our ancestors to become stronger, to be respected, so that foreigners may not enter the Romanian Countries as if they entered countries of slaves and dead people. . . ."[8]

Articles 42-45 of the Paris Convention provided "the legal basis" for the organization and reorganization of the army. They limited increases in military strength by one-third. Article 42 recorded "identical organization" with a view to the setting up of "a sole army" in case of need; the provisions of the following articles stipulated the fusion of the armies "whenever the internal security or that of the borders would be jeopardized," the appointment of a supreme commander under such circumstances and the placing of a blue stripe on the two flags as a mark of the unity of the two countries.[9] In other words, the Convention engendered the process of unification, but not that of reorganization and development to the extent desired by the Romanian nation. As in other respects, also, the Romanians were able to overcome this obstacle to the strengthening of the national army.

The consolidation of the armed forces did not, however, occur under favorable international circumstances. If support by France was helpful in many areas, the actions of the neighboring empires were, on the contrary, detrimental to any military Renaissance. Matters were further aggravated by the threats which faced the young national state, especially in 1859 and 1864, when troop concentrations on its borders seemed to herald repressive military intervention such as those of 1848-1849. The threats never materialized, partly because of provisions of the Convention which required the consensus of the Guaranteeing Powers for any intervention and partly because of the unflinching attitude of the Romanian United Principalities. "...If the Turk or German will be seized by a desire to enter the country," wrote the Bucharest newspaper *Dîmbovița* in the spring og 1859, "we must stop them at the border because we are sick of foreign locusts."[10] The camp at Florești, in the summer of 1859, or the "demonstration" made on the Danube in 1862[11] when the danger of foreign military intervention emerged because of an important shipment of weapons destined to Serbia transited through the Romanian territory, or again with Cuza's uncompromising attitude displayed in 1864[12] when the threat of intervention by the three big empires reemerged, compelled the same high powers to abstain from any action. The opposition of other powers to intervention contributed, of course, to deterring any action.

Reorganized in the period of the Organic Regulation, the national army was only a nucleus—its strength, combat capacity, equipment and armament were limited. Cognizant of the importance of the armed forces in the process of establishing and liberating the national state, Nicolae Bălcescu had dedicated, before 1848, tow of his first works to the army and to military history. In the next period, after the revolution, the revolutionary exiles (especially under the circumstances created by the outbreak of the Crimean War) devoted inordinate attention to the military factor and declared themselves in favor of organization of the resistance and of partisan warfare. Gheorghe Adrian even dedicated a special work to this problem envisaging also the support which the "entire nation" could give to the partisans—people hardened in battle.[13] Bolliac's attitude was also interesting; he favored participation by the masses and by Romanians outside the borders of the two Principalities suggesting the establishment of a larger army, initially of 30,000 men.[14]

Those who brought into being the national state, naturally favored the strengthening of the army. But to achieve that goal, they had to take into account the restrictions imposed by the Guaranteeing Powers and the relatively limited means at the disposal of the state. In his message of December 6/18 Prince Cuza revealed that he contemplated the creation of "strong effectives which in times of danger would be open to all Romanians called to defend the homeland."[15] Dimitrie Bolintineanu, in turn, spoke of the "armed nation," Ion Ghica had in mind a "general arming," and C. A. Rosetti wanted "every man" to be a "soldier."[16] In 1861, I. Missail declared for "an immediate introduction of military training for all classes of society," while Captain Petre Crăiescu wanted a national guard to comprise all citizens between the ages of 20 and 60 regardless of their qualifications.[17] As to future strengths opinions were varied; in an article issued in Dîmbovița in the spring of 1859, the number was placed at about 300,000 combatants;[18] in articles published in România militară in 1864, professional military men called for a force of between 100,000 and 200,000 men.[19]

The country's resources, however, were insufficient to support a standing army of that size. Instead, if the standing army—as Ion Ghica wrote—was to supply "special corps,"[20] —it had to be a people's army. A project of Gheorghe Adrian in 1858 recommended a standing army consisting of young men between the ages of 20 and 26, of militias organized in twelve territorial divisions (twelve infantry regiments, six cavalry regiments and six mountain battalions) which were to include young men who were not members of the standing army and men up to 34 years of age who had left its ranks, as well as a people's army, organized in three "classes" and including all citizens up to the age of fifty-six.[21] There were major differences of opinion in the political debates of the times related to the utilization of the masses; the conservative political leaders and even many of the moderate ones expressed great reservations in that respect. George Costaforu was reluctant to include in the army the "multidue" and the "masses" in the army of national guard—before the agrarian problem was settled. Dimitrie Văsescu openly expressed his concern over arming the "multitudes," particularly the peasantry, because of fears that then "the rural question will be solved not by legal means but by violence."[22]

But the Treaty and Convention of Paris stipulated that the Principalities' army was to engage not only in the maintenance of internal order but also in the guarding of the frontiers, a stipulation which gave impetus to the founders of the modern state for setting up the country's new armed forces. Partly due to the hostility expressed by the ruling Prince

and of Mihail Kogălniceanu toward the establishment of a national guard
as planned by the radical liberals,[23] the army was organized according to
the law of November 27/December 9, 1864 as a standing army of 19,345
men. Border-guard battalions and a *dorobanţzi* coprs which were to comprise 24,548 men were added to the standing army as was a force consisting of three "groups" of men aged 17 to 20 and 26 to 50 who were called
up for training and exercises.[24] "Our army," pointed out Alexandru Ioan
Cuza in his message of December 6/18, 1864, "has received a new law for
recruiting and organization with a view to protecting our budgetary resources and, at the same time, to enhance our defensive means."[25]

The entire society was subject to recruitment which caused Marsillac
to express enthusaistically, perhaps prematurely, for the genuine "egalit-
arianism" which would ensue.[26] Kogălniceanu was unenthusiastic about
the urban national guard, aware as he was that it would fall under the
influence of the radical liberals; he did, however, endorse the idea of
including peasants in the armed forces. In accordance with several ideas
of Cezar Bolliac, dating back to 1860, which called for the establishment
of two "legions" consisting of village *vătăşei* and of one "legion" of
forest guards,[27] in the summer of 1863 it proceeded to the military
organization of the *vătăşei*,[28] and in the autumn of the same year, by a
decision of the Council of Ministers, 4-8 guns were to be distributed to
each village council.[29] At the beginning of 1864, the commanders of
dorobanţi and gendarmes (in Moldavia) were ordered to provide instruction to villagers on how to use the weapons supplied to the villagers.[30]

The first order of business with which the national state had to cope,
however, was the achievement of complete unification of the armies of
the two Principalities. The establishment of a commission for unification of military uniforms, the fusion of the two armies in the summer
of 1859 in the camp at Floreşti, the appointment of a War Minister for
both Principalities (the first *common* minister), the establishment of a
common General Staff, the extension of the validity of the Wallachian
military penal code[32] and the like were only a few of the measures adopted even prior to the political-administrative unification of the two countries. The endowment of the units with new flags was also of capital
significance because on the occasion of their distribution on September
1/13, 1863, the ruling Prince stated that the "old flags recalled sad memories because they represented the separated countries."[33] It is certain

that the process of unification of the Principalities occurred most rapidly in the military field. The organization of the army was also concerned with modernization. Statutes for the commandant's offices were drawn up, military schools around all regiments were founded, ten thousand copies of a handbook by Lieutenant Pencovici devoted to the improvement of soldiers' knowledge were printed; in 1860, the first issue of the weekly *Monitorul oastei* which included studies on the martial arts appeard, and in 1864 the theoretical journal *România militară* was also published.[34] A new law on military promotions,[35] the establishment of major command posts in Bucharest, Jassy and Craiova,[36] the introduction of *dorobanți* and border-guards in Moldavia as well,[37] the creation of the Permanent Council on Military Training,[38] regulations for calling up the reserves and voluntary enlistment[39] were among the organizational and legislative measures which, especially during the last years of Cuza's reign, were classified as "radical transformations," by Ulysse de Marsillac[40] a few years later. Of course, the main achievement in the area of military organization was the law on the organization of the army, of November 27/ December 9, 1984.

The army had to reach the general European level of training and also had to rid itself of the limitation of its functions to internal matters alone. The conditions prevailing during the first half of 1859—the refusal of the two neighboring empires to acknowledge the new order in the Principalities and the concurrent outbreak of the Austrian-French-Piedmontese war—accelerated the process of military reorientation. As early as March 13/25, 1859 *Steaua Dunării, Zimbrul și Vulturul* reported foreign rumors on Romanian combat readiness.[41] One month later, in April 14/26, the concentration of the two countries' armies in a camp situated between Ploiești and Buzău was ordered.[42] Situated near the village of Florești, the camp—where over 400 huts were built—stretched for two kilometers in length and 300 meters in width. More than 11,000 soldiers from the standing army, *dorobanți* and border-guards gathered there. In addition to its external political-military aims, the camp at Florești represented an opportunity for the common training of the two armies, for the displaying of massive firepower (only within the regiment of musketeers every militaryman fired about 94 cartridges), for the standardizing of handling weapons and even for the staging of a "sham" war on August

23/September 4, 1859.[43] Although some unrest was recorded in the ranks of the "exchange" soldiers,[44] the profound significance of this camp was generally grasped by the army and by the entire nation. Not accidentally, Mihail Kogălniceanu wrote later, while emphasizing its international significance, that the camp at Florești "repelled an entire Austrian army on the battlefield."[45] Realizing the importance of this camp with respect to the unification, General Herkt stressed the fact that the military units of the two countries formed, since that moment, "the one and inseparable Romanian army."[46] But of special importance was the level of military training, of combat training with a possible outside enemy reached in that camp.

In the summer of 1862 after the Principalities' political-administrative fusion has been accomplished, General Ion Em. Florescu set up a new camp near the city of Bucharest, between Floreasca and Colentina. More important yet was the camp organized on the plateau of Cotroceni, in July-October 1863, where 8,500 soldiers were present, as well as two Serbian officers sent by Prince Mihail Obrenovici.[47] On September 1/13 the ruling Prince provided the units in that camp with new Romanian flags. On October 8/20 he announced that the "military exercises of the camp at Cotroceni had ended."[48] His remark that "military training had obviously developed"[49] was deemed highly significant.

The strengthening of the army, however, could not be fully realized without the training of a sufficient number of officers. Thus, the establishment of a military school for officer training was assigned high priority. Initially, the school was to function in Jassy, but later the decision was made to locate it in Bucharest[50] (as *Dîmbovița* had asked for in the summer of 1859).[51] On July 6/18, 1862[52] the unitary-centralized character of the school was agreed upon. In opening ceremonies the ruling Prince expressed his firm belief that the graduates would prove themselves "Romania's worthy sons."[53]

It was obvious, however, that the desired European level of training could not be achieved in Bucharest. That is why, on the occasion of his second audience to Napoleon III, Vasile Alecsandri received the Emperor's approval to have a few Romanian officers admitted ot the military schools in France.[54] The most gifted officers of Cuza's era thus attended Saint Cyr, Metz (engineering), Saumur (cavalry), and Brest (naval college). Also important was the participation by Romanian officers in military operations carried on in various places around the world. Five officers were sent to view the battles which were taking place in Marocco and eight to view the military operations related to the liberation of southern Italy. Others were sent to Algeria, to Mexico, and to the United States during the Civil War; moreover, a few participated in the large-scale maneuvers held by the French army at Chalons.[55] At least, with regard to the high echelons, one of the army's main organizers, General Florescu himself went to France in the autumn of 1864,[56] and in the summer of the coming year Colonel Duca was also sent there to study the organization of the gendarmerie and Colonel Logadi to familiarize himself with the war materials industry.[57]

During his first audience with Napoleon III, in February 1859, Vasile Alecsandri asked the Emperor send "officers-instructors for all the branches of the military art." Napoleon promised "to send officers of all arms as well as specialists to set up the factories and foundaries required by the army."[58] In the coming year, a French military mission in the United Principalities became a reality. A statement sent to Prince Cuza by the French consulate in Jassy concerning the French mission expedited matters, as did the introduction of the consul, Place, in France.[59] Napoleon III, however, did not satisfy Alecsandri's request that General Rose be appointed head of the military mission on the grounds that Rose was indispensable to France.[60] The leadership of the military mission was entrusted to Eugene Lamy, an experienced staff officer.[61] Lieutenant-colonel Lamy was accompanied by his brother, Paul Lamy, a mountain officer, by the artillery captains Guerin and Bodin, by the engineering captain Roussel and by the military subintendant, Gustav Le Cler,[62] who was assisted by the administrative adjutant, Serveille.[63] A decree of May 13/25, 1860 established the working conditions and aims of the French military mission.[64] The mission was to reorganize the command structure, the staff and the military administration; the chief of the mission had to deal with the unitary military school in Bucharest.[65] The French military mission remained in Romania until 1868. It assisted in the process of reorganization but was unable to resolve conflicts among Romanian officers anymore than it was itself immune from conflicts among its own members.

A special role was played by Le Cler who concerned himself with military logistics and military administration. The prevailing order based on the regulation of 1833, engenered abuses and unfair practices to officers especially to soldiers. Le Cler showed corps commanders had opportunities to enrich themselves at the expense and to the detriment of the national armed forces.[67] With respect to financial matters and the soldiers' pay, a letter dated February 17/29, 1863 is noteworthy. It was written by Lieutenant Eraclie Arion who informed Major Herkt, who at that time was on a mission abroad, that his regiment would not be able to pay his salary: "This moment there is a complete lack of money . . . public officials have not been paid since December."[68] Under those circumstances, partly derived from problems expressly related to the organization of the new national state and partly to improper administrative organization and controls, the Council of Ministers established a logistic corps on July 6/18, 1862.[69] The establishment of a system of military administration and of administrative officers, together with the introduction of French bookkeeping methods clearly contributed to the consolidation of the young army. The contributions of Le Cler and Serveille were indeed significant in this respect. However, their lack of tact and involvement in controversies with Romanian officers eventually led to Le Cler's premature recall[70] and to his writing, after his return to France, of a none-too-friendly book on Romania.[71]

One of the most important problems the United Principalities had to cope with was linked to armament. "In 1859," wrote Alexandru Ioan Cuza to the Vizier at the beginning of 1864, "I found the infantry armed with obsolete guns, the cavalry armed with lead swords, the artillery only with a few discarded pieces, the men dressed in uniforms which made every soldier look like a foreigner in his own country."[72] To improve that situation the United Principalities first sought the aid of France, the power which was mostly instrumental in the establishment of modern Romania.[73] In his first meeting with Napoleon III, Vasile Alecsandri received the Emperor's promise of a gift of 10,000 guns with percussion caps;[74] later on, that number increased to 25,000. Moreover, no payments were expected by France.[75] Cuza distributed older weapons to the village councils, and thus armed the villages, while he acquired 70,000 rifled guns from France for the regular army.[76] Concurrently a new artillery was set up. In 1863, twenty-four *Veuve Lachausser* cannons were bought from Belgium and another twenty-four were received as a present from Serbia.[78] Other cannons were also bought from France.[79] In 1864, as threats to the country's security became more serious, a grass roots movement for the financing of new purchases of cannons occurred.[80] The town of Brăila alone offered funds for six cannons[81] while hundreds of villagers provided money for the acquisition of both cannons and rifles. There were even cases when individuals provided large amounts for the purchasing of arms (I. C. Papadopulo and Procopie Filitti each gave 1,000 ducats for buying two cannons).[83] The reasons for mass participation were clearly expressed by the inhabitants of the Putna district who wrote Cuza that they were providing money for a cannon to allow him "to consolidate the people's independence, to assure its prosperity."[84] Over one million lei were sent to the Godillot company in Paris for armament purchases (a cannon cost 32,000 lei).[85] 10,000 tents were also bought and twelve ambulance services were organized.[86]

The creation of military workshops, a necessity for modern armies, was also significant. "The first condition for the existence of an army," wrote General Savel Manu to Alexandru Ioan Cuza, "is the state's ability to provide the means for its maintenance."[87] Several of the buildings of the Mihai-Vodă monastery were transformed into workships which made a large number of uniforms.[88] The first arsenal was opened in one of the houses at Malmeson.[89] Later, the arsenal on Spirei Hill was built and, in addition, also the gunpowder storehouse at Cotroceni and the gunpowder factory at Tîrgșor. A small foundary for shells was bought from Belgium.[90] As a result of the mission entrusted to Captain Herkt, sent for documentation to Belgium, the pyrotechnical factory was built on Spirei Hill; it became fully operational in the spring of 1861.[91] In July of the same year the ruling Prince was offered the first shell manufactured by this factory.[92] Two years later, after Herkt had paid a new visit to Belgium, the so-called "Artillery Establishment" were built on Spirei Hill, also.[93] They included old workshops as well as new ones. The workshops situated farther from Spirei Hill in Bucharest or in the country were eliminated.[94] The Artillery Establishments comprised the pyrotechnical works, a gunpowder factory, a foundary, mechanics', wheelwrights', and carpenters' shops and, most significantly, an arms factory. There, old flint guns were transformed into percussion guns and the weapons received as a present from France were rifled. In 1865 the first guns with Romanian-made caps were manufactured. Although it could not lead to serial production, this achievement was very important and promising for the following stage of development.[95] The Belgian Lieutenant

Boulanger assisted Major Herkt, the commander of the Artillery Establishments.[96] Among the shop foremen working in the Establishments there were some Frenchmen.[97] At Tîrgoviște, in the summer of 1864, "a foundary for cannons" situated "on the ruins of the ancient princes' palace in the town of Tîrgoviște"; were set up a decade later it was closed and transformed into an artillery depot.[98]

Works on the martial arts, or those referring to the army's organization reflected the profound transformations which were taking place in these years. Some of the writings were official manuals, some referred to the new law of recruiting,[99] to the new corps which had been set up,[100] to the uniforms,[101] others were translations or adaptations.[102] They dealt with other aspects of military issues and problems among the more important contributions were the work of George Adrian, written in 1858,[103] the works of Captain Petre Crăiescu—the first with a technical character,[104] and the second related expressly to the historical moment,[105] the balance sheet prepared by General Florescu in 1861,[106] and the works of Colonel P. Skeleti.[107] It should be noted that most of these books also had a political character reflecting the authors' views on national problems. A few of the writers, such as George Adrain and Crăescu, expressed the most advanced ideas of that time. But even moderates were concerned with the rejuvenation of Romanian military structures and bringing up to the levels of the more advanced European countries.

Toward the end of Alexandru Ioan Cuza's rule, the Romanian Army had become a modern army which would prove its valor only decades later. Everything had been reorganized and numerous new units and institutions had been set up.[108] Three territorial divisions, in Bucharest, Jassy and Craiova, comprised seven infantry regiments with garrisons in Bucharest (two), Craiova, Ploiești, Galatzi and Brăila, Jassy and Ismail, two cavalry regiments ("lancers") with garrisons in Bucharest and Jassy, an artillery regiment with the garrison in Bucharest where there were also a mountain battalion, the engineering battalion and the fire battalion were also located there. In Bucharest there was also the "Artillery Direction" comprising the arms manufacturing establishments, the workers' company, the pyrotechnical workshop, the carpenters' workshop, the smiths' workshop, the foundry as well as the arsenal. The gunpowder factor was at Tîrgșori but the "logistic command" was also in Bucharest. There was also a flotilla comprising 423 boats; a steamship had been ordered during 1859-1861.[109] The "School of fencing, gymnastics and of soldiers' sons" was located in Jassy. The gendarmerie was composed of six squadrons and two companies. The latter and three squadrons had their garrisons in Bucharest and Jassy and three squadrons were located in the country's eastern districts. The border guard consisted of ten battalions grouped in four inspectorates ("the inspectors"), and the *dorobanţi* comprised 30 squadrons responsible to three inspectorates. In addition, there was the Prince's staff, the two boards of the Ministry of War, the General Staff, the Permanent Council for Military Training, the Army's Advisory Committee, the Higher Commission on military endowment as well as the Corps' correction commissions. The army's sanitary corps, the military logistical corps and the administrative officers' corps completed the large number of units and organisms which comprised this young but unified, modernized and well-trained national army.

"When I was elected," wrote Alexandru Ioan Cuza to Napoleon III on October 1, 1865, presenting a suggestive balance sheet of his military achievements, "the United Principalities owned only 4,000 to 5,000 Russian guns from the time of Empress Catherine's rule and about ten worthless cannons of Turkish, Russian or Austrian origin. The gunpowder, projectiles, and the caps came only from Austria; we could not deliver a single fire without its permission. Today I have 70,000 rifled guns bought from France; the 25,000 unrifled guns which, due to your Majesty's generosity, have been distributed to the villages where I have set up a guard corps for the purpose of getting the rural population accustomed to weapons and of training it for the defense of its homes. My artillery has 72 rifled cannons built in France according to French models. If I found only some 3,000 men exclusively recruited from among the peasantry, badly armed, badly equipped, obeying only Russian or Austrian orders, today I have 12,000 border-guards; 8,000 *dorobanţi* on foot or on horse and a standing army of 20,000 men recruited from among all classes of society, well equipped, well armed, able to treble its normal strength through our double-reserves system and raised in the great school of France's military principles. I have set up a foundry, workshops for building and repairs where we manufacture our equipment, our shells, our gunpowder, our caps in a manner adequate for our needs. The army's bakery will complete the assembly of our establishments before long. These important achievements imposed, for a moment, great sacrifices on our country which thanks to the population's patriotic support we could support without burdening too much the state's budget."[110] It was a signifficent balance sheet which demonstrated clearly that Alexandru Ioan Cuza's rule represented a decisive turning point in the military history of modern Romania.

NOTES

1. *Puterea armată în România*, in "Românul" of January 8/20, 1864.

2. R. V. Bossy, *Agenţia diplomatică a României în Paris şi legăturile politice franco-române sub Cuza Vodă*, Bucharest, 1939, p. 169.

3. Ibid., p. 172.

4. General Herkt, *Cîteva pagini din istoricul armatei române*, Bucharest, 1902, p. 58; Gh. Smarandache, *Armata Principatelor Române în sprijinul Unirii*, in "Studii şi articole de istorie," VII (1965), pp. 393-400; Teodor Popescu, *Gîndirea social-politică despre înarmarea maselor oglindită în presa civilă, dezbaterile parlamentare şi legislaţia militară din timpul domniei lui Alexandru Ioan Cuza*, in *File din istoria militară a poporului român*, vol. I, Bucharest, 1973, pp. 69ff.

5. *Mesagii, proclamaţii, răspunsuri şi scrisori oficiale ale lui Cuza Vodă*, Vălenii de Munte, 1910, p. 105.

6. Cezar Bolliac, *Armarea*, in "Românul" of November 5, 1860.

7. "Curierul Principatelor Unite," no. 18, of July 9, 1859.

8. Radu Ionescu, *Guvernul şi armarea*, in "Reforma," no. 57, of August 1/13, 1860.

9. D. A. Sturdza and others, *Acte şi documente relative la istoria renascerei României*, vol. VII, Bucharest, 1892, pp. 312-313.

10. "Dîmboviţa," no. 55, of April 25, 1859.

11. In this "moral demonstration" were engaged an infantry regiment, a cavalry regiment and two artillery batteries. (R. V. Bossy, op. cit., p. 122).

12. The exchange of letters of January-February 1864 between the Grand Vizier, Ali Pasha and Prince Cuza is very self-evident; the Porte tried to "persuade" the United Principalities to give up the strengthening of the army because they were included "in the general guarantee of integrity of the Ottoman Empire" (Ulysse de Marsillac, *Histoire de l'armee roumaine*, Bucharest, 1871, pp. 85-100).

13.   Constantin Căzănișteanu, *Războiul de partizani în gîndirea militară românească din veacul al XIX-lea*, in *File din istoria militară a poporului român*, vol. 2, Bucharest, 1971, pp. 26-27, 28-32. For Adrian see G. Adrian, *Idee răpede despre rezbelul de partizani*, Bucharest, 1973, the edition under the direction of Major-General Constantin Antip, with a foreword signed by him.

14.   Constantin Căzănișteanu, op. cit., pp. 33-34.

15.   *Mesagii, proclamații, răspunsuri și scrisori oficiale ale lui Cuza Vodă...*, p. 20.

16.   Constantin Căzănișteanu, *Ideea înarmării poporului și a războiului popular în gîndirea românească de la mijlocul secolului al XIX-lea*, in *Oastea cea mare*, Bucharest, 1972, pp. 122-123.

17.   Maria Georgescu, *Problema cuprinderii maselor populare în sistemul de apărare a țării reflectată în programele revoluționare, unele proiecte și legislația anilor 1840-1877*, in *Oastea cea mare*, Bucharest, 1972, pp. 147, 150.

18.   "Dîmbovița," no. 69, of June 13, 1859.

19.   Teodor Popescu, op. cit., p. 70.

20.   Constantin Căzănișteanu, op. cit., p.123.

21.   Maria Georgescu, op. cit., pp. 149-150. Adrain expressed his opinions in the pamphlet "Memoire sur l'organisation de le force armee des deux Principautes Roumaines," Bucharest, 1858.

22.   Teodor Popescu, op. cit., pp. 78-79.

23.   Maria Georgescu, op. cit., pp. 155-158. The opposition unjustly accused the government that it intended to transform the army into a "great gendarmerie" (*La France, le Prince Cuza et la liberte en Orient*, Paris, 1864, p. 9). For the problem concerning the national guard see Maria Totu, *Garda civică în România*, Bucharest, 1976.

24.   Maria Georgescu, op. cit., pp. 158-159.

25.   *Mesagii, proclamații, răspunsuri și scrisori oficiale ale lui Cuza Vodă...*, p. 135.

26.   Ulysse de Marsillac, op. cit., pp. 117-120.

27.   Cezar Bolliac, *Armarea*, in "Românul" of November 1860.

28.   "Monitorul," no. 160, of August 19, 1863, pp. 657-658.

29.   Ibid., no. 192 of October 1, 1863, p. 801.

30.   "Monitorul oastei," no. 3 of January 14, 1864, p. 43. In Bucharest a "Societate de dare la semn" had been set up ("Monitorul," no. 188, of September 26, 1863, pp. 787-788).

31. Ulysse de Marsillac, op. cit., pp. 86, 96.

32. *Istoria României*, vol. IV, Bucharest, 1864, p. 319; "Monitorul oficial al Moldovei," no. 99, of September 26, 1859; Ulysee de Marsillac, op. cit., p. 102.

33. "Monitorul," no. 171, of September 2, 1863, pp. 709-710; *Mesagii, proclamații, răspunsuri și scrisori oficiale ale lui Cuza Vodă . . .*, pp. 89-90.

34. Ulysse de Marsillac, op. cit., pp. 101-105.

35. "Monitorul," no. 76 of April 4, 1863, p. 315.

36. Ibid., no. 202 of October 12, 1863, p. 841. See also the regulation of the new commands (Ibid., no. 241, of December 4, 1863, pp. 1009-1011).

37. Ibid., 1864, pp. 169-171.

38. Ibid., 1865, p. 239.

39. Ibid., pp. 285, 711.

40. Ulysse de Marsillac, op. cit., p. 100. For all these transformations see also Nomenclatorul comprising the laws issued in "Monitorul oastei," Bucharest, 1899.

41. "Steaua Dunării, Zimbrul și Vulturul," no. 52 of March 13, 1859, p. 201.

42. "Monitorul oficial al Țării Românești," no. 43 of April 20, 1859, p. 169.

43. For the camp see: Constantin Toderașcu, *Tabăra militară de la Florești, din vara anului 1859, începutul contopirii oștilor Principatelor Unite Române*, in *File din istoria militară a poporului român*, vol. I, Bucharest, 1973, pp. 49-68; Dan Berindei, *Frămîntările grănicerilor și dorobanților în jurul formării taberei de la Florești (vara anului 1859)*, in "Studii," X (1957), no. 3, pp. 114-133. With regard to the strength, "Dîmbovița" said it amounted to 12,000 men ("Dîmbovița," I (1859), p. 315).

44. Dan Berindei, op. cit., pp. 121ff.

45. M. Kogălniceanu, *Interpelațiunea privitoare la expulzarea românilor peste Carpați . . .*, Bucharest, 1886, p. 7.

46. General H. Herkt, op. cit., p. 66.

47. Ulysse de Marsillac, op. cit., pp. 120-126. For the camp of Cotroceni see also "Monitorul," no. 184, of September 21, 1863, p. 769; no. 191 of September 20, 1863, p. 797; no. 193 of October 2, 1863, p. 805;

no. 196 of October 5, 1863, p. 812; no. 199 of October 9, 1863, pp. 828-829.

48.   On October 3/15 took place general maneuvers in the perimeter Herăstrău, Floreasca and Băneasa, Ulysse de Marsillac, op. cit., p. 126.

49.   *Mesagii, proclamații, răspunsuri și scrisori oficiale ale lui Cuza Vodă*..., p. 91.

50.   Marcel Emerit, *Le dossier de la premiere mission militaire francaise en Roumanie*, in "Revue Roumaine d'Histoire," V (1966), no. 4, p. 581.

51.   *O idee despre armarea țării*, in "Dîmbovița," no. 69, of June 13, 1859.

52.   "Monitorul," no. 162, of July 25, 1862, p. 686.

53.   *Mesagii, proclamații, răspunsuri și scrisori oficiale ale lui Cuza Vodă*..., p. 78.

54.   V. Alecsanri, *Proză*, Bucharest, 1966, p. 576.

55.   Ulysse de Marsillac, op. cit., p. 106. In the summer of 1862 Lieutenant Iarca was to leave Algeria for Mexican battlefields (Arh. M.S.E., ms. 169).

56.   "Monitorul," no. 223 of October 6/18, 1864, p. 1034.

57.   Ibid., 1865, p. 547.

58.   V. Alecsandri, op. cit., p. 570.

59.   See N. Iorga, *Un projet de mission francaise en Roumaine (1860)*, in "Revue Historique du Sud-Est Europeen," II (1925), no. 4-6, pp. 94, 102. For the French military mission see in addition to the work by Marcel Emerit mentioned above, the study by General Radu Rosetti, *Relations entre l'armee francaise et l'armee roumaine*, in *Hommage a Monsieur de Saint-Aulaire*, Bucharest, 1930, pp. 93-104.

60.   V. Alecsandri, op. cit., p. 576.

61.   Marcel Emerit, op. cti., p. 579.

62.   Ulysse de Marsillac, op. cit., p. 104. R. V. Bossy, op. cit., p. 121.

63.   Marcel Emerit, op. cit., p. 583.

64.   "Monitorul oficial al Țării Românești," no. 120 of May 24, 1860, p. 497.

65.   Marcel Emerit, op. cit., passim.

66.   Ibid., pp.s581ff.

67.   Ibid., pp. 578-579.

68.   General R. Rosetti, *Lettres militaires roumaines 1862-1863)*, in "Revue Historique du Sud-Est Europeen," VI (1929), p. 165.

69. "Monitorul," no. 162 of July 25, 1862, pp. 685-686.

70. Marcel Emerit, op. cit., p. 583.

71. It is the work "La Moldo-Valachie. Ce qu'elle a ete, ce qu'elle est, ce qu'elle pourrait etre," Paris, 1866.

72. Ulysse de Marsillac, op. cit., p. 95.

73. With much ability Cuza remained, in 1864, the Grand Vizier of the fact that the Porte itself had asked for armament for itself. (Ibid., p. 96).

74. V. Alecsandri, op. cit., p. 570.

75. R. V. Bossy, op. cit., p. 120.

76. Ibid., p. 384.

77. P. V. Năsturel, *Contribuţiuni la istoria artileriei române*, Bucharest, 1907, p. 145.

78. General Radu Rosetti, op. cit., p. 165.

79. Ulysse de Marsillac, op. cit., p. 107.

80. See Constantin C. Giurescu, *Viaţa şi opera lui Cuza Vodă*, 2nd edition, Bucharest, 1970, pp. 227-228.

81. "Monitorul," 1864, p. 81.

82. Ibid., pp. 227-230.

83. Ibid., pp. 73, 181.

84. Ibid., pp. 575-577.

85. Constantin C. Giurescu, op. cit., p. 228.

86. Ulysse de Marsillac, op. cit., p. 114.

87. "Monitorul oastei," 1864, vol. I, p. 365.

88. Ulysee de Marsillac, op. cit., pp. 108-109.

89. "Monitorul oficial al Ţării Româneşti," no. 47 of February 26, 1860, p. 188; Etudes sur la Roumanie. Le pays. Les villes, Bucharest. Les etablissements militaires, in "Le Journal de Bucarest," no. 258 of February 16, 1873, p. 3.

90. C. Căzănişteanu, *Primele arme româneşti fabricate la manufactura de arme din Bucureşti*, in "Revista muzeelor," IV (1967), no. 3, p. 278; Gh. I. Popescu, *Evoluţia materialului de artilerie în decursul ultimilor 50 de ani*, in *Istoricul dezvoltării tehnice în România*, vol. I, Bucharest, 1931, p. 106.

91. C. Căzănişteanu, op. cit., p. 278.

92. Ibid.

93. Ibid., see also "Monitorul," 1864, pp. 815-816.

94. C. Căzănişteanu, op. cit., p. 278.

95. Ibid., pp. 278-280.

96. Gh. I. Popescu, op. cit., p. 106.

97. N. Stănescu, *Industria metalurgică, turnătoriile şi instalaţiile mecanice din România în ultimii 50 de ani*, in *Istoricul dezvoltării tehnice în România*, vol. II, Bucharest, 1931, p. 120.

98. M. Cioc, *Material de război*, in *Istoricul dezvoltării tehnice în România*, vol. II, Bucharest, 1931, p. 107.

99. *Instrucţiuni pentru recrutarea prin sorţi în Moldova*, Iaşi, 1860; see also E. Pencovici, *Recrutarea. Esplicarea legii. Introducere. Legea asupra recrutării. Esplicarea legii. Modeluri. Cerculare...*, Bucharest, 1862.

100. *Ordonanţa pentru admisii şi înaintiri în corpul de geniu din 14 septembrie 1859*, Jassy, 1859. For engineering also see Marin Mihalache, *Prima unitate română de geniu*, Bucharest, 1973.

101. *Descrierea uniformei şcoalelor militare, a şcoalei de medicină şi a companiei de infirmieri din Principatele Unite*, Bucharest, 1860.

102. Translations from the French became more common, one of the higher officers, I. Logadi became notable in that respect. Also, in 1857 Colonel Ioan Voinescu I published in Bucharest a substantial *Curs elementar de istoria artei militare. Ecstras din franţozeşte şi predat în şcoală.* (646 p. + VII pl.).

103. *Memoire sur l'organisation de la force armee des deux Principautes Roumaines Reunies*, Bucharest, 1858.

104. *Aşezarea trupelor pedestre pe două şiruri*, Jassy, 1860.

105. *Gardele naţionale şi independenţa României*, Paris, 1860.

106. /Ioan Em. Florescu/, *Expunere de îmbunătăţirile cele mai însemnătoare introduse în armata Principatelor Unite de la 24 ianuarie 1859-iunie 1861*, Bucharest, 1861.

107. *Cvestia armatei Principatelor Unite*, Jassy, 1860; *Ochire asupra bugetului militar din Moldova pe anul 1860*, Jassy, 1860; *Puterea armată în România*, Jassy, 1866.

108. I have used a valuable yearbook of the army, probably published in 1865, as it lacks the title page, neither the title nor the exact publication date can be ascertained.

109. Ulysse de Marsillac, op. cit., p. 107; on October 4/16, 1865 Colonel Petrescu was sent to Linz for the steamship ("Monitorul," 1865, p. 985).

110. R. V. Bossy, op. cit., p. 384.

Florian Tucă

ROMANIAN SOCIETY DURING THE WAR FOR INDEPENDENCE, 1877-1878

On the eve of the proclamation of Romania's full state independence on May 9, 1877, and throughout the national people's war for strengthening independence the Romanian society evinced, in an impressively unanimous way, full unity of will and action. Actually, what was the structure of Romanian society on the eve of the proclamation of Romania's full state independence and during the participation of the Romanian army in the 1877-1878 campaign?

The socio-economic transformations started as early as the eighteenth century, enhanced over the first half of the nineteenth century, ultimately led to major changes in the structure of the Romanian society, particularly after the making of the modern Romanian national state through the Union of the Principalities in 1859.

Essentially, the peasantry continued to form the largest class of Romanian society, the one which over the centuries bore the brunt of the battles fought for the preservation and assertion of the Romanian people's being, for the development of the Romanian nation, for liberty, independence and a better life, for the revolutionary transformation of the society. After the Land Reform of 1864, the condition of the peasantry had to some extent turned for the better; yet, although the peasantry continued to be the main producer of material goods, it felt most acutely the landlord's exploitation. In the circumstances in which winning independence became the topic of the day, the peasantry was to commit itself unreservedly to the struggle for the achievement of that century-old ideal of the Romanian people.

The development of industry eventually entailed an increase of the proletariat, which was to be ever more present on the country's social and political stage. As President Nicolae Ceauşescu underscored, "Ever since its assertion in history, in the second half of the nineteenth century, concomitantly with the development of the national forces of production, of industry, our working class manifested itself as a powerful revolutionary force of progress, as an exponent of the vital interests of the most advanced aspirations of the working people, as fighter for the attainment of the objective demands of development of the Romanian society—the building and development of the unitary national state, the winning and defense of its independence, the free assertion of our nation."[2] In the historical circumstances laborers, craftsmen and workers wholeheartedly supported the struggle of all Romanians, who actively joined in the fight for winning independence on the battlefield.

The bourgeoisie, which had asserted itself in the economic field especially over the fourth and fifth decades of the nineteenth century, and which was involved, due to its specific class interests in the political strife, would likewise play a major part in supporting the cuase of Romania's full independence. The bourgeois elements and the liberal boyardom, which once stood in the forefront of the 1848 Revolution, also militated for the making of the Romanian national state. Then, in the decade preceding the winning of the country's full state independence, they would stand out as partisans of the overt unbroken fight of the working masses in towns and villages for the attainment of Romania's independence.

In one way or another, the landed gentry, was also involved. Although the Land Reform of 1864 had to some extent proved injurious to its interests, while it itself had become a brake on the country's progress, on the whole the landed gentry had to acknowledge the development process of the Romanian modern state, and to join the efforts for regaining independence, the need of which was, however, conceived of in light of its own class interests.

Apart from those distinct classes, at the time the structure of the Romanian society consisted of various other social categories and strata, as for instance the intelligentsia, the clerkdom, and so forth. They, too, would impetuously engage, in different specific ways, of course, in the overall effort for obtaining full state independence.

Notwithstanding the variety of interests and aims, generally all the social classes and walks of life making up the Romanian society in the years previous to and during the War for Independence in 1877-1878 stood out as active forces in the winning of Romania's independence as independence satisfied their interests and aspirations, and was perceived as the only road to the country's social-economic development and progress.

The Romanian governments of the time took action in multiple directions for the achievement of that fundamental aim. Quite relevant in this respect is the energetic protest expressed by the Romanian government in 1876, ratified by the Parliament, against that stipulation in the Ottoman Constitution by virtue of which Romania was abusively included among the "privileged provinces" of the Ottoman Empire. Overtly declaring himself against such stipulations, Nicolae Ionescu, the then Foreign Minister, pointed out in the speech he delivered in Parliament that "both our older capitulations and the European international treaties ensure Romania a free, independent life."[3]

The proclamation of Romania's full state independence in 1877 was not an accidental fact, the result of some favorable international circumstances; instead, it was an dignified political act of the entire Romanian nation, actively and assiduously prepared and supported through diplomatic "work."[4]

Between 1871-1877, Romania made her presence felt in the international arena through political acts that clearly defined her individuality in international relations: the conclusion of the Romanian-Austro-Hungarian Telegraph Convention in Bucharest on August 8, 1871; the conclusion of a Romanian-Serbian Post Convention, again in Bucharest, on October 27, 1871; the establishment of the Romanian diplomatic agency in Berlin on May 6, 1872; the conclusion of the Romanian diplomatic agency in Rome on May 16, 1873, and of the Romanian diplomatic agency in St. Petersburg on March 24, 1876; the sanctioning of the Romanian-Austro-Hungarian Trade Agreement in Vienna, on June 10, 1875; the conclusion of the Romanian-Russian Trade and Navigation Convention on March 15, 1876, to list just a few of the Romanian political actions as a *de facto* independent state. But *de jure* sanctioning to that reality was essential.

In the circumstances of intense diplomatic actions initiated with a view to winning Romania's full independence, a Russo-Romanian meeting took place at Livadia, in the Crimea, on September 29, 1876, when the Romanian side approved in principle the passage of the Russian army through Romania's territory in the event of a Russo-Ottoman war. The opening of Romanian-Russian negotiations shows a clear understanding on the part of the Liberal Party, which had taken the helm of state on July 24, 1876, of the course of political-military developments in the context of a reopening of the Eastern Question, and also of the need to gain full independence by one's own forces in the looming military conflict with the Ottoman Empire, possibly through Romanian-Russian military cooperation.

The course of events was to point to an increasingly obvious fact, namely that the diplomatic demarches made for achieving independence did not arouse the anticipated response of the Great Powers. Consequently, the Romanian people and the state officialdom, now convinced that Romania would not be able to win independence without resorting to arms, concentrated their efforts on preparing the country from the military point of view as well. However, the Romanian government did not renounce diplomatic activity related to the securing of independence by concluding a military alliance with Russia, whose expansionist interests, as "heir" to the Ottoman Empire, aimed at the latter's weakening. As it happened, although the war unleashed by either empire had an unjust character, as a matter of fact aiming at a redivision in the area, Romania made use of it in her fight for winning independence.

As a matter of fact, the proclamation of Romania's full independence aimed at attaining some major political-strategic goals, such as: liberation from the suzerainty of the Porte, which had become obsolete in the new circumstances of Romania's development; removal of the danger of the Tsarist protectorate's asserting itself anew in the United Principalities; removal of the control of the seven Guarantor Powers, which had likewise become anachronistic, given the quick development and assertion of Romania both at home and abroad.

To this effect, on June 15, 1876, Mikhail Kogălniceanu, Romania's Foreign Minister, forwarded the diplomatic agents a memorandum of the Liberal Party, led by Emanoil Costache Epureanu, intended for the Ottoman government and the governments of the Guarantor Powers. The document demanded, among other things, recognition of the "Romanian state's individuality" and of the name of *Romania*, a fact implicitly entailing acknowledgement of Romania's independence. Seen against the ensuing events, the memorandum is indicative of Romania's endeavors to exhaust all peaceful means before becoming involved in armed conflict.

In the context of a rapidly-developing Balkan crisis, on June 18, 1876, Serbia and Montenegro declared war on the Ottoman Empire. Romania, comitted to a policy of benevolent neutrality toward Serbia allowed, notwithstanding Ottoman protests, the passage of groups of Serbian volunteers through her territory and the transit of weapons from Russia. Late in the year, however, events took a precipituous turn. A conference was held in Constantinople between December 11, 1876-January 30, 1877, where the representatives of the European powers tried to persuade the Porte to grant some liberties to the subject peoples. Planning to undermine the Conference, the Ottoman government led by Midhat Pasha proclaimed an apparently liberal constitution on December 11, calling Romania a "privileged province" of the Ottoman Empire. Given the obstructionist, even insulting, attitude of the Ottoman Porte, the Romanian Parliament protested vehemently on December 22-23, while the Prime Minister declared: "Never could the long sword of Bayazid and Mohammed reach Romania's mountains, where Midhat Pasha dares now to hit with his Constitution."[5]

Under the circumstances, on March 31, 1877, the Romanian government decreed general mobilization, and on April 1, the Council of Ministers, summoned in an extraordinary meeting, decided by a majority of pros the signing, first in Bucharest, of the drafts of a Romanian-Russian Convention by the representatives of the Romanian and Russian governments. On April 4, the Romanian-Russian Convention was signed in Bucharest, whereby the Russian armies were granted permission to pass through Romania's territory on their way toward the Balkans; concurrently, the Russian government pledged to preserve and defend the territorial integrity of the country and to observe the political rights of the Romanian state. That Convention, in actual fact a treaty concluded on equal footing by sovereign states, representated a major success of Romanian diplomacy.

On April 10, after the government had decreed general mobilization, Romania broke off diplomatic relations with the Ottoman Empire, and on April 29, as a result of provocative actions on the part of the Porte, which had started shelling the Romanian towns on the banks of the Danube,

the Deputies' Assembly passed a motion declaring that a state of war
existed between Romania and the Ottoman Empire. It is in theis context
that on May 9, 1877, the Deputies' Assembly, convened in a solemn meeting, proclaimed by unanimous vote Romania's full independence. Mikhail
Kogălniceanu, the Foreign Minister, proudly stated on that historic day:
"We are independent; we are a free nation. . . I don't have the least doubts
about it, and I am not afraid to tell you, the nation's representatives
here present, that we are a free and independent nation. We must show
that we are determined to concern ourselves with us, with our nation,
with the development of good moral and material conditions, and by no
means shall we be a threat to anyone else."[6]

The news of the proclamation of independence was greeted with
enthusiasm by the population. On hearing the news, the population
of Bucharest staged a manifestation unparalleled since that of 1859, the
year of the Union of the Principalities.

Documents from Romanian archives and newspapers show with luxury
of details that similar impressive demonstrations of full adherence to the
Parliament's decision occurred in many other towns, communes and villages, the Romanian territories under alien rule, included. Speaking of the
ebullience of he masses on that unforgetable day, T. C. Văcărescu wrote
down in his war reminiscences: "Every heart, all over the country, is
seized with unspeakable enthusiasm. The authorities and the constituent
bodies, the towns, villages, hamlets, in other words everybody, young and
old, is ready to make any sacrifice in order to support with the nation's
wealth, its gold and blood, the country's liberty and independence."[7]

The decision taken on May 9, 1877, by the Romanian legislative bodies
aroused feelings of deep satisfaction and approval with the international
progressive forces, with the peoples which, in their turn, were involved
in the national liberation fight, particularly those in Southeast Europe,
Serbians, Montenegrians, Croatians and Bulgarians. Speaking of Romania's
breaking off dependence relations with the Ottoman Porte, the Austrian
newspaper Der Osten carried in its May 10, 1877 issue, the following
lines: "The strings keeping Romania tied to Turkey for centuries are now
cut off. Romania is free and independent. Millions of Romanians in Transylvania, Banat, Bukovina turn a fraternal eye to the glorious fight of their
brethern."

What had been decided by the country's Parliament, the young and
vigorous Romanian army was to sanction on the battlefield beyond the
Danube through feats of valour and heroism.

As far back as January 1, 1877, due to a worsening in the international situation in Southeastern Europe, the country's government had taken some efficient measures for military developments. Eight dorobantzi (foot soldiers) regiments, two artillery regiments, etc. were created. Then, on April 6, 1877, mobilization of the standing army and of the territorial one with its reserves was decreed, a step which, though complex, was carried out quickly and accurately. Underlying the unanimity with which all the country's citizens answered the call-up order, *Telegraful* mentioned on May 8, 1877: "A fact which has filled our hearts with joy and hope for the triumph of the Romanian cause over the serious events we are now going through is the dispatch with which the reservists and the militia men ran, at first call, to arms. Hundreds of old reservists and soldiers on leave are gladly running from the remotest corners of the country toward the concentration point, ready to take up arms and rush against the Crescent, now threatening our borders."

Concluded on April 15, the mobilization brought under colors more than 120,000 people. The active army numbered 58,700 men, with 12,300 horses and 190 cannon, while the militia and town guard battalions reach 33,000 and 16,000 men, respectively; some 7,000 dorobantzi and calarashi (cavalry) were destined for border guard duty, order maintenance, administrative and quartermaster functions. The 1877 contingent about 14,000 men was being conscripted at the same time.

The Romanian forces guarded the Danube, along a 650km front, until the Russian army reached the river. Throughout that period the Romanian army ensured the defense of the national territory against a possible Ottoman invasion. Under protection of the covering operation carried out by the Romanian troops, the Russian military forces were able to move unhindered toward the front.

On July 18, 1877, the second battle of Plevna took place, ending, like the first one, that of July 8, in failure of the Russian troops. Under the circumstances, Grand Duke Nicholas, commander of the Russian armies in the Balkans, sent Prince Carol a telegram asking that the Romanian army cross the Danube and join in the efforts of the Russian army: "The Turks, mustering the largest number of troops at Plevna, are playing havoc with us. Please make fusion, demonstration, and, if possible, cross the Danube with your army, wherever you wish to."[8]

Considering the military situation south of the Danube and the serious implications its development might have had on Romania, the Romanian command decided to accept close cooperation between Romanian and Russian troops. As a result, on July 20 the 4th Division was ordered to move the bulk of its effectives south of the Danube with a view to co-operating with the Russian troops. Taking into account the operations the Romanian army was supposed to carry out south of the river, on July 23 it was divided into two distinct parts, namely: the *Operation Army*, made up of the II Army Corps (the 3rd and 4th Divisions) and the Reserve Division, boasting about 44,000 men, 7,000 horses and 110 cannons, and the *Observation Army*, consisting of two divisions, totalling around 11,000 men, 1,140 horses and 74 cannons.[9]

On August 20, the units of the Operation Army under the command of General Alexandru Cernat started the crossing of the Danube over a bridge built by the Romanian engineers and pontoneers at Siliștioara-Măgura. On the occasion, the Romanian Commander-in-Chief issued a high order of the day, read before the troops, which said: "Therefore, make the Romanian colors flutter again over the battlefield, where our forefathers were for centuries on end the champions of law and liberty. . . . So, forward Romanian soldiers, forward in manliness, and you will soon return to your folk, to your country, free through your own en-deavours, covered with the applauses of the entire nation."[10] Quite relevant, the crossing south of the Danube by the Romanian troops was attended by both the state officialdom—the government and the members of the Deputies' Assembly and of the Senate—and numerous inhabitants arrived from every corner of the country.

On the battlefields south of the Danube the Romanian soldiers fulfilled the expectations of the Romanian people. On August 27, by carrying a redan in front of Grivitsa 1 redoubt, the Romanian military actually went through the baptism of fire, and on August 30, during the third battle of Plevna, the Romanian troops, alongside the Russian ones, evidenced their combat qualities in conquering the Grivitsa 1 redoubt. In the life-and-death battle at Plevna the Romanian armed forces acquitted themselves nobly of their tasks. The order of the day issued by Prince Carol, Com-mander of the Western Army (made up of Romanian and Russian troops fighting on the front at Plevna) on September 5, addressing the Romanian fighters who had participated in the attack on August 30, 1877, read:

"You have proved that the ancestral virtues have not perished with the Romanian soldiers. Under brisk enemy fire you have valiantly defied death...the blood you shed shall forever uplift this country and sanction its independence."[11]

In the battle of August 30, 1877, the Romanian Army sustained heavy losses, the total casualties amounting to 19 dead and 34 wounded officers, and 2,511 soldiers dead and wounded.

In the attacks carried out on September 6 and October 7, designed to capture the Grivitsa 2 redoubt, the Romanian soldiers again covered themselves with glory, the toll being high this time, too: eight dead and 14 wounded officers, and 1,167 soldiers, dead and wounded, and two dead and 21 wounded officers, 964 soldiers, dead and wounded respectively.

In the ensuing period, the Romanian units were involved, alongside the Russian troops, in various other actions on the front at Plevna. These reached a climax on November 7-9, 1877, in the conquest of Rahova, a major pawn in the defensive system of the Ottoman troops on the Bulgarian theater of operations. In these fights, the decisive role was again played by the Romanian military, a fact pointed out by Grand Duke Nicholas himself, who addressed the commander of the Western Army in the following terms: "Allow me, please, to reiterate on this occasion too, that I have always been happy to acknowledge the bravery and the solid military qualities of the Romanian army . . . . The victory of Rahova belongs entirely to the Romanian armies."[12] The casualties sustained by the Romanians went up to four dead and four wounded officers, and 329 soliders, dead and wounded.

Following bitter fights jointly waged by Romanian and Russian soldiers, the Ottoman grouping at Plevna, which had tried to break through the blockade, saw itself compelled to surrender on November 28; many Ottoman troops, headed by their supreme commander, Osman Pasha, surrendered to the Romanians.

After that epoch-making victory, which was to mark a turning point in the course of the war, the Romanian army, reorganized, was to take part alone in the actions carried out on the front at Vidin. During December 1877-February 1878, the units of the Western Corps fought valiantly against the enemy and the bitterness of a hard winter. On January 12, the Romanian soldiers participated in the conquering of the localities of Tatargik, Inova, Rupcha and Smîrdan. The price was high in terms of casualties: five dead and six wounded officers, and 597 soldiers, dead and wounded.

On January 23, 1878, an armistice was reached in the Russo-Romanian-Ottoman war. Romanian troops entered Vidin and Belogradgik on February 12 and 13, respectively. With this, the national war for the Romanians' independence came to an end.

The fierce battles waged by the Romanian army at Grivitsa, Plevna, Rahova, Smîrdan and Vidin have been carved in the consciousness of the Romanian people as instances of heroism and sacrifice. "At Plevna, Rahova, or Palanka," the *Romanian Telegraph*, underscored in its December 29, 1877, issue, "the Romanians made proof that they are true descendants of their forefathers, that they know how to defend a cause, that they are a people of real men. And today no one dares make any distinction between Romanians: whether he is from Moldavia, Wallachia or Transylvania, when it comes to manly feats, the Romanian is as Romanian as can be."

The toll of the Romanian army's participation in the national war of 1877-1878 for full independence was high: 55 and 4,247 dead officers and soldiers; and some 20,000 other officers and soldiers contracted various illnesses.

Within the general effort of the Romanian people to secure full independence through the 1877-1878 war, the major contribution was made by the peasantry: by the peasant-soldiers on the battlefields, and by the people left behind, at home, who tilled the fields and made bread. "We rejoice and take pride," the newspaper *Românul* (The Romanian) of October 6, 1877, underlined, "in that the peasant, albeit the poorest of all, is, however, ahead of the others when it comes to making sacrifices for the common good."

The war for independence was supported, in part, by requisitions for the benefit of the army, an action regulated through the "Regulations on Military Requisitions." Covering a wide range of goods and services intended for the army (foodstuffs, fodder, clothes, animals and teams for transportation, billeting, sick assistance, etc.), the requisitions were provided mostly by the peasant masses. Apart from requisitions, the peasants contributed to the material efforts for the upholding of the war also through money donations, particularly for the purchase of arms, as well as through donations of food, fodder, clothes, sanitary stuff, etc.

Villagers collected and offered the state, individually or through many committees, important sums of money for the purchase of arms, food, clothes and of other materiel needed by the army. The dedicated contribution made by the peasantry to the war would be acknowledged by Prime Minister I. C. Brătianu himself. "I acknowledge," he said, "the sacrifices made by the Romanian peasant and what the country owes to him . . . because these days it has been precisely the peasant who confirmed what Mikhail Kogălniceanu had said in the ad-hoc Divan in Jassy, namely that the peasant is the pillar of the house."[14]

To the Romanian proletariat—born out of the economic and social-political realities in Romania at the end of the eighteenth century and in the first half of the nineteenth—the ideal of independence was a constant concern. Imbued with revolutionary ideas, with patriotic ideals, the socialists backed, alongside the entire people, the armed fight for the consolidation of independence. "Now, however," the gazette *Socialistul*, press organ of the Socialist Circle in Bucharest, declared on May 26, 1877, "spurred by the elan and the enthusiasm of past memories, the Romanians take up arms to defend their independence." Members of the socialist circles went to war as volunteers, in the heat of the confrontation with the enemy, or supported as best they could the war effort of the entire nation.

The military effort benefited by the workers' contribution. Those left at home made impressive efforts toward ensuring production of munitions, maintenance of transportation, manufacturing the equipment required by the army, equipping of hospitals and the like.

Documents of the time speak of donations made by the workers of numerous enterprises all over the country. For instance, the railway workers, at that time the largest contingent of the Romanian proletariat, collected and donated, large sums of money for the purchasing of arms and of goods required by the army. In turn, the workers dealing with bridge and road building collected money and objects also intended for those fighting on the front. The printers also ranked with those who felt bound to contribute, no matter how small their contribution, to the war effort. As a matter of fact, in the period under discussion, there were various workers' associations or laborers committees which offered the state sums of money for the conduct of the war.

The mass character of participation in the war effort was also evident through participation of other social categories and public organizations.

The town inhabitants—townsfolk, craftsmen, merchants, civil servants, employees of various private enterprises, the bourgeoisie and even the liberal landlords, played a major role in the winning of full independence by way of arms. The townsfolk set up an impressive number of committees for the relief of the army and of the wounded. In this respect, great response was aroused by the stirring appeal addressed to Romania's citizens through press articles. "Rally around the homeland's shrine, now in great peril!"—the newspaper *România liberă* (Free Romania) of August 17, 1877 said. "Let our body and soul be wherever the Romanian colors are! Romanians, come from all corners and unite under the colors!"

The efforts of the people in towns focussed on collection of funds for equipping the army with rifles and other war materiel, and donations of money and of various goods for the relief of the wounded and sick, and also of the families of those who had left for the front.

The committees for army relief found in all counties collected important amounts of money for the purchasing of arms. They were supported by civil servants, officials of communal and county councils, of tribunals, and of other local and central state bodies. In 1877-1878, tens and tens of such committees and associations were set up and worked all over the country—including the Red Cross Society, "Independence," "Providence," The Romanian Ladies' Central Committee in Bucharest, the Ladies' Central Committee in Jassy, the Central Committee for the Procurement of Arms. The Red Cross Society alone managed to collect 400,000 lei to be used for the relief of the wounded. Committees of coinhabiting nationalities in Romania, such as those of the Jewish and Armenian communities, or of the Magyar and German population, also contributed to that highly patriotic and humanitarian action.

The intellectuals—newspapermen, professors, teachers, physicians, men of culture, etc.—stood in the forefront of the fight for sanctioning independence on the battlefield. The journalists used the printed word to make the people's masses provide material support for the war; through press columns, they provided prompt and competent information as to the development of the campaign, eulogizing the gallantry and heroism of the Romanian soldiers engaged in bitter fighting against the enemy. In addition to the newspapers of the time, such as *Românul* (The Romanian), *România liberă* (Free Romania), *Telegraful* (The Telegraph), *Pressa* (The Press), *Timpul* (The Time), *Curierul de Iași* (The Jassy Courier), *Steaua*

României (Romania's Star), *Curierul de Galați* (The Galați Courier), etc., some new newspapers concerned themselves almost exclusively with informing the Romanian public opinion of the course of military events, such as *Războiul* (The War), and *Dorobanțul* (The Dorobantz).

To this end, one should add the publications issued in the Romanian provinces under foreign rule, such as *Gazeta de Transilvania* (The Transylvanian Gazette), *Telegraful român* (The Romanian Telegraph), *Familia* (The Family), etc.

Professors and teachers were also active in supporting the war effort. They established various committees for army relief, advocated the ideal of independence among the masses; taught love for one's homeland, for liberty and independence. In addition, teachers and professors donated a share of their salary, deposited monthly with the Independence society, or with the general equipping fund of the War Ministry, or with the Red Cross Society.

Physicians also made significant contributions to the war of 1877-1878. Many civilian physicans volunteered for the front to reinforce the military sanitary corps. Quite relevant in this respect is the petition of Dr. Nicolae Codreanu, a socialist militant, who asked to be detailed to an ambulance on the front. State hospital physicians lent a helping hand in the running of hospitals organized by the Red Cross or by other societies and organizations and also in hospitals set up durikng the campaign.

The men of culture or the scientists did not stand aloof from the efforts for the moral and material support of the War for Independence. Through lectures and other cultural manifestations they constantly expressed their commitment to the ideal of independence. On many occasions, public subscriptions were organized and the money thus obtained were donated for army or wounded relief purposes. The writers of the time used their pen in support of the independence ideal. The newspaper *Telegraful* carried in its issue of October 5, 1877, the article *A Few Historical Remembrances*, led by the great Romanian poet Mihai Eminescu, in which he pointed to the fact that the defense of the forefathers' land "has cost us rivers of blood, centuries of toil, our entire past intelligence, the most sacred torments of our hearts. The wounds of centuries of battles fought by our ancestors will not be healed, for, with our very hands, we shall open them now and forever." Praising the heroism evinced by the Romanian army on the battlefield, the same poet, who used to speak of independence as the "acme of our historical life," wrote in the newspaper *Timpul* of October 8, 1877: "the army, this only representative of the genuine Romanian people such as it is in the mountains or on the plains, still reminds us of past virtues." In turn, Vasile Alecsandri, another great poet of the Romanians, would regularly send poems to the review *Convorbiri literare* (Literary Talks), in which he praised the heroic virtues of the winners of independence. Moreover, at the request of public opinion, he wrote a play, *La Turnu Măgurele*. Alongside the writers, were the playwrights, musicians, and painters. Thus, for instance, Romanian painters of world renown, men like Nicolae Grigorescu, Sava Henția, Carol Popp de Szathmary, went to the front to immortalize on canvas, on the spot, scenes from the fight of the Romanian army.

During the War of Independence, when the whole nation was dedicating its effort to the sole imperative of victory, the women, in their turn, made the virtues of their forerunners shine again, through tenacious commitment to the great national ideal. The mass participation of the Romanian women, from all territories inhabited by Romanians, in the upholding of that just, war, fully enhanced the latter's popular and national character. The peasant women assumed the heavy burden of tilling the fields and thus provided food for the front. Moreover, tens of thousands of women were involved, through hundreds of committees set up to this effect, in collecting contributions destined to the army.

The first ladies' committee was set up in Jassy, on April 18, 1877. An appeal sent out by that committee published in *Curierul de Iași* of April 23, 1877–"The ladies of Jassy, true descendants of Stephen the Great's mother"–are hurrying to persuade their husbands and sons to do their duty now, when the homeland asks them to shed their blood; in their turn, they pledge to spare neither sacrifices, nor pains to alleviate war sufferings, being always by their side, with whatever help necessary."

It was not long before committees and societies in support of the war were set up all over the country, in which women contributed the majority such as in some of the Red Cross Committees in the county capitals. In this sense, noteworthy is the activity carried out by the ladies' committees and societies in Bucharest, Jassy, Sibiu, Cluj, Timișoara, etc.

Apart from ensuring the massive participation of women in supporting the war effort, the ladies who were members of such committees organized, most successively, the collection of contributions (money and objects) intended for the Army Sanitary Service, the relief of the wounded and aid to families. Moreover, on the initiative and with the help of some ladies' committees, hospitals and ambulances were set up, like those in Bucharest, Jassy, Craiova, Ploieşti, Piatra Neamţ, Tecuci, Turnu Măgurele, etc. In Bucharest for instance barrack-hospitals were organized in various parts of the town.

To the multiple efforts in support of the War of Independence of 1877-1878 one should add the contribution, by no means negligibel, of the younger generation, primarily by schoolboys and students. The youth took an active part in the nation's general effort for waging the war by organizing theatrical performances by circulating subscription lists, and by other means. Romanian schoolboys and students also fought in the front lines. Indeed, many young men lef their jobs or schools or universities to enlist as volunteers, as was the case of the printer Ştefan Georgescu, aged 18, from Bucharest, of high school pupil Ioan Pastia, aged 17, from Jassy, of young Constantin Popescu from Bukovina and of many others.

Influential in these respects was the decision of students of the Faculty of Medicine in Bucharest to volunteer for the Army Sanitary Service. The "group of 14 medical students," mostly socialists, is particularly noteworthy. Worth mentioning also is the fact that more than 500 students from Bucharest and Jassy sent a petition to the government, in which they asked that a battalion of volunteers be set up. In the winter of 1877 that battalion was trained in Bucharest. It should be said that Romanian medical students, members of the *Arboroasa* Society of Cernowitz, like schoolboys and students from Braşov, Sibiu, Timişoara etc also volunteered for the front.

These facts widely illustrated by the documents of the time, testify to the commitment of the entire Romanian society, to the war for Romania's independence. The statistical data of the epoch are revealing. Suffice it to give some general figures: the total value of the requisitions amounted to 11,227,089 lei; money donations from the population for army relief amounted to 427,137 lei, while voluntary contributions for the purchasing of arms, amounted to 1,212,661 lei. On the whole, the contributions made by the Romanian people to the war exceeded 100, 000,000 gold lei. These data aside, it should be pointed out that the war effort was supported with equal conviction by all Romanians. Manifestations

of fraternal solidarity reached a peak in 1877-1878, when Romanians
from the oppressed provinces regarded the war for independence as their
own cause. Therefore, the winning of absolute independence was the
result not only of the brilliant victories scored by the Romanian army
on the battlefields, but also of the efforts and sacrifices of the entire
people on either side of the Carpathians. It was the achievement of the
whole nation, of all Romanians. A reality, which *Gazeta de Transilvania*
put in a nutshell on June 2, 1877: "The cause of the Romanian soldier
is a general Romanian cause, his victory is that of an entire nation."

The winning of Romania's state independence, an event of historic
significance, spurred the national movement of the Romanians in the oppressed territories, because—to quote Sextil Pușcariu—"their hearts were
filled with confidence in their own forces," because they could "count
on the victorious arms of the heroes of Plevna." Romania's absolute independence sanctioned on the battlefield in 1877-1878 thus stimulated
the fight for the fulfillment of the lofty goal of the union of all Romanians in a single state, an ideal accomplished in 1918 through the resolute
and lucid action of the entire Romanian society, of the entire Romanian
people.

The historic act of winning Romania's full independence, like the
historic act of the Great Union of December 1, 1918 were thus not the
outcome of accidential events, of agreements reached at the negotiating
table. Rather, they represented the culmination and achievement of
the Romanian people's century-old aspirations for independence and
unity, of the dream for which generations of forerunners had sacrificed
their own lives.

NOTES

1. *Programme of the Romanian Communist Party for the Building
of the Multilaterally Developed Socialist Society and Romania's Advance
Toward Communism*, Meridiane Publishing House, Bucharest, 1975, p. 31.

2. Nicolae Ceaușescu, *Romania on the Way of Building up the Multilaterally Developed Socialist Society*, vol. 14, Meridiance Publishing House,
1978, p. 496.

3. *Monitorul oficial al României*, January 6, 1877.

4. In this respect, see: *Diplomația română în slujba independenței*

(Romanian Diplomacy in the Service of Independence), Editura politică, București, 1977; N.

Corivan, *Lupta diplomatică pentru cucerirea independenței României* (The Diplomatic Struggle for Winning Romania's Independence), Editura științifică și enciclopedică, București, 1977; Apostol Stan, *Grupări și curente politice în România între Unire și Independență* (Political Groupings and Trends in Romania between the Union and Independence), Editura științifică și enciclopedică, București, 1979.

5. Ion C. Brătianu, *Discursuri, scrisori, acte și documente* (Speeches, Letters, Papers and Documents), vol. II, part I, București, 1912, p. 252.

6. Mihail Kogălniceanu, *Opere* (Works), vol. IV, *Oratorie, II. 1864-1878* (Speeches), part IV (1874-1878), Editura Academiei Republicii Socialiste România, București, 1978, pp. 478-480.

7. T. C. Văcărescu, *Luptele românilor în resbelul din 1877-1878* (The Romanians' Fights in the 1877-1878 War), Bucharest, 1887, p. 61.

8. *Memoriile regelui Carol I al României (de un martor ocular)* (The Memoirs of King Carol I of Romania—by an Eye-Witness), vol. X, București, n.d., pp. 38-39.

9. General Radu Rosetti, *Partea luată de armata romănă în războiul din 1877-1878* (The Participation of the Romanian Army in the 1877-1878 War), București, 1926, p. 383.

10. *Documente privind istoria României. Războiul pentru independență,* (Documents on Romania's History. The War of Independence), vol. V, Editura Academiei R.P.R., București, 1953, pp. 544-545.

11. *Memoriile regelui Carol I,* vol. VI, pp. 79-80.

12. T. C. Văcărescu, op. cit., p. 474.

13. In this respect see: General-Maior Dr. Constantin Olteanu, *Masele populare și războiul de independență* (The People's Masses and the War of Independence), Editura militară, București, 1977, and *Masele populare în războiul pentru cucerirea independenței absolute a României, 1877-1878* (The People's Masses during the War for Winning Romania's Absolute Independence, 1877-1878), Editura politică, București, 1979.

14. I. C. Brătianu, *Acte și cuvîntări* (Papers and Speeches), published by C. C. Giurescu, vol. III (May 1, 1877-April 30, 1878), București, 1930, p. 155.

John E. Jessup

ROMANIAN SOCIETY AND THE INDEPENDENCE WAR OF 1877-1878

The year 1876 signalled the beginning of the centennial celebration marking the birth of the United States of America. It also was a time of decision for the people of the small European country of Romania that lay tucked away in a corner of the continent and obscured from western view by the clouds of more immediate and interest-consuming events closer to home. A new war was brewing in Europe that held portents of a global struggle and the great powers each behaved in their own fashions, as one might have expected, during the crisis.

But, as the disturbance was once again primarily the doing of Imperial Russia and the Ottoman Empire, the arenas in which the majority of the fighting would take place were, as they had been before, the Caucasus in the east, and the Balkans in the west. Romania was, thus, ideally located, as it had been on numerous occasions in the past, to be the theater of war in the west in what appeared to be a major effort on the part of Imperial Russia to once and for all settle the Eastern Question.

It was, therefore, of little real concern to the antagonists, and of even less interest to the other powers, that the people of Romania, and the rest of the Balkans as well, all of whom were in the Ottoman thrall, had aspirations of their own that did not include the seemingly constant disruption and destruction that attended the struggles of outside forces over their lands. The powers, therefore, averted their eyes and closed their

201

ears to the sights and sounds of these people for fear that any close attention might distract them from the more important task of assuring themselves a share of the spoils of war, whether or not they deserved it.

For the people of Romania, it was an entirely different matter altogether. For them, it was a matter of freedom and indpendence, and with good reason. This was an extremely critical period and Romania once again found itself caught in the middle of a situation not of its own making. Without question, if another war came, Romanian territory, lying on Russia's road to Constantinople, would be ravaged and Romanian lives lost. This, the Romanian government wanted to avoid, but the country was devoid of the means of controlling those colossal forces that surrounded it. That all of those giants, including Imperial Russia and Austria, had been among those who had guaranteed Romania's neutrality in 1856, so as to have a buffer between warring states, apparently did not matter for an instant where other interests were at hand, especially assuring one's fair share of the spoils when a moribund Ottoman Empire finally gave up the ghost.

Romania's position was anomolous, if not downright dangerous. While many jurists of the time saw Romania as a sovereign state, regardless of the tributary status it held to the Sublime Porte, the small Danubian principality required more in the way of protection than it alone could afford.[1] As the other countries of the region, Bulgaria, Serbia, Montenegro, and, until 1830, Greece, were in similar conditions of servitude to the Sublime Porte, only the Paris guarantors could protect it and this they had, in all respects, refused to do.

The danger to Romania lay in the fact that it was all but defenseless to prevent anyone from doing anything. If Russia, in the present situation, decided to march across Romania to the Danube, there was little Romania could do to stop it without the support of those great powers who had agreed to protect its neutrality. Similarly, if war did come and Turkey moved first, crossing the Danube to meet the Russians somewhere south of the Prut, on Romanian territory, it was again powerless to prevent it. In either case, Romanian territory and its inhabitants would suffer the devastation incident to the fighting that would take place.

By the end of 1876, it had become evident that none of the powers, including Germany, even though a Hohenzollern sat upon the Romanian throne, was disposed toward fulfilling their obligations regarding Romanian neutrality.

Romania's options were strictly limited and there was very little time to choose. There were but three choices, however: to cooperate with Russia, to cooperate with the Ottoman Empire, or to remain neutral. If Romania happened to choose the wrong side, the country would suffer in the aftermath. The Turks would visit a terrible scourge on a vanquished Russian ally who had treacherously abandoned its allegiance to the Porte. A victorious Russia might, on the other hand, simply occupy and plunder an active Danubian ally of the Turks. There was no real alternative at that juncture, except to declare Romania neutral and await the outcome of events over which the government had no control.

There had been very few times since the beginning of their nation almost two millenia earlier that the Romanian people had been left to choose their own way. Indeed, there were few examples up to that moment when the Romanian people were not under one alien overlordship or another, and, since the Ottoman Empire had expanded its domain into the Balkans and had finally overcome the Moldavians and Wallachians, in the fifteenth century, there had been few, if any, respites for the Romanians in which to savor the joys and sorrows of freedom. Because of this long standing suzerainty to the Sublime Porte many, who did not understand or appreciate the almost continuous struggle put up by the Romanians and the other Balkan peoples against the Ottomans for their freedom, chose to see them as weak supplicants capable only of servile acquiescence to the will of others. It is not surprising, therefore, that there was something less than overwhelming external support for the Romanian cause in 1877, when the people sought to throw off the Ottoman yoke. The general lack of foreign support and sympathy had the effect of further strengthening the resolve of the Romanians to depend upon themselves for their deliverance.

Yet, in accepting the notion that the time of deliverance was at hand in 1877, the Romanians found themselves divided as to what to do and over how to go about the whole affair. More than that, there were few in Romania who understood the amount of sacrifice that would be involved in insuring the country's independence.

Except for the tribute which had to be paid, Romania was literally independent as it was—independent, that is, without the rights that normally attend that condition. Romania did have diplomatic agents at a number of courts of Europe. Indeed, a diplomatic representative was even maintained in Constantinople itself, but the tiny principality was denied the right to chart its own course, wherever that course might take the Romanian people.

It was also true, however, that, on the eve of war, these discussions were over the best course of action to follow in those perilous times. Without question, the vast majority of the people of all stations would have preferred that Romania remain neutral. A people ennured by centuries of assault will not willingly court disaster through overt action, regardless of the stakes, and it was only through the maneuverings of a small group of dedicated men, including the reigning prince, Carol, who understood that liberty could not be purchased by inaction, that independence was finally achieved. Those Romanians who did counsel caution during the crisis were grouped around the Foreign Minister and did so because they clearly understood that Romania would be the first country to suffer, and they were the ones who wanted the nation's neutrality guaranteed, even though that status was not as clearly defined as it should have been by the great powers at the 1856 Paris conference.[2] There was, however, no real difference between this and and the other sides' position in the discussions over what course to follow.

Even though one group counseled restraint, while the other, focussed about the prince and several of his chief advisors sought for active participation in the forthcoming conflict as a means of guaranteeing their freedom, the two principle groups understood that the initial responsibility of a neutral state was its abstention from any hostility toward its neighbors. At the same time, both sides agreed that one of the chief duties of a nation, regardless of its status, was to prevent violations of its own territory through the hostile acts of others. If this meant war, then Romania was prepared to fight, in the meantime, the nation would remain neutral.

In the ensuing struggle between the Serbians and the Turks, and during the period of the Ottoman's gratuitous brutality of the Bulgarian Christians, Romania kept to its neutral position, but its course went apparently unnoticed by the great powers, and none of them openly declared themselves ready to protect the principality. Rather, many of the powers, particularly Austria, heaped considerable abuse on the Romanians for doing for itself what those who had solemnly sworn to uphold the treaty refused to do. Abandoned as it was by the great powers, some questioned openly whether, given Romania's semi-independent status, it did not have the right to seek those arrangements with anyone who was willing and able to help protect the country.[3]

This notion of self-determination was best expressed sometime after the events had transpired, by the noted British military historian Colonel Sir Henry Montague Hozier, when he wrote: "The conduct of the young Romanian people was criticized with some severity by the European press. It is easy, however, when people are free, to counsel patience to those who are not."[4] Indeed, the Romanians were impatient as their position became more dangerous by the day. If Romanian neutrality could not be maintained, then which way should the nation move? Romania might have informed either Constantinople or St. Petersburg of its willingness to cooperate under given sets of circumstances; but which one should they trust? There is little or no evidence to indicate that any serious consideration was given to supporting the Turks—that had been tried in the past and had failed to produce any lasting benefits. Yet, few, if any, Romanian officials trusted the Russians. This political decision-making process was underway when the Constantinople meeting of the great powers closed in January 1877, without achieving any success. Europe girded for war.

In full appreciation of the precariousness of their position the Romanians had not relied on words alone but had, over a period of months, taken a number of steps to prepare their military forces, such as they were, to take to the field.

The Romanian army was brought into the modern age through the efforts of, first, Prince Cuza and, then Prince Carol. The reorganization and reequiping of the forces was a time-consuming and expensive proposition, but it went on despite some opposition in the parliament. Even though there were debates, often heated ones, both sides of the chambers understood the gravity of the situation. The preparations went on even though Romania's national debt was almost $40 million dollars in 1874, and would grow even larger in the ensuing half-decade.

By May 1877, Carol had assumed personal command of the army, ostensibly for the purpose of carrying out extensive maneuvers but, in reality, the move was made to solidify the national leadership.[5] Carol's reign to that time had been marked by considerable partisan animosity and by financial problems that he had, to a large extent, inherited from the foregoing administration. On more than one occasion, Carol had threatened to resign and leave what appeared to be a thankless office. By the young Hohenzollern, who had slipped through Austria in disguise in 1866, after his election to the Romanian throne, had instead, stayed on and had persisted in his program to strengthen the army and, in doing so, probably saved his adopted country from continued bondage.

The Romanian society of the period contained all of the elements found in other, similar national states in Europe. The largest segment of the population was the peasantry whose condition varied widely as one traversed the land. In some areas, especially in eastern and southeastern Romania, the peasants were extremely poor.[6] The villagers were characterized as being content with little, and fancying that the Romanian principality of Wallachia, in which they lived, was the whole world. Yet, while this national awareness existed, visitors to the region commented that not one "inhabitant seem[ed] to know anything of the country ten miles beyond his own village."[7]

The entire countryside was, by no means, in this same degraded condition. Other sections were pictured as containing clean, neat villages, where the peasants were cheerful and friendly. As a common characteristic, the peasantry was imbued with a stubborn and independent attitude that was, without question, inculcated by the constant struggle for survival, not only against the elements, but also against the stream of foreign invaders who used the lands of Romania as a battleground or as a passage way in the series of conflicts that plagued Central Europe in its role as the arena for the contest of strength between the great powers of Europe and the East.

The vast majority of the peasantry were members of the Romanian Orthodox Church, one of the branches of Eastern Orthodoxy, that was generally considered the national church.

There was a landowner class that had survived the 1864 land reforms and still managed to mantain many of the old feudal ways, but in many ways these gentry were only little better off than the peasants themselves. This upper group in the Romanian society strata performed their societal role amost entirely in agriculture as there was little entrepreneurship outside the cities.

There was a very clear demarcation between life in the village and life in the town, an abyss, one writer called it, that separated the "semi-barbaric" villagers from the industrious tradespeople of the towns and lesser cities.[8] The townsfolk had schools to which they could send their children, a luxury not often found in the countryside, where, more often than not, children were sent to the fields, when old enough and strong enough to help maintain the precarious existence of the family and the village. Even so, in a population of between four and one-half million and five million, less than 85,000 children were in primary schools at the outbreak of the war.[9]

Life in Bucharest was another matter altogether, as the Romanian capital was known, even at that juncture, as "Paris in the East."[10] In 1876, the city was populated by one-quarter million people, having grown from one hundred thousand souls in about 150 years, despite the ravages of war, foreign occupations, and pestilence.[11]

At that point in history, Bucharest was four days travel from Paris by the most direct train route through Austrian Bukovina to Vienna, by way of Lemberg and Cracow. And it was by this route, most likely, that most sons, and possibly a few daughters, of the Romanian upper classes traveled to France to be educated. A French education was the mark of a gentleman and the French language served as the *brassard* of the gentile class of Romanian society. During the last decade before the war, the German tongue had also gained some favor because of the election of a Hohenzollern to the throne. Romanian was spoken by the gentry only when protocol required, as when at one of the ministries, or when dealing with the lower classes.

The visitor to Bucharest was at once struck by the incongruity of broad boulevards and spacious hotels reminiscent of Paris, but with hints of Turkish architecture showing at every corner. Restaurants that served the best in French and Austrian cuisines also had the most palatable of Turkish dishes on their menus. The average food of the peasants, on the other hand, in one of the more deprived districts, was black bread, cheese, and coarse hominy. Meat apparently was available, but was either too expensive, as some would say, or way, according to others, too much trouble for the peasants, who were probably unfairly judged as, "generally too lazy to prepare it."[12]

The peasantry formed the backbone of the country, however, as a true working class had not yet developed, even though some commerce existed in the cities and towns. It would be from this class, the tillers of the soil and the hewers of wood that the army would grow. By the Law of 1864 modified in 1876, all able-bodied males who were "ative" inhabitants of the country, and who were between 20 and 50 years of age, were required to be enrolled in the standing army or its reserves, the territorial army or its reserves, the militia, or the town or rural guards (*gloatele*).[13] This, according to the literature of the time, constituted the means whereby, "a national army comprising all the social elements," was raised.[14] As one might suspect, the system, although unique in many aspects, was based on the Prussian *Landwehr* model with which Prince Carol no doubt felt most comfortable and which best suited the needs of Romania's situation at the time. To build this military force required a great deal of time and effort and not a little sacrifice on the part of the people.[15]

In general terms, it is difficult to assess the mood or attitude of the common people of Romania during this period. Internal retrospective reporting tends to show a mass of patriotic enthusiasm for the course charted by the Romanian government, but some foreign observers viewed the situation somewhat differently. A dispatch from the rather optimistic London Standard of May 9, 1877, reported that Romanian public opinion over the issue of the declaration of independence was more "resigned" than changed, but that the events on all sides were simply too strong for those who opposed so drastic a change.[16] It is clear, then, that opposition did exist to the government's course that may have transcended the issues raised by the Kogălniceanu forces who counselled temperance. Without question, also, the events, as they transpired, such as the Turkish artillery bombardment of Calafat, reported on May 8, 1877, only helped still those voices that might otherwise have been heard. If for instance, the public could have been heard, would there have been an alliance with Russia? One foreign journalist reported this point as follows:

> It would have been impossible at the outbreak of hostilities for the Romanian Government to induce the people to accept an open alliance with Russia, but step by step they have been moving steadily forward, using every argument and inducement. They have succeeded in arousing sufficient feeling to enable them to call out the militia . . . the war party has carried to day.[17]

It is difficult, therefore, to know what the people thought, although the actions taken by the government appear to have been the correct ones. And, once again, the reaction of the outside world to Romania's charting of its own course only tended to mute even further any real public opposition to the government's actions.

When the declaration of Romanian independence was finally achieved— the decision was not unanimous, but those opposed were very few in number, a kind of euphoria swept the land that was reinforced by a number of other events. For one thing, the first Russian units to pass Bucharest carried standards bearing the double Greek cross used to symbolize the religious nature of the war with which the devout Romanians could easily identify and within which cause they could easily join.[18]

A second event was the alliance between Romania and Russia which while abhorrent in one sense did add an atmosphere of legitimacy to the Romanian claim of independence. Had the Romanian people known what lay ahead for them in their dealings with the Imperial Court in St. Petersburg, any elation that might have come from the notion of an alliance would have been quickly disapated. As it was, however, the alliance was entered into with forebodings, but also with the resolve to live up to the obligations the arrangement required.[19]

The last event of importance here was the reaction of other European powers to the idea of an independent Romania. The vilification heaped upon the Romanians, especially by the Austrians, could not have but helped strengthen the Romanian determination to continue its struggle, for surely they must have know that Vienna was also interested in aggrandizing the two provinces of Wallachia and Moldavia as they had taken Transylvania in earlier times.

It was in this setting the, that Romania went to war to secure its independence. The only real question that remained was whether or not the Romanian army could or would fight.

The answer to this question lay at the very core of the concept of Romania as a free and independent nation, and its solution rested upon the very nature of the Romanian people. It was a difficult question at the time, and it is no easier to understand today than it was a century ago.

There was actually very little known about Romania until no more than a few decades before those fateful months in 1877. Only during the

Crimean War period did western journalists devote any time to explaining about the Romanian people. When the specter of war again loomed over the Danube in 1876 and 1877, foreign journalists, military observers and others with or without bona fides descended on the region to take advantage, as one young British officer put it, "of seeing real war (which) is not an every day occurrence."[20]

From these sources, the only objective view of Romania and its people can be achieved. There is much written by the Romanians about themselves concerning their own history and this is only right and proper. But, as is so often the case, native reports develop a reality of their own that the prism of time only tends to intensify regarding what is good and to diminish what is not too good. It becomes, therefore, a matter of judgment as to what to believe. Even in the most blatantly biased commentaries, there are kernels of information that help explain how the Romanian people played out their roles in this drama.

Almost to a man, the foreign correspondents denigrated the Romanian army and its soldiery. The London Daily News correspondent, discussing the efficiency of the Romanian Corps of Observation stationed at Guirgevo noted that the Minister of War thought it would be a good thing to exercise the troops and accustom them to the sounds of war.[21]

The army of Romania was made up of three elements, the leadership, the officer corps, and the line. At the apex of the structure was Carol I, Prince of Romania, and it was with and from him that the Romanian army of 1877 seemed to grow and flourish. Carol was a Roman Catholic and the son of Prince Charles Anthony of Hohenzollern-Sigmaringen. When he arrived in Romania in 1866, following his election as ruling prince, following the ouster of the famous hospodar, Alexander Cuza, he spoke no Romanian and was very much the stranger in a strange land. Before 1877, Carol was not always a popular ruler because of his German background and some of his policies. This dislike was especially true during the course of the Franco-Prussian war of 1870-1871, when Romanian sentiments favored the French.

Above all, however, Carol was a soldier; as a Prussian officer he had fought in Denmark in 1864. His first and most important task in Romania was to continue the building of a viable military force on the groundwork laid out by his predecessor, Prince Cuza. Carol was characterized as a "heavy, sleepy-looking German, with a seat on his horse like a salt-sack attached to two poles."[22] Yet it was his labor, without much help, according to one not altogether sympathetic source, that reconstructed the army which would soon be called upon to prove itself in battle, and in doing so, would secure a nation.

The second group, the officer corps, in 1877, came largely, but not exclusively, from the upper classes. In previous times, especially under the *Reglement Organique*, only the sons of the noble or privileged class could be commissioned. Even so, the officer's numbers were small, as was the overall strength of the army, and, therefore, the commissioned ranks maintained a rather singular social character. Officers were considered to be either combatants, who were assigned to the combat arms, or "assimilated," which designated those officers assigned to the more administrative and logistic functions. There was a rather distinct differentiation between the two types of officers as the combatants could order, while assimilated officers could not. Many officers in the Romanian army were graduates of foreign military academies. Officers in the standing army and the territory forces were accorded the same status. After 1872, militia officers had equal rights and the same obligations as the regular and territorial officers when called up for training or emergencies.

The officer corps came in for its share of scrutiny by the foreign correspondents and observers, much the same as Prince Carol. On one occasion, Carol was reported to have reviewed his troops in a blue uniform, "ablaze with decorations," but, the correspondent went on:

> How can I do justice to the officers, except to say that they are, emphatically, a "thing of beauty and a joy forever." At first sight the traveler is dumbstruck and is inclined to fancy either that the Army is exclusively composed of Captains and Lieutenants, or that the number of privates should be estimated by hundreds of thousands. One meets few privates . . . but is elbowed at every step by some gorgeous creature in gold lace, buttons and auguillets, with a little cloth let in to keep the ornaments together . . . . [23]

Whatever contempt the correspondent may have shown in his description of the Romanian officers he had encountered, was dissipated when he took the occasion to again comment on the officers some three weeks later:

It is somewhat the fasion during our war in America to ridicule well-dressed officers, who were called 'popinjays' and other contemptous names, but the experience abroad has seemed to prove that sloven-liness is not a certain guage of ability, and that both chiefs and soldiers are not only more healthy but fight better when they are clean and tidy.[24]

To Richard Graf von Pfeil, a Prussian officer in the service of the Russian tsar, the Romanian officer—and the soldier as well—were reminiscent of the French, but pleased him, "more by their bearing and dress."[25] Salusbury reported on more substantive matters:

Be it observed, the Roumanian officer when he makes a campaign, does so in the most luxurious style possible...yet it can be laid to their credit, ...that their steel has proved no less keen, their valour in the field none the less conspicuous.[26]

Salusburg was particularly impressed by the friendliness he felt from the Romanian officers with whom he served.

Of particular importance was Salusbury's comments on the decorations worn by many Romanian officers that identified the fact that they had taken part in campaigns with foreign armies at some point in the past. This fact is almost entirely overlooked in other western sources but is extremely important as it tends to mitigate the apprehensions of many who wrote about the lack of experience of the Romanian army.

I notice a fact which, were it unexplained, would puzzle any who think, that as this is the first war in which Roumania has been engaged this century, the officers of her Army, must therefore, be un-tried in the lessons of campaigning—on many a jacket do I see the tokens of service in the field, war medals and decorations of honour gained in battle. The explanation is that the officers...have been permitted to accompany and serve with foreign armies in their campaigns...it cannot be denied that the great, and best school of war is the European Continent, and that lessons....[27]

The third element of the army was the enlisted soldier. Indeed, the backbone of the Romanian army, much the same as it has been in all armies at almost any point in history, was the infantry soldier. The infantry was considered the basis of the army and was composed of the infantry of the line (composed of the standing infantry formations) and the *dorobanți*, the infantry of the territorial army. In counting the common soldier, however, one cannot forget the cavalrymen, artillerymen and all the other branches in which men served. But even more important in understanding the full impact of the situation brought about by the impending struggle in 1877 on the Romanian societal structure was the role played by the militia and town guards.

The militia was comprised of all able-bodied men, organized into two classes, who were not in either the standing or the territorial army, and who had to serve until their 38th birthday. They were required to equip themselves, although arms and ammunition were furnished by the government, and their training was supervised by cadres from the standing and territorial formations located in the vicinity of the militia unit's home base. Without question, the efficiency and effectiveness of these units varied with the locale, their commanders, and the type of training they received. That they were available and ready when needed was, of course, made apparent by their performance as a part of the Operational Army during the war.

As might have been expected, many disparaged the Romanian soldier, much the same as criticism was heaped on his officers.[28]

The significant fact was, of course, that, regardless of the biased reporting of some correspondents, no one took the Romanian army very seriously and it was, therefore, a more simple task to find faults, real or imagined, than to discover the strengths exhibited by the young army. "The truth is that criticism," wrote Carroll Tevis, "except as to appearance should be cautious regarding the Roumanian. . . . How they will prove under fire no one can say until they have been tried."[29]

And, again as with the officers, the dress and appearance of the common Romanian soldier took on unwarranted importance. Boyle, again writing with more sarcasm than seemingly necessary, stated:

> The smart look of a soldier depends immensely on his costume, and the Roumanian is most fortunate in this respect. His cap is a strange

construction of black sheepskin with a turkey feather in its side,
fastened with a ugly badge. There could not be a headdress less
martial or less becoming. The great coat is always worn, with dirty
white trousers outside the clumsy boot. . . regiment's reserves are
still provided . . . with sandals . . . it must be admitted that the
Roumanian soldiers do not look "smart" at all.[30]

Carroll Tevis, on the other hand, writing with more military experience
than journalistic savvy, wrote about the same Romanian soldier saying
their appearance and outfit were excellent and, "if they are as good as they
look, Romania has cause to be proud of her Army."

They must be, in any case, superior to the Turks, if they have as
much courage as they have military instruction and, although there
may be the natural hesitation of young troops to face the music in
their first engagement, we ought remember that they are the direct
descendants of those Dacians who furnished the bravest gladiators
in the sports of Imperial Rome.[31]

The situation in Romania in July 1877 was a paradox. The country
was on a wartime footing and much had been asked of its people, yet
". . . on one murmured against the extraordinary requisitions that were
made."[32] No one really complained too loudly about anything because
independence was at stake. But the idea of freedom and the prospect
of offensive action across the Danube were two entirely different matters;
at least in the minds of those of lesser station than the Prince and his
immediate advisors. The various artillery duels across the Danube had
shown that Romanian artillery was a match for that of the Turks, and
that the Turks had no compunctions about firing into the territory of
their former satrapate.

However, in the middle of July, with the heavy Russian casualties and
signs everywhere that all was not well with the Army of the Tsar south of
the Danube, rumors about impending action by the Romanian Army were
everywhere. As yet, however, the Russians had shown no inclination to
ask for help from the Romanians. Neverthelss, the rumors created exactly
the wrong atmosphere for Carol who was trying to negotiate an honorable
role for the Army, one that would bring an "acknowledgment of the absol-

ute independence of Romania."[34] That these negotiations were going on prior to the first two battles at Plevna seems obvious, and many Romanians in high places were afraid the Prince would affect some sort of agreement with the Russians without recourse to the Chamber for consultation and approval.[35]

When the Grand Duke's telegram arrived Carol was, therefore, caught on the proverbial horns. There was a commercial and financial crisis at home, his army, doughty as it was, was not really prepared, and the Russians, feared as friends and dreaded as enemies had still not clarified the Romanian position. The Russians had, after the second defeat at Plevna, cried for help and Romania was about to answer that plea, but at what price?

What transpired next was summed up in Carroll Tevis' dispatch of August 20:

> The hitherto despised Roumanian Army, so sneered at by the Russians a few weeks ago, is about to play an active role in the great drama, provided the Grand Duke will consent to its separate action under its own Commander in Chief, Prince Carol. If not, the troops will be withdrawn from the right to the left bank, where they will maintain a strictly defensive attitude as frontier guards, and the sovereign will return to Bucharest, declining all future co-operation with the Russians. On Friday (August 17) this result of the late negotiation at the imperial headquarters appeard probably. . . . But a great many things may change in six and thirty hours. A satisfactory compromise has been effected [sic] and the embryo heroes have orders to. . .win their laurels by an attack on the left flank of the Army of Osman Pasha, commanded by the Prince in person.[36]

Thus, the fledgling army of Carol was moved to join the battered Army of the Tsar at Plevna. In doing so, Carol notified his people that the "fate of Romania is become more critical. . .we are compelled to cooperate with the Russian Army in order to hasten the end of the war at all costs."[37] There was no praise forthcoming from the Russians, however, and, if anything, Russo-Romanian relations worsened. What had before been the humiliation of having to deal with the Romanians was now a necessity. All the effusive cordiality that had gone on before between the Grand Duke Nicholas and Prince Carol was now in the past.

To accept the help of Roumania was for the Russians to confess
in the face of Europe that they had been grossly deceived, and had
not men sufficient to continue the war. The animosity of the chiefs
extended to the soldiers. . . . Russian pride was thus obliged to give
way, and Prince Charles at last attained his point.[38]

What happened after this point is history. The Romanian Army went
to Plevna, to the right wing of the Russian Army to the east of the town.
There on September 11, 1877, two battalions of Romanian militia along
with one battalion of Russian troops, in a last desparate assault just as
darkness fell, stormed and took one of the redoubts, Grivitza No. 1. As
the story thus far has been told to a large extent in the words of those who
were there, it is only fitting that their comments tell the last chapter.

Lieutenant Francis V. Greene, United States Military Attache with the
Russian Army at Plevna reported that, "a battalion of Romanians under
Major Popescu rushed forward without firing a shot." Greene went on:

> They got into the ditch in large numbers before the Turks saw them,
> and there they actually killed the men in the counterscarf galleries
> by firing through the loopholes from the ditch. They then climbed
> over the rampart which was much beaten down, by the artillery fire,
> and after a hand to hand bayonet fight in the dark they drove the
> Turks out and held the redoubt.[39]

Caroll Trevis, Special Correspondent of the *New York Times:*

> . . . the behavior of the Roumanian troops was excellent . . . cour-
> age and recklessness of danger, among both officers and men, they
> have given most satisfactory evidence . . . the despised Moldo-Walla-
> chian Militia has merited well of their country, and have showed
> themselves to be far better soldiers than the much vaunted Russians
> who faltered a good deal in the last days' fighting and whose of-
> ficers not infrequently set a very bad example.[40]

Frederick Boyle, British Newspaperman expelled from the front by the
Grand Duke:

Amongst the events of this war which should have a permanent result is the discovery that Roumania possesses soldiers who will fight.
The Turks knew, or might have suspected it, had they searched their
own annals, but to Austria and Russia, yet more to the world at
large, the revelation was quite a surprise.[41]

Archibald Forbes, Correspondent of the *London Daily News:*

. . . the work was finally catpured at seven P.M. Four guns and a
standard were the trophies of the feat of arms . . . to my surprise,
when I reached the Plevna Valley this morning, I beheld a flag-staff
up, defiantly exposing the Roumanian flag, in that hitherto dreaded
Grivica [sic] Redoubt.[42]

Wentworth Huyshe, Special Correspondent of the *New York Herald* in
Constantinople:

The survivors sullenly come up out of the valley of death. But what
is that yonder, over the Grivitza redoubt? The Roumanian flag![43]

Lieutenant General Valentine Baker Pasha, Imperial Ottoman Army,
defender of Constantinople:

The despised Roumanian army had come up to the assistance of the
Russians, and there can be little doubt that its arrival saved the
Muscovite forces from a disastrous issue of the whole Danube cam-
paign.[44]

Again, Carroll Tevis:

So many centuries have passed without any warlike deed to place
to the credit of Roumania that the world has taken up the undeser-
ved opinion that the nation was lacking courage, and that the money
spent in the education of its officers and the organization of its
Army had been wasted in vain. And yet they fight well these so-
called holiday soldiers and nothing can be more heroic than their
conduct since they have taken the field.[45]

The war was far from over for the army and the people of Romania. Much hard fighting at Rahova and Vidin still faced the now-blooded Romanians and there would be more than enough casualties to touch every corner of the nation. And even after the fighting had ended, Romania still had to face the betrayal of Alexander II, the Tsar-Emperor of all the Russias and the equally callous treatment of all the other great powers of Europe, all of whom, it would seem, were more interested in aggrandizement than in fulfilling their obligations to the numerous small countries stuck away in corners around the continent.

Yet, for Romania, and its aspirations for independence, the issue had been settled at Plevna. At that small Bulgarian village, the army that everyone said would fail proved to the world, and, indeed to itself, that soldiering is not made up of fancy uniforms, rigorous deference to rank and cruel discipline alone, but is also the result of devotion to a cause that most of those who served did not really understand. Five hundred years of servitude may have dulled the ability but not the ardor for freedom. As with any army, it is likely that the Romanian soldier would have preferred to be elsewhere, to be doing other things. Yet, faced by a brave enemy and backed by a recalcitrant, but equally brave ally, and mocked by a world that did not fully appreciate the reach of desire, the Romanian soldier rose well above the occasion and proved himself beyond any question to be among the very best. No people could ask more of their sons.

NOTES

1. The tribute amounted to about $190,000 per annum based upon the 1876 value of the American dollar.
2. *New York Times* (hereafter *NTY*), January 8, 1877, 5/4. See also *NYT*, May 15, 1877.
3. Ibid.
4. Henry Montague Hozier, ed., *The Russo-Turkish War: Including an Account of the Rise and Decline of the Ottoman Empire, and a History of the Eastern Question*, (London: Mackenzie, 1878), p. 606.
5. See *NYT* October 24, 1876, which places date of assumption of command in October 1876.
6. Edward King, "In Roumanian Land," *Lippincott's Monthly Journal* XXI (May, 1878), p. 538.
7. Ibid.
8. Ibid., p. 539.
9. *Edinburgh Review*, CCCIII (July, 1978), p. 101; see also King, p. 539.
10. The city was also called "The City of Pleasure," and "The Wanderer's Paradise."
11. The plague had last striken Bucharest in 1813, when in less than six weeks, 70,000 had died.
12. King, p. 538.
13. The law, passed in February of 1876 covered both general and compulsory military service and came close to being a form of universal military service. See *Monitorul oficial*, No. 51, 5/7 March 1876, pp. 1297-1303. For the earlier laws that affected the army see *Monitorul Ziar oficial al Romaniei*, No. 162, 17/29 July 1868, pp. 975-978; *Monitorul oficial*, No. 79, 7/19 April 1872, p. 497; *Monitorul oastei*, No. 14, 1/13 June 1874, pp. 597-608.
14. Cf. Nicolae Iorga, *Razboiul pentru indendenta Romaniei*, (Bucharest: Actiunile diplomatice si stari de spirit, 1927), p. 137.
15. Report from London, *NYT*, May 3, 1877.
16. *NYT*, May 9, 1877.
17. Dispatch of the Bucharest Correspondent of the London Times, *NYT*, May 10, 1877.
18. *NYT*, May 14, 1877.
19. Hozier, p. 606; see also State Department Dispatches, Atkinson to Evarts, No. 174, May 10, 1877 for a perception of the alliance from St. Petersburg.

20.   Major W. G. Knox, R.H.A., "Personal Reminiscences of the Turco-Russian War, 1877-78," Lecture given to the Aldershot Society, No. IX, October 4, 1878, p. 3.

21.   *NYT*, May 17, 1877.

22.   *NYT*, May 27, 1877.

23.   *NYT*, May 27, 1877. The correspondent is Carroll Tevis, a United States Military Academy graduate who served as a general officer in the Union Army during the American Civil War. For a complete account of the Romanian army's uniforms see Captain Philip H. B. Salusbury, "With the Roumanians in the '77 Campaign," *United Services Journal* DCX (September 1879), 208-209 and DCXII (November 1879), 327.

24.   *NYT*, June 17, 1877.

25.   Richard Graf von Pfeil, *Experiences of a Prussian Officer in the Russian Service During the Turkish War of 1877-78*, trans. by Colonel C. W. Bowdler (London: Edward Standford, 1893), p. 29.

26.   Salusbury, DXCI (October 1879), p. 204.

27.   Ibid.

28.   Frederick Boyle, *The Narrative of an Expelled Correspondent*, (London: Chard Bentley, 1877), pp. 414-16.

29.   *NYT*, May 27, 1877.

30.   Boyle, pp. 416-17. It is obvious that Boyle is describing a militia soldiers uniform, or possibly that of a dorobanti.

31.   *NYT*, May 27, 1877.

32.   Hozier, p. 606.

33.   *NYT*, July 3, 1877, p. 1.

34.   *London Times*, July 31, 1877, p. 9.

35.   *NYT*, September 7, 1877, p. 1. See also Hozier, p. 607 for an explanation of an incident that led to the withdrawal threat.

36.   *London Times*, September 11, 1877, p. 5; September 12, 1877, p. 5; *NYT*, September 17, 1877, p. 1.

37.   Hozier, p. 607.

38.   Report No. 6 of Lt. F.V. Greene, Official Dispatch No. 219, Baker to Evarts, St. Petersburg, September 24, 1877. (Greene is apparently in error as to the composition of the force that made the final attack, as in his report he says two regiments of Russian troops were also present).

39.   *NYT*, October 4, 1877, p. 5.

40.   Boyle, p. 411.

41.   Archibald Forbes et al., *London Daily News: Correspondence of the War Between Russia and Turkey*, 2 vols. (London: Macmillan, 1879), p. 485.

42.   Wentworth Huyshe, *The Liberation of Bulgaria: War Notes in 1877,* (London: Bless, Sands and Foster, 1894), p. 107.

43.   Baker Pasha, p. 359.

44.   *NYT,* October 27, 1877, p. 1.

Gheorghe Zaharia

EPILOGUE: THE HISTORIC PERSPECTIVE OF THE GAINING OF INDEPENDENCE

The gaining of independence in 1877 stimulated the development of the nation and of the national state under favorable conditions. Two aspects of this phenomenon are rooted in the historic perspective. The first was the accelerated rhythm of the multilateral development of all aspects of socio-economic and political life. In this respect suffice it to point out the remarkable achievements in industrialization recorded by the end of the nineteenth century, the progress realized in the search for a solution to the agrarian problem—which included *inter alia* the bloody peasant revolt of 1907—which entailed the diminution of the latifundia of the big landowners, and as a result of industrial development, the expansion of the ranks of the proletariat and the establishment of the workers' first political party of their own since 1893, the Social-Democratic Party of the Workers of Romania.

Second, the Romanian society having benefited from the attainment of state independence sought, at once, the attainment of the revolutionary goals of the "Forty-eighters" to wit, the reconstitution of the ancient home of the Dacians through the union of all Romanians into a Romanian state. This second aspect, in particular, had a powerful impact on the military. Yet the expansion of the army in both terms of structure and manpower, the constant modernization of armaments—primarily through acquisitions from abroad—and the evolution of military doctrine, which took advantage

223

of the experience gained during the war of 1877-78 and of the technological achievements of the period, were not a function of any aggressive designs entertained by the Romanian state. On the contrary, a sensible assessment of European political realities prior to World War I, the very location of Romania with respect to the two powerful enemies of the Habsburgs and of the tsars, demanded first of all the consolidation of the Romanian state to safeguard itself against possible attempts at domination by its neighbors. Such apprehensions, for instance, were reflected in the secret treaty of alliance with Austria-Hungary in 1883 which, however, did not become effective in 1914.

The outbreak of World War I raised the possibility of the repetition of the achievement first realized by Michael the Brave in 1600. The Romanians instanctively understood that the attainment of complete national unity had to be achieved then or never. But they also understood that prudence and intelligent political and military actions were a prerequisite. The realism of the leaders and the pressures exerted by the people—as most clearly expressed in the public opinion and the views of all political organizations, socialists, liberals, conservatives—made for Romania's entering the war on the side of the Entente. The results are well known. The Romanians in all provinces inhabited by them expressed freely and unequivocally their determination to be united unreservedly and forever with the homeland. The treaties of peace concluded at the end of World War I, which were to constitute the so-called Versailles system, confirmed this great achievement, the product of the efforts and sacrifices of the entire society.

The determination of the Romanian nation to safeguard national independence and sovereignty during the interwar years is well known. So is the determination of the post-World War II Romanians for indeed the legacy of the gaining of state and national independence in 1877 is permanently embedded in the history of the Romanians.

Nicolae Ciachir

MILITARY COOPERATION BETWEEN ROMANIANS AND THE PEOPLES TO THE SOUTH OF THE DANUBE DURING THE OTTOMAN PERIOD

Nowadays, in the southeast European area there are seven states—Romania, Yugoslavia, Bulgaria, Greece, Albania, Turkey and Cyprus—whose inhabitants have taken an active part in developing civilization in the area. Their contribution to the development of the production forces, as well as the achivements of the Dacian, Hellenic, Thracian, Illyrian, Roman and Byzantine civilizations—whose nucleus had been formed, for its greatest part, in southeaster Europe—provided a common denominator between the Balkan feudal states in the thirteenth and fourteenth centuries. Those relations grew ever stronger in the second half of the fourteenth century concomitantly with the emergence of the Ottoman danger.

The Romanian people, preserver of the Dacians' tradition of liberty, but also of the Roman order and steadfastness, has known how to cope with the many waves of the migratory peoples, which overran this rich land for a century, and by using military and diplomatic skillfulness, how to withstand the subsequent attacks of the two neighboring feudal states: Hungary and Poland.

On the eve of the Turkish conquest—started with the occupation of Gallipoli (1354), a major strategic point on the European coast of the Dardanelles—feudal parcelling had grown in scope in the Balkan states. The Byzantine Empire, Serbia, Bulgaria were divided into numerous small states—principalities warring with each other—while the first self-dependent

225

Albanian feudal state (Arberia), which had shaken off Byzantine rule, as well as the small Montenegro (Zetta), because of their small territory, their geographical location and demographic resources were unable to offer major resistance to Ottoman expansion.

While the "Byzantine Empire was completely unable to withstand the new attackers, and if the capital, strongly fortified on the land and most difficult to storm from the sea, could repulse the Ottoman attacks for as long as a century, this was due to its location rather than to the bravery of its defenders,"[1] the Turks met with strong resistance on the part of the peoples in East Europe. "These peoples were, in the order in which they opposed, with their chests, the yataghans of the Crescent: the Albanians, the Serbians, the Bulgarians, the Romanians and the Hungarians. They made up those concentric walls which the Turks had to break in order to penetrate the European citadel."[2]

A brilliant military success scored by Wallachia in 1369 against certain Ottoman actions carried out north of the Danube enhanced Prince Vlaicu's prestige in Southeastern Europe. Upon the express request of the Serbians, Romanian detachments took part in the battle of Chirmen, on the Maritsa River, in 1371, on the side of Tsar Vukashin and Prince Ugliesha. But the battle would be eventually won by the Ottomans, Vukashin was killed during the fight, and a number of Serbia counties were forced to acknowledge the Ottoman authority; the Ottomans laid waste to almost the entire Balkan peninsula.

As an outcome of the defeat sustained at Kossovopolje (1389), where the Christian forces (Serbians, Bosnians, Croatians, Albanians and, according to Ottoman sources, Romanians, too), were deciminated, Serbian became a vassal of the Ottomans and, a few years later, the Bulgarian tsars' states were turned into Turkish pashaliks (Tîrnovo and Nicopolis in 1393 and Vidin in 1396). The hopes of the Balkan peoples were then pinned on the Prince of Wallachia, Micrea the Old (1386-1416).

It is not by mere chance that at Nicopolis (1396) Mircea succeeded in saving part of the Christian effectives, that he regained Dobrudja in 1404, or that the battle of Rovine (1394) became deeply imbedded in Balkan folklore. His gallantry, his skillful diplomacy, his reputation as a good organizer, acknowledged by both his friends and his enemies, made them consider him the "bravest and most clever of all Christian princes,"[3] while the Balkan people joined his military forces, thereby enabling him to continue the armed struggle against the Ottomans.

The successors of Mircea the Old—Dan II, Vlad Dracul, Vlad the Impaler—continued to fight against the Ottomans, facing the enemy on battlefields north and even south of the Danube. It is for that reason that Balkan folklore calls Dan II "the brave" and Vlad Dracul, alongside the troops of Iancu of Hunedoara, reached as far south as Sofia (1443), Varna (1444), etc. or Vlad the Impaler faced successfully the very conqueror of Constantinople.

In his *Hronica Românilor și a altor neamuri* (A Chronicle of the Romanians and of Other Peoples) Gheorghe Șincai points out the cooperation between the Albanian Skanderbeg and Iancu: "being in the Turkish camp, he not only let John of Hunedoara know about the Turks' movements, but also left the Turkish camp with a number of faithful soldiers; he drafted several letters as if they had been written by the Sultan, and in this way, by cunning, he occupied almost the entire Epyrus and his native stronghold, Kruja."[4] Nicolae Iorga drew a parallel between the struggle waged by Moldavia under Stephen and the actions carried out by Skanderbeg in Albania in the second half of the fifteenth century: "The troops which attacked Stephen at Vaslui had come from Albania, and Soliman Pasha had just left the command of the troops there to come and fight in the narrow valleys of Vaslui against the Moldavian armies. Skanderbeg was dead at the time of the attack on Moldavia, but his nationals were still fighting. The endeavors of one peope, under its own, Moldavian flag, and of the other people, to defend Scutari against the development of the Ottoman Empire in the fifteenth century, are justly paralleled."[5]

The conquest of Constantinople in 1453 and the dismemberment of the Byzantine Empire were of utmost importance to the Ottomans, as the city was a famous stronghold and a major commercial and cultural center, lying at the crossroads of two continents. "On conquering the capital of the Ceasars"—the Turkish historian Halil Inalcik shows—"Mohammed II considered himself the legitimate descendant of the Roman emperoors. He thus synthetized in his very person the monarchic Islamic, Turkic, and Byzantine traditions, founding an empire that would last for more than four centuries."[6]

In 1459, the Ottomans abolished Serbia as a state by turning her into a Turkish pashalik, and in 1463, they conquered Bosnia, the Greek principality of Morea and the Duchy of Athens. In 1475, they occupied the mighty stronghold of Caffa (in Crimea), until then a possession of the

Genoese, and the 160 Moldavians found there were beheaded; they also
occupied Mangop, where Alexander, the brother-in-law of Stephen the
Great, was ruling. The same year (1475), the powerful Khanate of the
Tatars in Crimea, likewise ruling over southern Russia up to the Dniester
acknowledged Ottoman suzerainty. Being of the same religious faith—
Mohammedan—and closely related by language and origin, the Tatars of
the Khanate of Crimea were to enjoy a privileged situation and would
assist the Ottomans many times, and thus pose a serious threat to the Romanian countries, Moldavia in particular. In 1479, the Ottomans occupied
anew the largest part of Albania, which had been liberated during the era
of Skanderbeg (George Kastriotti), and in 1482 Herzegovina, too, was incorporated into the Ottoman Empire. Likewise, in 1499 the remaining
territories of Montenegro were occupied and included in the newly-found-
ed sanjak of Skadar. By 1500, almost the entire Balkan Peninsula had been
incorporated into the Ottoman Empire, and, as a consequence. Europe,
Italy, and North Africa was opened to ambitious sultans.

At that historical juncture, when almost the entire Balkan Peninsula
and a great part of Hungary had been turned into Turkish pashaliks, the
Romanian countries—lying north of the Danube—managed to maintain
through military resistance and diplomatic skill, a large degree of domestic
autonomy, to preserve their state institutions and yield several territories
(Giurgiu, Turnu, Brăila, Dobrudja, Chilia, Cetatea Albă, Tighina, etc.)
to the Turks. Moreover, it should be noted that after part of Hungary
became a Turkish pashalik, Transylvania managed to avoid a similar fate,
to proclaim herself an autonomous principality, and acknowledge the
suzerainty of the Porte. Thus, "the Romanian people—unlike the other
peoples of the Danubian basin which had been integrated into the Ottoman Empire or into the Habsburg Empire—succeeded in maintaining
its state autonomy. As an outcome of the determination with which it
had defended its homeland, our people succeeded in concluding treaties
with the Ottoman Empire, already in the times of Mircea the Old, stipu-
lating the obligation of the Porte to respect the country's organization, not
to interefere in its internal affairs, and even pledge to defend the country
against foreign attack."[7]

As a consequence, many Balkan people took refuge in the Romanian
lands. Whether they settled in Wallachia, Moldavia or Transylvania, whether they were boyars or monks, townsfolk or peasants, soldiers or craftsmen,

they were granted asylum and the possibility of work. As soldiers, they fought most bravely with the troops commanded by Stephen the Great, Prince John the Valiant, Michael the Brave and other princes.

As a matter of fact, the Romanian prestige in the Balkans was high from as early as the reigns of Mircea the Old, Stephen the Great, Michael the Brave, Matei Bassarab, Constantin Brîncoveanu, influential princes, good managers and able diplomats, and especially skilled in the art of warfare.

If we think of the uncertainties of the fifteenth century in Southeastern Europe, we can hardly imagine a fourty-seven year-long reign as that of Stephen the Great. At the time, Spain was just unified, England—involved in the Wars of the Roses—watched the Ottoman expansion with indifference, France, exhausted by the Hundred Years' War, was striving to strengthen the central power during the reign of Louis XI (1461-1483), while the German states prompted future Pope Pius II to say: ". . . the disunited will never show a united face." Hungary, Poland and the Venetian Republic were indeed interested in checking the Ottomans, but thought that the danger could be thwarted through diplomatic arrangements alone.

"On fighting for the independence of their countries," the historian C. C. Giurescu pointed out, "all great princes of the Romanian countries also harbored the conviction that they were fighting for the defense of the entire Christendom, of South-East Europe in particular."[8] On the eve of the battle of Călugăreni Michael the Brave would declare that he went to battle . . . with this poor country of ours, to be a shield for the entire Christendom."[9]

One should also add the fact that, although in the sixteenth century the Ottoman Empire was still expanding, centralization became an obvious political goal of the European states, and the naval defeat sustained by the Ottomans at Lepanto (1571) showed that the Turks might not only be contained but also defeated. Moreover, the Ottoman Porte had a tendency to ignore the letter of treaties, even those concluded with friendly countries. Reigning princes, vassals of the Ottoman Empire, were never secure in their positions, the sultans' firmans notwithstanding, even if they had scrupulously paid the tribute and met all other obligations. And that insecurity became greater after the death of Soleiman the Magnificent (1566) when the Ottoman Empire became increasingly less powerful in all, including the military, fields.

After the brilliant victory scored by Michael the Brave at Călugăreni (1595), the Wallachian prince encouraged an uprising of the Balkan population against the Ottoman Empire. Even after the first victories, ". . . the Bulgarians approached him, through their messengers, telling him that more than 30,000 people would be on the ready in the forests, waiting for him."[10] The advance of Michael the Brave south of the Danube, when he reached Plevna, the Balkan Mountains and even beyond, coordinated with the "first insurrection of wider scope of Tîrnovo" (1598),[11] challenged the Porte's domination. Thogh put down, the insurrection helped the Bulgarians in that they acquired experience in guerilla warfare which they would use against the Ottomans.

In the first quarter of the seventeenth century, the French gentilhomme Charles Gonzaque, who considered himself a descendant of the Paleologues, planned an anti-Ottoman European coalition which was to include all southeastern European leaders and in which the Romanian princes were to be assigned a leading role. In 1614, a secret general Balkan conference was held in northern Albania, attended by representatives of Albania, Greece, Bosnia, Serbia, Dalmatia, Bulgaria, Herzegovina and Macedonia, whose purpose was to launch a general insurrection which would expel the Ottomans from Europe and deliver Constantinople. The insurrection relied on the assistance of the princes of Wallachia and Moldavia, who were supposed to take their troops south of the Danube, to move on to Adrianople and join forces with the other insurgents. Even though the projected insurrection did not materialize, Ottoman documents reveal that between 1618-1630, many groups of outlaws coming from Wallachia, Transylvania and the provinces south of the Danube, were active in the Kriva Palanka, Sofia, Bitolia, Djuma-Pazar, and other areas.

In Tîrgoviște, prelate Petar Parchevich, a subsequent Catholic archbishop of Bulgaria, unveiled to the Wallachian Prince Matei Basarab the plans of an anti-Ottoman crusade, which was to involve Poland, Austria and Venice and in which the Romanians would be assigned a leading role. This project alos was not implemented, primarily because of Austria's and Venice's reticence.

In the seventeenth and eighteenth centuries, Matei Basarab, Serban Cantacuzino, Constantin Brincoveanu and Dimitrie Cantemir, with the knowledge of such leaders of the Christian peoples of the Balkans, conceived of various forms of anti-Ottoman cooperation; when their actions proved unsuccessful, as in the case of the Bulgarian insurrection of 1688 (in the Chiprovets area), refugees were granted asylum and privileges by the Romanian princes.[12] Thus, the anti-Ottoman struggle in the Balkans gained in intensity, with Romanians, and especially, Wallachian support. In Bucharest, the turning of the eigtheenth century "witnessed the most fervid diplomatic activity in South-East Europe,"[13] during the rule of Prince Constantin Brîncoveanu. Brîncoveanu realized that the destiny of his country, surrounded as it was by enemies, had to rely not only on military forces as such, but also on the power of diplomacy, which had to be informed, flexible and ubiquitous.

In a memorandum sent by Brîncoveanu to Russia on the involvement by the tsar in a war against the Ottoman Empire, he indicated that not only by Wallachian and Moldavian troops, but also troops recruited from among the Balkan peoples, would participate in the conflict. Only a few years earlier, Prince Serban Cantacuzino, engaged in anti-Ottoman negotiations with the Habsburgs, had stated that all Balkan peoples, Serbians, Bulgarians, Macedonians, Albanians and all the other Greek populations, would join the Romanians.

It is a known fact that toward the end of the eighteenth century the decline of the Ottoman Empire had become irremediable. The two empires in the area, the Austrian and the Russian, attempted to dismember the Ottoman Empire by military means. Under the circumstances, the peoples of southeast Europe staged uprisings against the Porte, and participated in warfare alongside Russian and Austrian troops. The Romanians cooperated with the other Balkan peoples in most of the Russo-Turkish and Austro-Turkish wars waged in the eighteenth century and during the first part of the nineteenth century. The insurrectional movement of the Balkan peoples, as clearly shown by the Yugoslav historian D. Djordjevic, played a major role in the strategy of anti-Ottoman coalitions, as the rising autochthonous bourgeoisie was readying revolutions for national emancipation.

The Serbian insurrection (1804), enjoyed the support of the Romanians, Prince Constantin Ipsilanti aided it first by diplomatic means, and, subsequently, provided it with victuals, arms and men. The French consul to Bucharest informed Paris on the fact that the Romanians applauded the insurgents' successes and openly wished that "Serbia should free herself from the Ottoman Empire."[14] Since the metropolitan bishop of

Bucharest had frequent contacts with the Russian consul in Vidin and had made several visits to the camp of the Serbian insurgents in Belgrade, the French diplomat suggested to Talleyrand that he should appoint a consul in Craiova, so that Paris may be better and more operatively informed of developments in the Balkan Peninsula.

The chronicler Naum Rîmniceanu recorded that Prince Ipsilanti, enlisted in his army many Balkan peoples such as Serbians, Slavonians and Christians; Serbian historiography likewise recorded that the Wallachian prince provided the Serbians with "powder and munitions for 50,000 rifles and ten or twelve old cannons."[15]

The Serbian uprising was a genuine bourgeois-democratic revolution (1804-1815), which paved the way for the establishment of the modern Serbian state. The Serbian revolution generated peasant movements in the Vidin area and in other parts of Bulgaria, which were supported by Romanians, as well as actions by *armatoles* and *klephts* in the Olympus Mountains, in Montenegro and in Northern Albania.

After the otubreak of the Russo-Turkish war in 1806, Ipsilanti became ruler of both Romanian Principalities with Russian support, and began to recruit Romanian peasants for his army. Ipsilanti also commissioned officers, from lieutenant to general, and his forces were joined by many Balkan peoples, the so-called units of "Macedonian dragoons."

Concurrently with the advance of the Tsarist and Habsburg empires toward the Balkans, the Romanians, alongside other Balkan peoples engaged in organized actions against the Porte. These culminated in the Romanian revolution led by Tudor Vladimirescu (1821), and the Greek revolution triggered off in Peloponnesus, in mainland Greece, and in the islands. Many Balkan people joined the army of Tudor Vladimirescu and Romanians, particularly many Macedonians (Vlachs), such as those of the Pyndus Mountains, took part in the fight for the liberation of Greece, south of the Danube. "Those armatoles or chieftains were all of Romanian origin, whom the Turks had found, since they first set foot in Europe, on the peaks of the mountains, in villages or cities that seemed to be hanging from the skies rather than lying on earth . . . in their mountain gorges where they lived they had all preserved almost complete independence from the Turkish power."[16]

As far as the Romanian revolution of 1821 is concerned, several things should be emphasized. It was carried out in the complex aftermath of the unrest in Southeast Europe, in close relationship with the Hetairia, which planned to stage a general insurrection which would force the Ottomans to disperse their forces between the Romanian Principalities, Serbia, Montenegro, Greece and the troops of the rebellious Ali Pasha of Janina. While the Hetairia confined itself with the fighting for national emancipation, with a view to ensuring Greek preponderance, the revolution led by Tudor Vladimirescu had a comprehensive program of national and social reorganization and opposed any form of national discrimination or subordination.

In a collection of documents published in Yugoslavia in 1969, Omer Nakichevic shows that the revolutionary movement which spread all over the region of Kossovo in 1822 had been triggered off a year before by the Romanian people.[14] A number of Turkish documents brought to light by the historians of Skopje reveal the fact that Hurshid Ahmed Pasha, the governor of the vilayet of Rumelia, ordered subordinate Ottoman authorities to suppress as quickly as possible the forces of the rebellious Ali Pasha of Janina and to act rapidly against the Greeks to prevent expansion of the Wallachian insurrectional movement.

As an outcome of both the Romanian revolution and the Greek one (1821-1829), the political situation in the Balkan area witnessed a number of changes, stipulated in the Treaty of Adrianople (1829), concluded after the Russo-Turkish War (1828-1829), in which thousands of Romanians had fought alongside Bulgarians, Serbians, Greek, Montenegrians and Albanians. The Treaty of Adrianople brought recognized autonomy to Serbia, Greece and the Romanian Principalities. As far as the Romanians were concerned, it stipulated, in addition to an independent domestic administration, the removal of Ottoman monopoly and full liberty of trade. The former Turkish rayahs on the left bank of the Danube—Giurgiu, Turnu and Brăila—were to be restored to Wallachia, and their fortifications were to be dismantled, while the Moslems possessing immovable property were to sell it to the native inhabitants in eighteen months' time. Pursuant to the same treaty (Article 10), the Porte had to delegate a number of representatives who, along with those of Russia, France and England, were to clarify the situation of the Greek people. Thus the Treaty of London (1830) was concluded, which stipulated full independence for Greece, an event of major political significance for southeastern Europe, as it stimulated the aspirations of other Balkan peoples for complete emancipation from the Ottomans and of the Greeks for national unity.

The revolutionary events which took place in southeastern Europe in 1848 should be linked to the general revolutionary movements of that year which shook almost the entire continent to its very foundations. Speaking of the spreading of the bourgeois revolution in Europe, Engels stated that: "Starting in 1789, the front of the revolution would advance without interruption. Its last outposts were Warsaw, Debreczen and Bucharest."[18]

The Romanian revolution was particularly remarkable in that among the participants were to be found many Balkan people, especially Bulgarians and Serbians. At the same time, the Bulgarian population in Romanian villages joined the Romanian peasants in opposition to the landed gentry. The Bulgarians sought to emulate the Romanians and launch an insurrection in the Rahova and Vidin areas but they were unable to do so because of Ottoman and Tsarist opposition.

The Eastern crisis which led to the Crimean War, did not resolve the issue of liberation of the Balkan peoples inasmuch as the Paris Treaty of March 1856 maintained Ottoman suzerainty over the Romanian Principalities, Serbia and Montenegro, and the subordination of the other territories of the Balkan Peninsula.

Romania, Serbia and Montenegro pursued the common goals of ending Ottoman suzerainty, removal of Habsburg rule over territories singled out for eventual incorporation into national states and lending assistance to the Balkan peoples under direct Ottoman rule. The support of Greece was also sought inasmuch as Greece herself wanted to regain parts of Epyrus, Macedonia, Thessaly and many of the islands still under alien rule. Meanwhile, the territories still under direct Ottoman rule of the Porte, such as Dobrudja, Macedonia, Bulgaria, Bosnia, Herzegovina, Albania, the Sanjak of Novi Bazar, parts of Old Serbia, parts of Epyrus, Thessaly, Cyprus, etc., engaged in various forms of actions designed to secure national independence.

If during the Middle Ages many Balkan inhabitants—Greeks, Serbians, Bulgarians, Montenegrians, Albanians—moved into the Romanian countries which had retained domestic autonomy and state institutions, now as the emergence of Balkan states occurred, significent population movements were recorded. Thus, Romanians of the Dobrudja, Macedo-Romanians of Macedonia, Bulgarians, Orthodox Albanians looked for asylum in Romania, whereas the people living in Old Serbia, Bosnia, Hercegovina, the Sanjak of Novi Bazar, the Slavs of Macedonia, the Bulgarians of the western provinces and some Albanians looked for asylum in Serbia and Montenegro, while the people living in Epyrus, Thessaly, Cyprus, Crete, etc., were to take refuge in Greece, as many other Balkan people settled in Russia and other European centers.

The Romanian people's struggle for union, the election of Prince Alexandru Ioan Cuza in both Principalities (1859), and the unification of the administration of the Romanian state (1862) were well received by the peoples of the Balkan Peninsula. "The long-waged, common struggle against foreign domination, for freedom and national independence, has laid the basis of a lasting friendship among the Balkan peoples."[19] As early as April 14, 1859, the consul of France accredited to Belgrade informed Paris that the "example set by the Romanian Principalities fosters general unrest," and added in an ensuing report, that following the Romanians' example, the Skupshtina intends to refuse to pay the tribute.[20]

Romania's readiness to allow the transit of arms from Russia in 1862, which enabled Serbia to equip her army with modern armament was considered by the Serbian government as an act of "great courage and of utmost usefulness." It strengthened the relations between Serbia and Romania leading to the establishment of formal diplomatic relations through the setting up of standing agencies in 1863. In 1868, the two states concluded at treaty of alliance designed to faciliate their proximate independence.

Around 1870, Montenegro too was anxious to establish a Balkan league with Romania, Serbia and Greece. The Prince of Montenegro told the Romain diplomat, Theodor Văcărescu that Romania should lead the alliance since she was the "largest, the most prosperous and the richest nation"[21] in the Balkans. A Romanian initiative in this respect—Prince Nicholas maintained—was justified by both Romania's geographic location and her national homogenity.

During the armed conflict between Montenegro and the Ottoman Empire in 1862, the Serbian-Turkish war of 1862-1867, the crises in Crete, Epyrus and Thessaly of 1866, the revolt of Hercegovina and Bosnia in the summer of 1875, the Bulgarian uprisings of 1875-1876, or the war waged by Serbia and Montenegro against the Ottomans in the summer and autumn of 1875, the Romanian press was overtly sympathetic to the struggle of the Balkan peoples, denouncing the Ottoman Empire, despite the latter's being the suzerain power.

It should be emphasized that, while the Balkan refugees, especially the Bulgarians and the Orthodox Albanians, were granted asylum by Romania and enjoyed freedom despite the fact that many a time the Porte sought their extradition, Ottoman subjects were subject to constant abuses. In this respect, a diplomatic note revealed: ". . . while the foreign governments ensure their subjects an efficacious protection, the subjects of the Supreme Power are faced with the painful need of appealing to other nationalities in order to protect trade and themselves against hindrances and vexations."[22]

In another document, the general governor of the Danube vilayet (Tuna) would protest against the fact that a number of Ottoman subjects on Romania's territory were ill-treated by Bulgarians, without the Romanian authorities taking any measure whatsoever. Likewise, in 1875, a few Ottoman subjects in Romania complained to the Ottoman general consul in Bucharest about the fact that, although they produced passports, they were arrested and ill-treated by the police of Alexandria.

At the time of the Eastern crisis, reopened in 1875 through the uprisings in Herzegovina and Bosnia, Romania while declaring herself neutral during the initial stage of the fighting, supported the struggle of the Balkan peoples by granting asylum and in many cases also material assistance to Serbian and Bulgarian refugees in 1875-1876. Romania's approval of the transit of volunteers, arms, munitions, victuals and sanitary items from Russia to Serbia entailed repeated protests from the Ottoman government and the suspicions of almost all Great Powers, which wished the status quo to be maintained in the Balkans. The Bulgarians' fight for the liberation of their homeland enjoyed broad support from Romanian authorities and public opinion. The detachment led by Hristo Botev was organized on Romania's territory, wherefrom it launched its heroic action south of the Danube.

At the same time, the Romanian, Serbian, Montenegrin and Greek diplomats were anxious to prevent the replacement of Ottoman rule by that of Austro-Hungary or Russia should the Ottoman Empire collapse altogether. The actions of the Great Powers since 1856 revealed the Powers' selfish interests and basic opposition to the total political emancipation of the Balkan peoples.

Romania's neutrality during the early years of the Balkan crisis was of a tactical nature. A military solution of Balkan and particularly Romania's problems was however envisaged as maybe seen in a letter Prince

Carol sent to his father in August 1875, in which he said: "The Christian East has had quite enough of Turkish administration. . . . High diplomacy is hopeless in the Eastern Question, which can be solved only in the East, even through war, with the participation of the peoples directly involved."[23] In the same letter, Carol showed that given the complicated situation prevailing in the Balkans, Romania had to strengthen herself from economically and militarily points of view in order to be able to cope with any contingency.

In this respect, Serbia's consul in Bucharest informed Belgrade in 1875 that Romania was making military preparations and that, by the spring of 1876, she would be able to muster 50,000 able-bodied soldiers. Romanian public opinion was increasingly in favor of participation in the war, alongside Serbia and Montenegro, to secure the country's independence. "Here everybody is against the Turks and the public spirit calls for a war"—Carold recorded in his memoirs.

Concurrently with the strengthening of her military capacity, Romania sought to secure independence by peaceful means. The rejection of diplomatic moves and the military defeat of Serbia in the autumn of 1876 prompted the search for an agreement with Russia. Romanian political leaders, particularly the liberal government of I. C. Brătianu, realized that the states and peoples of Southeastern Europe would not by themselves be able to defeat Ottoman armed forces, all the more so as the Porte was supported by certain Great Powers which wished to maintain the Ottoman Empire's territorial integrity.

Tsarist diplomacy succeeded in having the five Great Powers (England, France, Germany, Austria-Hungary and Italy) sign, alongside Russia, the London Protocol of March 31, 1877, whereby the Porte was compelled to undertake reforms, or failing to do so, risk war with Russia acting on behalf of Europe. Romanian diplomacy was also successful because the Romanian-Russian Convention of April 4, 1877 stipulated that the country's integrity would be respected. Following the conclusion of the convention, the Romanian government became actively involved in the Balkan crisis; a state of war with the Ottoman Empire was reached on April 29, 1877. On May 9, 1877, the Romanian Parliament broke off relations with the Porte and proclaimed Romania's independence.

The Romanian army, of some 40,000 men, was sent across the Danube, and fought alongside the Russian army and Bulgarian volunteers—at

Grivitza, Plevna, Rahova, Smîrdan and Vidin. "The blood shed by the Romanian soldiers at Grivitza, Rahova, Smîrdan"—points out the Bulgarian historian Hristina Mihova "strengthened the unity and friendly relations between the Bulgarian and the Romanian peoples in their fight against Ottoman rule."[24] The Greek newspaper "Stoa" eulogized the Romanian army, considering it ". . . a model worthy of being immitated by the Balkan peoples."[25]

The fall of Plevna—regarded by Russian and Ottoman documents as the turning point of the war—had a profound impact on events in southeastern Europe; it prompted, inter alia, Serbia's reentry into the war. In ordering this action, Prince Milan stated: "on the battlefield we shall find the brave Russian army, covered with heroic glory; we shall find our Montenegrin brothers and our brave Romanian neighbors, who crossed the Danube and went to fight for the independence and freedom of the oppressed Christians."[26]

The war of 1877-1878, which brought together on the battlefield Romanians, Serbians, Montenegrins, Bulgarians, insurgents from Bosnia and Hercegovina, volunteers from Macedonia, Epyrus, Thessaly, and Russians was the most significant stage in the struggle of the peoples of southeastern Europe against Ottoman rule which resulted in the securing of the state independence of Romania, Serbia, Montenegro, and the establishment of the Bulgarian autonomous principality. A basis for future progress and cooperation, if not the realization of all expectations of the peoples of the Balkans, was thus achieved by 1878.

NOTES

1. A. D. Xenopol, *Istoria Românilor din Dacia Traiană* (A History of the Romanians in Trajan's Dacia), Third Edition, I. Vlădescu, ed., București, 1927, III, p. 76.

2. Ibid.

3. Leunclavius, *Historia musulmana Turcorum de monumentis ipsorum exscriptae*, libri XVIII, Frankfurt, 1591, col. 418.

4. Gh. Șincai, *Hronica Românilor și a altor neamuri* (A Chronicle of the Romanians and of Other Peoples), II, Iași, 1853, p. 4.

5. N. Iorga, *Albania și România* (Albania and Romania), Vălenii de Munte, 1916, pp. 4-5; see also N. Iorga, *Breve historique de l'Albanie et du peuple albanais*, București, 1919.

6. H. Inalcik, *L'Empire Ottoman*, in "Les peuples de l'Europe du sud-est et leur role dans l'histoire (siecle XV-XX)," Sofia, 1966, p. 21.

7. Nicolae Ceaușescu, *Romania on the Way of Building up the Multilaterally Developed Socialist Society*, vol. 14, Bucharest, Meridiane Publishing House, 1978, p. 295.

8. C. C. Giurescu, *Premise istorice ale redobîndirii independenței poporului român*, (Historical Premises of the Regaining of the Romanian People's Independence), in the volume *România în războiul de independență* (Romania in the War of Independence), București, 1977, p. 15.

9. P. P. Panaitescu, *Documente privitoare la istoria lui Mihai Viteazul* (Documents on the Reign of Michael the Brave), București, 1936, p. 14.

10. A. D. Xenopol, *Istoria Românilor din Dacia Traiană*, V, p. 194.

11. B. Cvetkova, *Les Bulgares et la situation politique internationale au XVIIe siecle*, in "Revue bulgare d'histoire," nr. 2/1978, p. 27.

12. Nicolae Ciachir, *România în sud-estul Europei. 1848-1866* (Romania in South-East Europe. 1848-1866), București, 1968, p. 7.

13. V. Cîndea, D. Giurescu, M. Malița, *Pagini din trecutul diplomației românești* (Pages from the History of Romanian Diplomacy), București, 1966, p. 169.

14. *Documente privitoare la istoria Românilor, Hurmuzaki*, (Documents on the History of the Romanians, Hurmuzaki), vol. XVI, *Corespondență diplomatică și rapoarte consulare franceze. 1603-1824* (French Diplomatic Correspondence and Consular Reports. 1603-1824), București, 1912, p. 609.

15. Greg. Iakchitsch, *L'Europe et la resurrection de la Serbie*, Paris, 1917, p. 33; see also Andrei Oțetea, *Tudor Vladimirescu și revoluția din 1821* (Tudor Vladimirescu and the 1821 Revolution), București, 1971, p. 95.

16. A. D. Xenopol, *Istoria Românilor din Dacia Traiană*, IX, p. 33.

17. Omer Nakicevici, *Revolt i protesni mars stanovnika Kosova 1822 godine*, Priștina, 1969, p. 3.

18. K. Marx, F. Engels, *Opere* (Works), vol. IX, București, 1969, p. 35.

19. Ceaușescu, op. cit., vol. 13, Bucharest, p. 42.

20. Archive of the History Institute, Belgarde, mark I, XXVII, inv. no. 59/26, dispatch sent from Belgrade on April 14, 1859, and inv. no. 59/47, dispatch of August 13, 1859.

21. Bucharest State Archive, Royal Family Stock, file 7 (1872), pp. 21-22.

22. Bucharest State Archive, Ministry of the Interior Stock, Administrative Division, file 3/374 (1870), p. 2.

23. King Carol I, *Acte şi cuvîntări* (Papers and Speeches), vol. I, p. 430.

24. Hristina Mihova, in Sbornik Statii, *Osvobojdenieto na Bălgaria ot tursko igo (1878-1958)*, Sofia, 1958, p. 217.

25. "Familia" (Budapesta) of October 16, 1877.

26. *Documente privind războiul pentru independenţă*, vol. VIII, p. 43.

Ştefan Pascu

THE ROMANIAN ARMY AND SOCIETY
1878-1920

The victorious conclusion of the War for Independence and the ensuing recognition of Romania's new state by Europe's powers created a new framework for the functioning of Romania's armed forces. The fundamental political purpose of the national armed forces was the defense of the indepenedent state's integrity. However, external trends designed to make Romania into a potential theater of war for the benefit of certain foreign powers, jeopardized Romania's independence. Indeed, international political and military developments, occurring toward the end of the nineteenth century and the beginning of the twentieth exacerbated such potential dangers: the aggressiveness of the Great Powers increased concurrently with the real development of capitalism in Europe and North America, with the increase in multilaterial competition among the developed countries and the emergence of an economic and technological gap between developed and underdeveloped countries and the corollary attempts of the former to render the latter into colonies. These factors were of decisive importance in the armament race which gained momentum by the turn of the century and which anticipated military confrontations of unprecedented magnitude. All processes defined the Marxists as engenderers of the imperialist stage of capitalism threatened the general peace and the existence of small and medium-sized nations. Romania's geographic location invited the power's interest; they were covetting its

241

natural resources, including petroleum; at the same time, the country's status was jeopardized and realized its strategic position along the roads of expansion into the Balkans and to the Straits of the Black Sea. The Romanians in those years were concerned with safeguarding the state's inviolability and sovereignty, in the period and with the liberation of the Romanian provinces that were still under foreign domination, their military prepardness and activities after 1878 reflected these goals.

In Transylvania, in the period following 1877-1878, the national struggle involved resistance to the policy of denationalization. The aggravation of oppressive nationality policies resulted in the closing of the ranks of the leading groups of the Romanian bourgeoisie. In May 1881, at Sibiu, the National Romanian Party was established under the chairmanship of George Barițiu, Vicențiu Babeș and Ioan Rațiu. The program of the Party assigned priority to regaining the autonomy of Transylvania, obtaining the right to use the Romanian language in administration and justice, appointing Romanian officials in proportion with the size of the population, and so forth.

Of overwhelming importance in the struggle of the Romanians of Transylvania to secure union with Romania was the memorandum of 1892. The memorandum sent to the Court of Vienna attested to the strength of Romanian national feelings, demonstrated the irreconcilable opposition of the masses to the regime of national discrimination. The political trial initiated by the Magyar government against the signatories of the Memorandum, which took place before the Cluj Tribunal between April 25/May 7 and May 13/25, 1894 resulted in the sentencing of the signatories to long prison terms. The ideas of the Memorandum, however, could not be eradicated particularly as its goals were embraced by the Romanian masses.

In the period 1878-1900, the Romanian press in Transylvania voiced the people's aspirations for national and social liberty, as well as the interests of the Romanian bourgeoisie a part of which oscillated between nationalist positions and class collaboration with the Austro-Hungarian bourgeoisie. *Observatorul* (The Observer) founded in 1878, *Transylvania, Gazeta Transilvaniei* (The Transylvanian Gazette) and many other publications supported the Romanians' struggle for unity. Romanian culture in Transylvania, devoid of state support, continued to develop especially within

ASTRA (The Transylvanian Association for Romanian Literature and the Education of the Romanian People).

The national movement of the Romanians in Bukovina, where the Habsburg occupation made desperate efforts to stiffle the Romanian spirit also gained in intensity in those years. At Cernăuți, the foundation for a cultural association *Reuniunea română de lectură* (The Romanian Reading Society) was laid in 1860; in 1864 that association became *Societatea pentru literatura și cultura română în Bucovina* (Society for the Romanian Culture and Literature of Bukovina). From 1897, when the "Society" acquired a printing press, to 1916 it published nine magazines, twenty newspapers and numerous books.

In Maramureș, also following several attempts in the 1870s to establish Romanian cultural societies, the *Reuniunea docenților greco-catolici români din Maramureș* (The Association of Romanian Greek-Catholic Deans of Maramureș) was set up in 1883 with the aim of raising the economic and cultural status of the peasantry.

Nor did the Romanians of the Banat and Crișana remain inactive. When ASTRA was set up they envisaged the establishment of a Romanian cultural association. It was founded in Arad and its work was intensive and successful. The Transylvanian ASTRA itself greatly valued the creation of branches in Banat, Crișana and Maramureș.

At the beginning of the twentieth century, the Romanian people intensified their struggle for liberation from the Dualist rule, for union with the independent state of Romania. Ștefan Bethlen, the Hungarian governor of Transylvania himself wrote that "it is difficult to imagine the spiritual influence exercised by the existence of the independent Romanian state on the Romanian souls. . . . As the prestige of independent Romania grew in the eyes of the Romanians from Hungary, their policy became bolder. They have in view that the territory which they inhabit may at a favorable moment be united with the Romanian kingdom."[2]

Although the Romanian governments, because of their policies, were faced with numerous internal socio-economic and political problems— especially after the great peasant uprising of 1907—they indirectly or tacitly encouraged the people's aspirations for unity. Romania's adherence to the Triple Alliance was an obstacle to its overtly supporting the unionist struggle of the Romanians in Transylvania.

The evolution of social-political life in the Austro-Hungarian dualist monarchy before World War I brought out the artificial character of the

Austro-Hungarian state, the imminence of its breaking up under the pressure of the people's struggles for liberation from the domination of the monarchy, for their inclusion in national states or their union with co-nations in existing states. In response to these pressures the tendency was virulently manifested, in Hungary, to consolidate the levers of domination over the oppressed peoples. Under the circumstances, the National Romanian Party renounced its tactics of political "passivity" and engaged in resolute actions for expediting the struggle against national persecution. In the 1905 program of the National Party the formula of "regaining the autonomy of Transylvania," which existed in the old program adopted in 1881, was abandoned in favor of the more comprehensive goals of securing recognition of the political individuality of the Romanian people and ensuring the Romanian's ethnic and constitutional development.

The socialist organizations and the trade-unions of Transylvania were particularly significant instruments of political and patriotic education of the working people in the struggle against socio-economic exploitation and national oppression. In these respects the party of the workers met and cooperated frequently with the Romanian National Party. "We admit," wrote the paper of the Romanian socialists (*Adevărul* of December 9, 1906) in addressing the leaders of the National Party, "that you are today the only ones in the Diet who carry out a genuinely democratic struggle. . .let us join our forces and start the struggle which will save the entire people from the slavery and misery in which it is living." In 1907, during the campaign for universal suffrage, the socialists asked that "these two parties be one and fight shoulder to shoulder, with mutual brotherly trust for securing universal suffrage."[3]

Because of such political activity, despite the negative attitude of the authorities and the discriminatory character of the electoral law itself, the National Party was able to win in 1905, 1908 and 1910 elections, 8, 14 and 5, respectively, seats in the Parliament of Budapest. Among those elected were Vasile Lucaciu, former militant in the Memorandist movement, Ștefan Ciceo Pop, Iuliu Maniu, Aurel Vlad, Ioan Suciu, T. Mihaly, to name a few.

International developments of the period 1911-1913 (Italo-Turkish war, the Balkan wars) brought about a reorientation of Romania's foreign policy marked by increasing coolness toward the Central Powers. Moreover Romanian public opinion was profoundly hostile to the foreign policy pursued by Austria-Hungary. Under these circumstances, the ruling circles in Bucharest, seeking closer relations with the Entente powers, asked the Vienna government to give careful consideration to its relationship with the Romanians of the Empire. This led to the beginning of negotiations between the Hungarian governments of Lukacs and Tisza and the Romanian National Party in 1912-1914. Although the demands of the Romanian National Party were rather moderate (universal suffrage, proportional representation, higher education in the Romanian language, etc.) they were all rejected by the authorities with the formula "after good relations are established between Magyars and Romanians."[4]

The outbreak of the First World War confronted the Romanian forces which militated for the Great Union with new and intricate problems. Between 1914-1916, Romania pursued a neutral policy. Both the Triple Entente and the Triple Alliance sought to attract her in the war on one side or the other. The Romanian government and other outstanding Romanian statemen, however, believed that Romania's participation in the war had to be contingent on the securing of assurances, based on treaties, that the country's national aspirations would be fulfilled. In the sumer of 1916, the Entente wought an immediate commitment as it promised its support for the liberation of Romanian territories under Austro-Hungarian domination.

Consequently, on August 17, 1916, Romania concluded a political treaty and a military convention with France, England and Russia. The Great Powers acknowledged Romania's right over the Austro-Hungarian provinces inhabited by Romanians and drew up the new frontiers. Romania was granted equal rights with the Allies in all matters concerning preliminary and actual peace negotiations. The three Great Powers recognized Romania's difficult military situation and agreed to facilitate Romania's cause by unleasing concurrent offensive operations on the Russian-German and Salonica fronts; moreover, Russian forces, amounting to one Army Corps, were to operate alongside Romanian units in the southeastern part of Romania. Finally, the powers were to supply the Romanian army with adequate armaments.

Under the circumstances, on August 27, the Romanian plenipotentiary in Vienna delivered the Romanian declaration of war to the Austro-Hungarian Empire. It pointed out that "Romania . . . finds itself compelled to enter the war on the side of the Great Powers, which secured the achievement of her national unity."[5]

The mass of the Romanian army was concentrated in the west of the country along the mountain range of the Carpathians. The Romanian headquarters had mobilized 1,083,000 men out of which 562,000 were combat troops located as follows: 420,000 men on the Carpathian front and 142,000 on the southeastern front.[6] The armament of the Romanian forces was inferior to that of the enemy.

On the very day that war was declared, Romanian troops were ordered to carry out military operations across the Carpathians. Concurrently, the Romanian army had to fight on the second front, in the Dobruja. The first clashes on the southeastern front took place in the vicinity of the town of Turtucaia, where the Romanian troops were defeated by the German-Bulgarian forces. The defeat lowered the morale of other Romanian forces operating between the Danube and the Black Sea. However, when the enemy assumed the offensive in this area as well, the Romanian troops—and the two Russian and one Serbian division fighting alongside them—reorganized themselves and staged a powerful counteroffensive. The counteroffensive, coordinated with one to cross the Danube through Flămînda, and attack the left bank and encircle the enemy between the Danube and the Black Sea had to be abandoned after Romanian troops had crossed the river and established a bridgehead on the right bank because of the enemy's advance on the Carpathian front. On that front, the enemy assumed the offensive designed to enter the Romanian plain along the Danube and toward Bucharest, Ploiești, Focșani, and Bacău while a simultaneous German-Bulgarian offensive across the Danube, through southern Romania was to encircle a great part of the Romanian army.

Although superior in number and equipment, the enemy forces faced stiff resistance in the Carpathian passes where the first and the second Romanian armies staged two counteroffensives. The Romanian actions in the Oituz, Slănic, Uz and Trotush valleys arrested the enemy's offensive.

On November 23, 1916, as the German-Bulgarian troops forced the Danube at Zimnicea and advanced toward Bucharest, Romanian forces gave a good account of themselves. They retreated to avoid encirclement and fought on the Olt-Neajlov-Argeș line; after the collapse of that line, they continued their resistance on the Cricov river, on the surroundings of Rîmnicu-Sărat and then on the Sireth river and around the town of

Focşani. During the first part of January 1917, the German offensive was completely arrested by Romanian and Russian forces on a front stretching from the maritime Danube, Nămoloasa, the lower Sireth Valley, around Oituz and further on, to the north, to the range of the Eastern Carpathians.

For Romania, the campaign of 1916 had ended in temporary defeat as much of the country's territory was occupied by foreign forces. To survive, the Romanian state had to make enormous efforts and sacrifices in all fields.

During the winter and spring of 1917, Romanian military leaders reorganized and endowed the Romanian army with armament and supplies received from the Western Allies through Russia, trained the army with the assistance of French officers who had come to Romania in October 1916 as part of the French Military Mission and improved the army's morale. At the same time, Romanian authorities and sanitary services fought the outbreak of typhus which killed thousands of people, so that by the sping the epidemic was eradicated.

In 1917—the peak year of the First World War—both belligerent sides made great efforts in pursuit of a final victory. On the Romanian front, 1917 recorded three great decisive battles for the destines of the Romanian nation, the battles of Mărăşeşti, Mărăşti and Oituz.

The forces which were to confront each other during that summer were the 6th Russian, the 1st Romanian, the 4th Russian, the 2nd Romanian and the 9th Russian armies on the one side, and the 3rd Bulgarian and the 9th German armies, the "Ruiz" and "Gerock" groups, the 1st Austrian and the 7th Austro-Hungarian armies on the other side. Both sides had offensive plans. The Russian and Romanian commands intended to crush the main part of the enemy's forces in the Focşani region, then to chase the enemy out of Romania, and then, through a joint action with the allied forces from Salonica, they would force Bulgaria's withdrawal from the war.

The Romanian-Russian offensive was staged on July 22, 1917 with a powerful artillery bombardment carried out in the area of the 2nd Romanian and 4th Russian armies. The 2nd Romanian army was to crush the enemy positions and advance beyond the Putna river valley. In that manner they would support the operations of the 4th Russian army, which was to reach the river Milcov and from there, together with the 1st Romanian army, to deal a decisive blow to the enemy in the Focşani area.

The Romanians attacked on July 24, 1917 at dawn, near the village of Mărăşti with three divisions. By evening, the Romanian divisions conquered the first enemy strongholds, the foremost enemy defensive positions in the area. The Russian divisions on the left of the 2nd Romanian army scored a similar victory. The next day, pursuing the offensive, the Romanian troops met strong resistance only in the central hills in the center as the German units on the flanks hastily retreated. In the Mărăşti area, the large Romanian units waged continuously battles until July 30, 1917 when they reached the Putna river valley from its passage in the plain to its springs in the mountains, and in the north to the peak of the Măgura Caşinului mountain. Thus, the battle of Mărăşti came to an end.

Although it was not carried to conclusion, serious losses were inflicted on the enemy. The enemy was forced to cede an area of thirty-five kilometers side by twenty kilometers deep leaving thousands of dead and wounded. The Romanian troops alone took 2,800 prisoners and seized large quantities of armament and ammunition, including sixty-nine cannons and mine throwers. The Romanian forces themselves lost over 1,300 dead and had some 3,000 wounded.[7]

After the stopping of the battle of Mărăşti and of the Russian-Romanian offensive in general, the German Command attempted to put into practice its own offensive plan for the summer of 1917. It sought to encircle the Russian-Romanian forces in the area and crush them through a blow dealt from the northwest, in the direction of Focşani-Mărăşeşti-Adjud, in conjunction with another attack, which was to start in the mountains, on the Oituz valley to Tîrgu-Ocna-Adjud. The German armies were then to occupy all of Moldavia, and thus force Romania's withdrawal from the war, and after that, by means of a joint operation with Austro-Hungarian forces from the Bukovina front, to push back the Russian forces to the east and conquer Odessa.

The offensive started on August 6, 1917 at dawn, along the river Sireth by five divisions of the 9th German army which faced two Russian divisions. It was preceded by a massive bombardment involving all sizes of cannon, which in the last stages made use of poison gas. The attack lasted the entire day as the German divisions penetrated the Russian defenses. The following day frequent attacks and counterattacks succeeded one another. In the ensuing two days (August 8 and 9, 1917), the 9th German army moved against four Romanian and Russian divisions but the Romanian troops held their ground.

In writing on those battles and of the hopes of the German side to score a decisive victory, the Austrian newspaper *Neue Freie Presse* of August 9, 1917 pointed out: "We are fighting in southern Moldavia against the majority of the Romanian reorganized army. Through the clash of great masses, the fight between us and the Romanians begins to assume a decisive nature. This can be only gladdening for us. The victory over them, which can no longer be delayed, will be the more decisive."[8]

The enemy's views also reflected the fact that starting on August 8, 1917, the battles on the Mărășești front were coordinated with a German-Austrian-Hungarian offensive in the Eastern Carpathians, along the Oituz, Slănic and Cașin river valleys. The battles in the Oituz area were characterized by powerful bombardments, infiltration of enemy lines, flank attacks and frequent counterattacks, under the circumstances. In spite of their numerical superiority, the enemy forces failed to penetrate the Romanian defenses by more than one to three kilometers.

On August 10 and 11, the battles of Mărăști and Oituz reached their climax and forced the adoption of new tactics. Two days before, the Romanian-Russian command decided to engage in a counteroffensive. August 19, 1917 was the most difficult and bloodiest day—the decisive day of the great battles of Mărășești and Oituz. The German headquarters, aware of the exhaustion of its forces, decided to throw the last reserves into the battle to secure the long-awaited victory. But that strategy failed as the German forces were unable to stage a meaningful offensive.

The same situation prevailed also in the Oituz area, where, after one day of battle, the German troops advanced only about one kilometer and only on the Oituz valley. Elsewhere, all enemy attacks were repulsed. Thus, the enemy's offensive on the Romanian front in the summer of 1917 ended in complete failure.

These three battles, and Mărășești in particular, were the fiercest on the Romanian front and entailed serious consequences for the war as a whole. The bitterness and bloodletting was attested not only by their duration but also by the size of the forces involved and by the enormity of casualties. Romanian statistics record for the Mărășești battle alone, the loss of 27,410 Romanian fighting men (5,125 dead, 12,467 wounded, 9,818 mission—many of them also dead). It is reasonable to assume that the enemy, who carried out the offensive suffered equal or greater losses.

The German offensive was carried out in a small sector but with huge forces while the Romanian defenses proved their prowess. The deployment of troops in depth (sometimes on four or five lines) and the positioning of the forces allowed the Romanians to launch constant counterattacks. "The adversary's resistance, and in particular that of the Romanians"—said the German General Kurt von Morgen—"was uncommonly fierce, and materialized in counterattacks during the sixteen days of battle. The majority of these ended in bayonetting which inflicted heavy losses."[9]

The Romanians made masterful use of their reserves in blocking the enemy's advance after every breakthrough. Another characteristic feature of the battles was the extensive useage of artillery by both sides. For instance, at Mărășești 1,820 cannons and mortars (of which 696 were Romanian and Russian and 1,028 German) were engaged in a single day over a period of two hours, with the Romanian artillery alone firing 19,000 shells.

The most relevant feature of these battles was the heroism of the Romanian forces determined first to resist and then to win at all costs. That heroism was appreciated by foreign leaders and newspapers. "The Romanians fought successfully and even the Germans were surprised at such heroic resistance"[10] Lloyd George, the British Prime Minister, pointed out in 1917. "The Romanians"—stated a Russian newspaper—"are brave and they fight like lions. . . . They die but do not surrender. They fight fiercely for every inch of their land as the she-wolf when her last whelp is taken from her."[11] The British newspaper, The Times wrote: "The defense of the front north of Focshani was the most brilliant deed of arms ever performed by the Romanians."[12]

The victory scored by the Romanian army and the Russian troops in the Mărăști, Mărășești and Oituz battles thwarted the enemy's plan to achieve a junction with his forces in the Bukovina and Galicia and to expand his conquests to the East. By inflicting heavy losses on the enemy and thus preventing him from pursuing continuous massive military operations in Romania, the Romanians upset German military strategy and, above all, secured Romania's continuing existence as a state.

Important changes took place in the Entente toward the end of 1917. On November 7, in Russia the Bolshevik revolution broke out, which not only brought on a profound social and political change in Russia and put an end to the war, but also had a profound impact on the international scene. On November 21, 1917 the government of the new Russian state suggested a general truce to the Central Powers and one month later, peace negotiations were undertaken which ended with the Treaty of Brest-Litovsk on March 5, 1918. Under the circumstances, Romania was left alone to confront a militarily superior enemy. Unable to secure outside help, the Romanian government was obliged to ask for a truce and to engage in peace negotiations. Romania concluded the truce on December 9, 1917. On March 2, 1918, the truce was denounced by the Central Powers which forced Romania to sign a preliminary peace treaty and on May 7, a separate peace treaty. That onerous treaty was never ratified by the Romanian parliament and was, in fact, annulled by subsequent events of the same year.

The war waged by Romania entailed great human sacrifices and huge cultural and material losses. About 300,000 Romanian soldiers and civilians died in combat or through epidemics. The war, and especially the enemy occupation and war debts, financially exhausted the country. Thus, the consequences of the war were bitterly felt for many years after the termination of hostilities.

As the war progress, the principle of self-determination, enunciated by the Russian Revolution of 1917 and by President Wilson in January 1918, became of paramount importance. It was upon that principle that "the Moldavian Autonomous Republic of Bessarabia" was proclaimed in the autumn of 1917. It was also upon that principle that soldiers' councils were organized, that a "Country's Council" was elected as a representative assembly which on March 27/April 9, 1918 decided on Bessarabia's union with Romania.

Under the circumstances, the collapse of the Habsburg Monarchy appeared imminent. The political leaders of the Romanians in the Monarchy thus concentrated on attaining their ultimate goal of union with Romania. The Committee of the Romanian National Party met on September 24, 1918 and decided to resume militant activities and reestablish links with the social-democratic leaders. The meeting of October 16 of representatives of the Romanian National Party and the Social-Democratic Party decided on common action through the foundation of the Romanian National Council. The decision of the two parties' representatives was also influenced by European developments in general, and especially those in southeastern and eastern Europe, as well as by the establishment of the National Council of Romanian Unity in Paris, a body acknowledged by the allied powers as representatives of Romania's interests and by the manifestation of the emigrant Romanians in Austro-Hungary who, acting as a National Assembly also on October 6, in Iași demanded on their behalf and on behalf of the "Subjugated brothers at home, who were unable to demonstrate freely" that they be released from the yoke of Austro-Hungarian Monarchy, since they were determined to fight by all means for the creation by the Romanians of a unitary, free national state, according to the Treaty concluded by Romania with the Entente powers in August 1916.[13]

Under the circumstances, the representatives of the Romanian National Party of Transylvania met in Oradea, on October 12. The participants, by virtue of the inherent right of each and every nation to freely dispose and decide by itself on its fate, declared that "the Romanian Nation of Hungary and Transylvania" claimed the right to decide by itself its status among the free nations.

The decision made in Oradea, which meant the proclamation of the Romanian Nation's right to self-determination virtually stood for a declaration of separation of Transylvania from Hungary. The declaration also called for the convening of a national assembly.

Parallel actions occurred in Bukovina, a parallelism limited not only to synchronization of actions but also of political programs. A major political rally took place in Chernowitz, on October 27, at which a Constituent Assembly was established and a National Council, a representative body of the Romanians in Bukovina was chosen. The first decision of the Constituent Assembly was "Bukovina's integral union with the other Romanian countries into an independent national state in full solidarity with the Romanians in Transylvania and Hungary."[15]

Three days later, on the night of October 30-31, a "Romanian National Council" was set up in Transylvania, which was to rule that province for one month." "The Revolution has triumphed. The Romanian National Council has been set up"—proclaimed *Adevărul*, the newspaper of the Romanian socialists. The Council consisted of six representatives of the Romanian National Party and of as many representatives of the Social-Democratic Party.

To "guide" the revolution it was necessary to achieve a new political-administrative organization in Transylvania and Bukovina. To this end, from its very inception, the Central Romanian National Council set up a central military organization, the Romanian Central Military Council, which was entrusted with the securing of peace and order. The Central Romanian National Council and the Romanian Military Council governed the territories inhabited by Romanians through regional and local organizations subordinated to it: the Romanian national councils and the Romanian national guards. These democratically-elected bodies were set up almost everywhere during the first half of November.

On November 5 the struggle for union received encouragement from Washington. The government of the United States and President Wilson lent their support to the Romanians' aspirations by assuring them that "Romania's integrity, freedom and independence is a point of honour to the allies," that the allies would back "Romania's national claims."[16]

By mid-November, the success of the people's revolution in Transylvania and Bukovina appeared certain. The National Central Romanian Council, representing "the Romanian nation's sovereign will" in Transylvania, advised the local national councils of the decision that in all counties inhabited by Romanians elections would have to be held within 12 days to select delegates (deputies) "to the Romanian Great National Assembly" which was to be called soon. The elections would be held according to "the rules of universal suffrage," as the assembly would have "to represent in a most dignified and happy manner all our democratic strata,": intellectuals, peasants, workers, merchants and industrialists. The instructions governing the designation delegates or deputies were in conformity with those principles. The representatives were to be the bishops of the two Romanian denominations; the archpriests of the same; two representatives of each cultural society; two representatives of each women's organization; one representative of each school; two representatives of each teachers' organization; two representatives of each national and county guard, two representatives of each craftsmen's organization; the delegates of the Romanian Social Democratic Party, as representatives of the workers; two representatives of the students; five representatives of each constituency inhabited by Romanians.

Considering these decisive actions for Transylvania's union to Romania, "The Great Council of the Romanian Nation of Hungary and Transylvania," which was another name for the Central Romanian National Council, addressed on November 18 a manifesto "to the peoples of the world," printed in Romanian, French and English. The Romanian nation, "the embodiment of the most consumate democracy" pledged not to oppose other nations, but to secure full national freedom for everybody, to organize its free and independent state upon the principles of democracy, ensuring equal living conditions to all.[17]

On the day when Transylvania started their travel to Alba Iulia, on November 28, the People's Congress of Bukovina was meeting at Chernowitz. As in the case of Transylvania, the elections of delegates abided by democratic principles: 74 Romanian delegates, 13 Ruthenian delegates, 7 German and 6 Poles were elected in keeping with the ethnical configuration of Upper Moldavia. Another five *de jure* deputies were added. Besides the official delegates, others thousands of residents of Bukovina representing all social categories and nationalities, proceded toward Chernowitz, where the People's Congress was to meet.

Following the wise, well-thought out and responsible speech of the President, Iancu Flondor, "The General Congress of Bukovina, embodying the supreme power of the country and being invested with law-making power, in the name of national sovereignty, decides for the unconditional and eternal union of Bukovina to the Kingdom of Romania."

After three days in Alba Iulia the union of Transylvania with Romania was accomplished. 1,228 elected delegates or deputies, plus several tens of alternates brought with them instructions from their constituents to vote for the eternal and unconditional union of Transylvania to Romania.

On the eve of the Assembly, political leaders, "the wise" of the nation, as their contemporaries put it, debated in detail the draft resolution that was to be prevented to the Assembly. The next day, Sunday, December 1, at about seven in the morning, "endless lines of people" made their appearance. At ten o'clock, the members of the National Romanian Council and the bishops mounted on the improvised stage in the hall of the Casino henceforth called the Hall of the Union to the audience's tremendous cheers and ovations. The festive speech was delivered by Vasile Goldis. At the end of his address, Goldis submitted for approval to the Great National Assembly the decision for Union: "The National Assembly votes for the union of the Romanians of Transylvania, the Banat and the Hungarian Country and of the territories inhabited by them to Romania." When Vasile Goldis read out the first point of the decision, "the whole attendance answered with a thunder of applause."[18]

The territories united to Romania were granted provisional autonomy until the meeting of the Constituent Assembly elected by universal suffrage; all coinhabiting nationalities were granted full national freedom and equal rights, the right to instruction, administration and trial in their mother-tongues, to be part of the law-making bodies and to participate in the governing of the country in proportion to their size; equal rights and full freedom to all religious denominations; full accomplishment of a genuinely democratic regime in all domains of public life; direct, equal and secret universal vote, for both sexes aged at least 21; full freedom of the press, of association and meeting; free propagation of thought; radical land reform, giving the peasant the possibility to hold as much property as he and his family could work; the securing for industrial workers of the same rights and advantages as provided by law in the most advanced industrial states of the Wests, and so forth. The National Assembly expressed the wish that the Peace Congress achieve the communion of free nations, so that freedom and justice may be ensured for all nations, big and small alike, and in the future war should be ruled out as a means of settling international affairs; the National Assembly greeted the liberation of the nations subjugaged until then by the Austro-Hungarian Monarchy (Czechoslovak, Yugoslav, Austrian, Polish and Ruthenian); the National Assembly paid pious homage to the brave Romanians who shed their blood for the accomplishment of the national ideal; the National Assembly thanked all allied powers who fought for the salvation of civilization.[19]

After other official addresses, G. Pop de Băsești submitted for approval to the Assembly the Decision which was unanimously approved with great enthusiasm. Thus, the President could solemly announce that "The National Assembly of the Romanian people of Transylvania, the Banat and the Hungarian lands received the resolution advanced through Vasile Goldiș in its entirety and so, the union of these Romanian provinces to the motherland is decided for all ages to come."

To secure implementation of laws and of constitutional principles in the Romanian territories united to Romania until complete unification of the institutions could be achieved, the assembly elected a "Great National Council" endowed with the prerogatives of a provisional legislative assembly, which consisted of 212 members. The following day, December 2, the Great Council elected the President of the Great Assembly, Gheorghe

Pop de Băseşti, as President of the Legislative Body; he was to be assisted
by four vice-presidents and six notaries (secretaries). A provisional government called the Ruling Council, made up of fifteen departmental heads
(ministers) was then elected with Iuliu Maniu as chairman.

Convinced as they were of the irreversible character of the historical
process that ended with the Great Union, aware of the superiority of the
new, democratic rule, and of the equal rights granted in all spheres of
activity, the coinhabiting nationalities acknowledged, one by one, the
decisions of union to Romania of the Romanian territories formerly under
foreign domination.

Meanwhile, the Peace Conference in Paris was trying to find solutions
appropriate for settling world affairs in the postwar era. The proceedings
were painstaking and slow. A historian of the peace conference, D. A.
Pollar, rightly stated that "it is easier to destroy than to build" and that
"it takes wise people and long efforts to entrench peace in place of war."
It was only on June 28, 1919, that the Versailles Treaty was ready for
signing, in the Hall of Mirrors of the Palace of the Sun King, by the representatives of the "allied and associated powers" (France, England, Italy,
the United States and Japan) on the one hand, and of Germany and Austria-Hungary on the other hand. Based on the general framework provided
by the Versailles Treaty, special treaties were then concluded at Saint-
Germain with Austria (September 10, December 18, 1919 respectively),
at Neuilly with Bulgaria (September 27, 1919), at Trianon with Hungary
(June 4, 1920) and at Sevres with Turkey (August 10, 1920).

Thirty-two delegates, from as many countries, participated in the Peace
Conference. The Romanian delegation, led by Prime Minister I. I. C.
Brătianu, claimed for Romania the status of ally by virtue of Romania's
sacrifices during the war and of the treaty concluded with the allied
powers on August 17, 1916, which stipulated that Romania would participate in peace making "with the same rights as the allies."[20] As that
clause, as well as other official assurances given to Romania by the allied
governments at the end of the war were ignored and, moreover, as the
allied powers sought to ascertain certain rights over the conduct of Romania's internal affairs, the Romanian Prime Minister left Paris in protest
and tendered his resignation. The governments that followed in Romania
adopted a similar course which eventually forced the allied powers to
yield to Romania's demands. Brătianu thus negated the concept according

to which the smaller European countries had only marginal control over their own destiny, a fact noted by the American historian S. Spector.[21] The Saint-Germain Treaty then confirmed the decision of the Chernowitz national assembly of November 28, 1918 on Bukovina's union to Romania. The conclusion of the Trianon Treaty was more difficult. "Minute and well thought out researches" were necessary, confessed British Foreign Minister Arthur Balfour, "with the sincere wish to establish just frontiers for all parties." The result of these "minute and well thought out researches" and of the sincere wish to establish just frontiers, was Hungary's giving up "all rights and titles" to "the territories beyond Hungary's frontiers" and her acknowledgement of those territories' union to Romania. A commission of delimitation, made up of representatives of the allied powers, of Romania and Hungary, spent twelve months in studying the documentary evidence on the basis of which the "equitable and practical" setting of the frontiers was achieved. The conclusions of the commission are comprised in the letter of Alexandre Millerand, President of France and, as such, President of the Supreme Council of the Peace Conference, who pointed out that "the treaty is a work done with great endeavour and seriousness," as the authors made efforts to know in depth the realities in Central Europe and the claims of nationalities, of their century-old injustice, objectively pondering over everything that might be a right of Hungary.[22] The authors of the treaty took account of the "will of the peoples" which, long oppressed, joined their Italian, Romanian, Yugoslav and Czechoslovak brothers. And one of the most important experts, Charles Seymour, affirmed that where the ethnical criterion was inconclusive, the balance leaned slightly toward the old ruling nationalities, the German and the Magyar. Another important expert, Joseph Rudinsky assessed the treaties as "a work demanded by historical justice, as a quite necessary condition for the smooth running of the mechanism of peace."[23]

The treaties of Saint-Germain and Trianon confirmed the historical justice done in Chernowitz and Alba Iulia on November 28 and December 1, 1918. These treaties meant international recognition of the justness of the Romanian people's decision.

After several exchanges of letters between A. Vaida-Voievod, Prime Minister and head of the Romanian delegation to the Peace Conference, and Chicherin, Commissar for Foreign Affairs of Soviet Russia, designed

to establish "peaceful relations and advantageous links to both parties,"
to solve "by good understanding all litigations" between the two parties,
the Peace Conference signed, in October 1920, a special document, which
was ratified by Great Britain, France, Italy and Japan, which recognized
Bessarabia's union to Romania. In 1933, the United States acknowledged
it also.

The protracted and irreversible process of union of all territories inhabited by Romanians into a single unitary, national and independent
state, was thus ratified and consacrated and juridically sanctified, through
the internationally recognized principles of the people's right to self-
determination, observance of the ethnic realities and of existing laws
by "the tribunal of the peoples," the Paris Peace Conference.

NOTES

1.   I. Papp, *Procesul memorandului românilor din Transilvania. Acte
și date*, vol. I-II, Cluj, 1933-1934.

2.   Stefan Pascu and Miron Constantinescu, editors, *Desăvîrșirea
unificării statului național român. Unirea Transilvaniei cu vechea Ro-
mânie*, București, 1968, p. 97.

3.   *Adevărul*, September 20, 1907.

4.   Ștefan Pascu, *Marea Adunare Națională de la Alba Iulia*, Cluj,
1968, pp. 242-243.

5.   *România în războiul mondial 1916-1919*, vol. I, Bucharest, 1934,
p. 8.

6.   Constantin Kirițescu, *Istoria războiului pentru întregirea României*, ed. II, vol. I, Bucharest, 1925, p. 192.

7.   Lieutenant-Colonel Alexandru Ioanițiu, *Războiul României
1916-1917*, vol. II, Bucharest, p. 314.

8.   *România*, I, nr. 209, September 7, 1917.

9.   Kurt von Morgen, *Meiner Truppen Helden Kampfe*, apud Al.
Ioanițiu, op. cit., p. 347.

10.   "România," I, nr. 180, August 11, 1917.

11.   Apud *Apărarea patriei*, August 9, 1967.

12.   Ibid.

13.   Ștefan Pascu, op. cit., pp. 317-319.

14.   *Românul*, VII, nr. 1, October 26/November 7, 1918.

15. I. Nistor, *Unirea Bucovinei. 28 noiembrie 1918. Studii și documente*, Bucharest, 1928.

16. V. Stoica, *In America pentru cauza românească*, Bucharest, 1928.

17. *Românul*, VII, no. 10, November 7/20, 1918.

18. V. Netea, *O zi din istoria Transilvaniei. 1 Decemrbie 1918*, Bucharest, 1970.

19. Ștefan Pascu, op. cit.

20. I. Ionașcu, P. Bărbulescu, Gh. Gheorghe, *Tratatele internationale ale României 1354-1920*, Bucharest, 1975, pp. 410-412.

21. A. Gianini, *L'Unita nazionalle della Romania alla Conferenza della pace*, in *Studii sulla Romania*, Napoli, 1923; Sherman David Spector, *A Study of the Diplomacy of Joan I. C. Brătianu*, New York, 1962.

22. G. Sofronie, *Principiul naționalităților, în tratatele de pace din 1919-1920*, Bucharest, 1936, p. 191.

23. I. Rudinsky, *La revision du Traite de Trianon*, Paris, 1933; Ch. Seymour, *La fin d'un Empire; le debris de l'Autriche-Hongrie*, in *Ce que se passa reelement a Paris en 1918-1919*, Paris, 1923, pp. 86-88.

24. E. Campus, *Recunoașterea pe plan internațional a desăvîrșirii unității statale a României*, in "Studie. Revistă de istorie," no. 6/1968, pp. 1165-1183.

Mircea Muşat

MILITARY FACTORS AND NATIONAL DEVELOPMENT: THE IMPACT OF FOREIGN PRESSURES

Many archeological vestiges and written sources of antiquity speak of the Geto-Dacians located in the Carpatho-Danubian-Pontic area. History has recorded the flourishing centralized and independent Dacian state led by Burebista, one of the most significant figures in the history of the Romanian people and one of the great rulers of antiquity.

Burebista's epoch paved the way for that of Decebalus, the king of the Dacians, who had to face the Romanian Empire. Thus, the first century A.D. marked the beginning of struggle for the defense of a well-defined territory, which were to become, what Mihai Eminescu, the most outstanding poet of the Romanians, was to call the fight for independence, the "acme of our historical life."

In the fourth-tenth centuries, that is at the time when the territory of Romania was crossed by migratory populations, the continuity of the Romanian people was preserved and strengthened without interruptions, leading to the setting up of Romanian feudal states on the entire territory of former Dacia.

The historical process of the establishing of the centralized Romanian feudal state, as a result of the development and unification of the principalities on the entire territory of Romania, was hindered by both the domestic centrifugal tendencies, through the process of feudal division characterizing the whole of Europe at the time, and the vicissitueds of the ever present foreign danger. Starting in the tenth century, after their settling in the Pannonian Plain, groups led by Hungarian kings began the conquest of Transylvania. The Hungarians secured control over parts of Romania's northwestern territory (Transylvania) only in the late thirteenth century and at the beginning of the fourteenth century. This notwithstanding, even in the ensuing period the Romanians of Transylvania managed to preserve their organization in "lands," perpetuating the Romanian spirit in that region. Organized, for the social point of view, in village communities, the Romanians formed compact masses—lands—in all parts of Transylvania. Documents of the time, those belonging to Hungarian kings included, speak quite often of *terra Blachorum* (the Land of the Romanians). The Oaş, Lăpus and Sălaj Lands, the Haţeg Land, where voivode Litovoi ruled, or the Maramureş Land, where Romanian principalities were ruled by the Dragoş and Bogdan families, are examples and proof of a continuing Romanian political tradition in Transylvania. Under the circumstances, the administrative organization of Transylvania differed from that of the rest of the Hungarian feudal state, preserving an autochthonous form of organization—the principality run by a voivode —common to the other Romanian countries as well. Late in the fourteenth century, Roman Muşat called himself "Voivode of the Moldavian Land from the Mountains up to the Black Sea Coast."

However, the Romanian countries, which had just organized themselves into independent feudal states, had to cope with the danger coming from the south—the Ottoman Empire—which after having conquered the entire Balkan Peninsula and turned the territories of the Bulgarian and Serbian tsars into Turkish pashaliks, was now bordering on the Romanian countries. In 1417, despite the victories scored by Mircea the Old, the Ottoman Empire managed to detach from Wallachia the territory lying between the Danube and the Sea—Dobrudja—which remained under Ottoman rule until 1878.

The joint resistance of the Romanian countries to the Ottoman danger, the victories won during the reigns of Mircea the Old, Iancu of Hunedoara, Vlad the Impaler, Stephen the Great and of some other princes allowed the Romanian countries to conclude several agreements and treaties with the Porte as far back as the fourteenth century, whereby the sovereign power of the princes was acknowledged, while the Ottoman Porte in return for a tribute paid by the Romanian rulers, pledged to ensure the independence and territorial integrity of the Romanian countries. Even later, in the mid-sixteenth century, when the political and economic pressure of the Ottoman Porte on the Romanian countries intensified, the Romanian countries maintained their administrative autonomy, by virtue of the above-mentioned political treaties, the so-called "Capitulations," and were run according to their own laws and customs, and enjoyed the privileges acknowledged by those official documents. In this respect, the treaty concluded by Wallachia, Moldavia and the Ottoman Porte in 1511 stipulated: "The Porte acknowledges Moldavia as a free, unsubmitted country. The Christian faith, observed in Moldavia, shall never be infringed upon or hindered. . . . The Porte pledges to defend Moldavia against anyone who might attack her, preserving her previous status, without harming her or letting her ever to be subject to the least partition. Moldavia shall be ruled according with her laws and customs, without the least interference by the Porte. The princes shall be elected by the people and sanctioned by the Porte to rule for as long as they live. The princes shall rule over the entire land of Moldavia. . . . "[1]

The division of the Romanian people into several countries during the Middle Ages could not undermine its unity, expressed by common language and culture, by similar economic, social and cultural structures throughout the territories inhabited by Romanians. Within that framework, the Romanian countries maintained close permanent economic, political and military relations, with their domestic organization, the princedom, high offices, justice, army, and all other feudal organizations were identical or almost identical everywhere. The people kept the old generic name—Romanian—for all the inhabitants of the homeland, even if, in addition to that name other names were also used, taken from geographical zones, rivers or mountains. Such names as Muntenians (inhabitants of Muntenia-Wallachia), Moldavians, Oltenians (inhabitants of Oltenia), Transylvanians, or *bănăţeni* (inhabitants of the Banat), *maramureşeni* (inhabitants of Maramureş), *bucovineni* (inhabitants of Bukovina), *dobrogeni* (inhabitants of Dobrudja),and, within these categories, some even more particular names such as *moţi* (inhabitants of the Apuseni Mountains), *vrînceni* (inhabitants of Vrancea), *bîrseni* (inhabitants of Bîrsa Land), and so forth, all belonging to the historical category of the Romanian people.

The beginning of the sixteenth century marked a new stage in the offensive launched by the Ottoman Empire toward the heart of Europe.

Following the battle of Mohacs (1526), the Ottoman forces crushed the Hungarian army and abolished the Hungarian Kingdom. A couple of years later (1541), the Porte turned Central Hungary into a pashalik with its capital city in Buda, while the former principality of Transylvania was given a new organization, as a principality which no longer depended on the Hungarian Crown, but was a vassal of the Ottoman Porte. It is worth mentioning that the setting up of that autonomous principality had been facilitated by the military expedition of Petru Rareș, Prince of Moldavia, in Transylvania, by the existence of permanent economic exchanges between all Romanian provinces, by their joint military actions and, particularly, by the community of language and culture of the Romanian provinces. As for the Banat and a certain part of Crișana, in 1552 the Turks turned them into a pashalik with its capital in Timișoara.

During that difficult stage in its history, the Romanian people sought to survive, to cope with those difficult external circumstances by all means at its disposal. Prince Neagos Basarab (1512-1521) advised his son to love his country and not to let her fall into enemy hands, "for you better to die in honesty than live a bitter shameful life."[2] It is in the same spirit that Iliaș Rareș, Prince of Moldavia (1546-1551) and son to Petru Rareș, expressed his love for his forefathers' land: "We wish to preserve Our father's land; we will be kind with the kind, but will always oppose Our enemy."[3]

Symbolically, the Romanians, during the reign of Voivode Michael the Brave, achieved in 1600, the first political union of the Romanian countries within frontiers delimiting the greatest part of the territory of former Dacia. After Michael the Brave, the idea to rebuild the Dacia of old, of the union of the Romanian countries within their natural frontiers, became a dominant element in the political, diplomatic and military plans of many princes, including Gheorghe Stefan, Matei Basarab, Serban Cantacuzino, Constantin Brîncoveanu, Gabriel Bethlen, Mihnea III, Gheorghe Rakoczy II, and many others.

Starting with the second half of the seventeenth century and the beginning of the eighteenth, when the Ottoman Empire was declining, while Austria and Russia were on the rise, the Romanian countries assumed greater interest for the three great powers. The Ottoman Porte attempted many times to solve its military and political difficulties at the expense of the Romanian people frequently violating the obligations it had assumed through "Capitulations," and even ceding Romanian territories. This prompted certain Romanian princes to seek alliances with the Tsarist Empire, while Tsarist Russia assumed ever more the title and right of "protector" of peoples under Ottoman domination. Thus, in 1656, during the reign of Gheorghe Stefan, in Moldavia, and of Tsar Aleksei Mikhailovich the first political treaty far between Moldavia and Russia was concluded. In the first article of the treaty, "Russia pledged to observe the dignity and ways of Moldavia, such as they had previously been when that country was not a vassal of the Turks, namely without encroachments on her policy and administration;" the article went on to say that "Gheorghe Stefan, the Prince of Moldavia, shall rule for as long as he lives, while his successor shall be elected from among the native inhabitants."[4] In other words, Russia pledged to observe the independence of Moldavia against any interference by the Ottoman Empire.

Likewise, the stipulations of the treaty concluded by Dimitrie Cantemir, the Prince of Moldavia, with Peter the Great, Russia's Tsar, on April 13, 1711, were based on the same principles. The two leaders acted toward one another as sovereigns of two independent states: Peter the Great did not negotiate with Moldavia's prince through the agency of the Porte, but recognized Cantemir as the absolute ruler of the country. "According to the older rules of Moldavia"—Article 6 read—"the entire state power shall rest with the prince." At the same time, in Article 11, Russia admitted that "By virtue of its old rights, the Principality of Moldavia borders on the Dniester river, Kamenica, Bender (Tighina), with the whole territory of Bugeac, the Danube, Muntenia (Wallachia), the Great Duchy of Transylvania and on the territory of Poland in keeping with the above delimitation."[5]

The increasingly obvious decline of the Ottoman Empire in the early eighteenth century allowed the Habsburg Empire to start its own offensive against the Ottomans, overtly aiming at the Romanian countries. In 1686, as a result of victories won over the Turks, the Austrian army penetrated into Transylvania, imposing on Prince Mihail Apafi the Treaty of Blaj, in pursuance of which the Austrian army had to be provided for in Transylvania for "winter stay." Subsequently, in 1688, as a result of the policy of force promoted by the Habsburgs, the Transylvanian Diet "willingly" renounced the suzerainty of the Porte and accepted the "protection of the Emperor" in Vienna. Thus, Transylvania became a province of the Habsburg Empire, "legalized and sanctioned" from the political-juridical point of view by the Diploma of Leopold I, a "document" by which the Austrian emperor became also prince of Transylvania. The Porte accepted the new status of Transylvania bu the Peace of Karlowitz (1699), following which Transylvania "formally" passed under the rule of the Habsburg Empire, thus changing Ottoman domination for Austrian occupation. After the Austrian-Turkish war of 1716-1718, Oltenia was annexed by the Habsburg Empire for a period of twenty-one years (1718-1739), while the Banat would remain under Habsburg domination until 1918.

In the second half of the eighteenth century, the conflict of interests of the great empires had reached its pinnacle, jeopardizing the existence and national being of the peoples of Central and Eastern Europe. The first to fall prey was Poland, partitioned by Prussia, Austria and Russia in 1772, after that it was to be Moldavia.

At the end of the Russo-Turkish war of 1768-1774, won by the Tsarist Empire, Austria mustered her army and assisted Turkey during the negotiations, so that Russia should not obtain too significant an advantage. As a reward for the help extended, resorting to the most unfair political manuevers and the most object corruption, the Habsburgs asked the Ottoman Porte that a frontier rectification be made in South Galicia under the pretext that they needed a strip of Romanian territory to link Galicia, which they had occupied in 1688, to the Habsburg Empire. By submitting a forged map to the Porte, the Habsburgs eventually succeeded in annexing a much larger piece of territory from northern Moldavia. The cession was agreed upon at Palmuta on the Dniester in 1775, and was formally incorporated in the peace treaty singed by Austria and the Ottomans at Shishtov in 1791, whereby Austria took possession of the northern part of Moldavia, that territory included the former capital of feudal Moldavia, Suceava. Initally, the Habsburg government called the new territory "Austrian Moldavia," soon, however, to obscure the annexation, Austria changed its name to "Bukovina," after the name of the beech forests of Cosmin. Until 1786, Bukovina was kept under Austrian military administration, while in the ensuing period it was annexed to Galicia, as a more administrative unit of that province.

In 1806 a new Russo-Turkish war broke out for supremacy in the Black Sea and the Danubian basin. With the signing, on May 28, 1812, of the

Bucharest Peace Treaty by Russia and Turkey, the almost six-year long war between the two empires ended; Romanian military units of *pandurs* (among them, Tudor Vladimirescu) had also participated in the war, on the side of the Russian armies, in the hope that upon termination of the conflict their country would be given its independence. The vague promises made by the Tsarist Empire were, however, designed to justify the war against the Ottoman Empire and the corollary military occupation of the Romanian Principalities as well as to induce the Romanians to join the war against the Porte.

In May 1812, Napoleon I started his campaign against Russia and the Tsarist government hastened to conclude the Peace of Bucharest, on May 28, 1812, contenting itself with taking the eastern part of Moldavia, between the Pruth and the Dniester, which it incorporated into Russia under the name of Bessarabia. By the Peace of Adrianople of September 14, 1829, concluded after the Russo-Turkish war of 1827-1828, Russia also annexed the Danube Delta, the Serpents' Island and the three counties of southern Bessarabia: Ismail, Cahul and Cetatea Albă (Ackermann).

Throughout that most difficult period in its history, the Romanian people were faced with the encroachments of foreign empires and with the dire consequences of such actions. Starting in the fourteenth century, the sacking of the Romanian people by foreign powers can be inferred from documents. An analysis of the evolution of the tribute paid to the Porte from the conclusion of the first treaty between Muntenia and the Ottoman Empire until 1877 reveals the loss of Romanian wealth as quantities of gold and other goods were received by the Ottoman Empire. All in all, the tribute paid by the Romanian countries (Muntenia, Moldavia and Transylvania) to the Ottoman Empire amounted to the sum of 1,066,305,780 lei gold,* or the equivalent of 341,021 kgs. of gold.

It should also be pointed out that in 1417 the old Romanian territory located between the Danube and the Black Sea-the Dobrudja-was occupied

---

* The transformation of currency units into lei gold were made on the basis of the following average equivalencies: 1 Ducat = 10 lei gold; one country red coin = 1 Ducat; 1 Florin = 10 lei gold; 1 Asper = 1 lei gold. The equivalent in gold was reached by using 1 leu gold = 0.3225 grams of gold.

by the Ottoman Empire, and the occupation lasted until 1877, while a series of major cities on the Romanian bank of the Danube, such as Giurgiu, Turnu, Brăila, Chilia, Tighina, Cetetea Albă had been turned into rayahs and pashaliks by the Ottomans.

By occupying Transylvania (1687-1918), the Banat (1718-1918), Oltenia (1718-1739) and Bukovina (1775-1918), the Habsburg Empire took from Romania more than 2.45 billion lei gold, or 875,500 kgs. of gold, through taxes, military contributions in money or in kind, through work on military constructions.

Between 1769 and 1854, when Muntenia and Moldavia were occupied for various periods of time, by the Tsarist armies, significant material assets or obligations went to the Tsarist Empire. The obligations in money and in kind incurred by Moldavia and Muntenia reached the sum of 200 million lei gold, or 64,516 kgs. of gold. It should also be noted that the Moldavian territory lying between the Pruth and the Dniester, called Bessarabia, was incorporated into the Tsarist Empire in 1812.

The numerous wars between the great empires also affected the material well being of the Romanian people. Located in an area of continuous conflict among the Ottoman, Tsarist and Habsburg Empires, the Romanian lands were frequently turned into battlegrounds, or were compelled to provide for the troops of one or another of the empires in that occupied them. The Romanians paid obligations in money and in kind, were subjected to plunder, their towns were set on fire—the damages incurred cannot be estimated.

As the eighteenth century progressed so did the aspirations of the Romanians for a better life, for liberty, for unity and for independence. Highly significant for the Romanian people's fight for social and national liberty was the peasant uprising led by Horea, Cloșca and Crișan in 1784. Later, everything that had accumulated throughout "eighteen centuries of endeavor of the Romanian people for progress"—gallantry, courage, wisdom, military and diplomatic knowhow, the desire for liberty, the craving for independence, the wish reassert their rights over ancestral Dacia—was embodied, through the personality of Tudor Vladimirescu and the generation of the revolutionaries of 1848, in the century-old aspiration to achieve "independence outside and within the country."

Despite the overt hostility of the Great Powers, the Romanians registered a major victory on January 24, 1859. "A golden day of the century," as it was called by contemporaries, the Union of the Principalities, achieved by what Mihail Kogălniceanu called the "energetic act of the nation," was the acme of an objective historical process. Centuries of sacrifices and unbroken efforts dedicated to the liberty and progress of the homeland thus led to the historic act on May 9, 1877. That day, expressing the will and aspirations of the entire Romanian people, the Parliament proclaimed, by unanimous vote, the absolute independence of the country. The resounding victory scored by the Romanian people on May 9, 1877, aroused a positive response in the southeastern European and Balkan area, where the Serbians, the Montenegrins, the Croatians, the Bulgarians and others were engaged in battle designed to eliminate foreign domination.

After the war, the old Romanian territory between the Danube and the Black Sea—Dobrudja—was reunited with Romania. However, the Great Powers severed from Moldavia's body the counties of Cahul, Ismail and Cetatea Albă, which were incorporated into Russia.

The Union of 1859 and the gaining of state independence in 1877 opened a new stage in the Romanians' political and national movement, in the economic, social and cultural life of the country. The ideas of national liberty was readily adopted by the progressive bourgeoisie political forces, by cultural associations, by the press, and by Parliament; its implementation became a matter of primary concern. The struggle of the Romanians in territories under foreign domination for political, economic and cultural rights gained in intensity. The Romanians' socio-economic and political development revealed the inexorable need for the Romanian nation to achieve state unity, to free all Romanian provinces under alien rule, and unite them with the mother-country. Romania participated in World War I to achieve the union of all Romanians into an independent state. The collapse of Tsarism and the triumph of the socialist revolution in Russia ushered the fight for freedom and self-determination of all the peoples of the world.

The fight of the Romanian people likewise belonged to the people's movement for national self-determination and removal of foreign domination. It had a broad, bourgeois-democratic character, involving the working class, the peasantry, the intelligentsia, and other social and political forces. On March 27, 1918, for the above-mentioned reasons and in the given historical context, Bessarabia was united with Romania. In the

Romanian provinces in Austria-Hungary, the news of the victorious revolution in Russia spurred on the fight for national liberation. The decline of the Austro-Hungarian monarchy precipitated late in 1918, the union of Bukovina and Transylvania with Romania.

On November 15/28, 1918, the Congress of representatives of the population of Bukovina decided unanimously "The unconditional union, for good and all, of Bukovina with Romania, within her former frontiers."[7]

On December 1, 1918, 100,000 people, workers, peasants, intellectuals, and craftsmen gathered on Horea's Field, near Alba Iulia. The assembly convened on December 1, 1918, adopted the historic "Declaration of Alba Iulia," whereby the Great National Assembly solemnly proclaimed "The Union of Transylvania and of the Banat with Romania for all centuries to come."[8]

History shows that the achievement of the unitary national state was long in the making. Underscoring the historical circumstances in which that process was achieved, President Nicolae Ceausescu pointed out: "Therefore, the formation of the unitary Romanian national state is not a gift, it is not the result of international conferences; it is the result of a tireless struggle for unity waged by the most progressive forces of society, by the broad masses of the people, a natural outcome of the historical, social and national development of the Romanian people."[9] The Peace Treaties of Saint-Germain (1919), Trianon (1920) and Paris (1920) gave international recognition to a *de facto* situation created by the actions of the people.[10]

NOTES

1. Apud A. D. Xenopol, *Istoria românilor* (A History of the Romanians), vol. IV, Third Edition, Editura "Cartea românească," București, /f.a./, p. 214.

2. *Învăţăturile lui Neagoe Basarab către fiul său Theodosie* (Neagoe Basarab's Teachings for His Son Teodosie), a text chosen and selected by Florica Moisil şi Dan Zamfirescu, Editura "Minerva," București, 1970, p. 281.

3. Nicolae Iorga, *Scrisori de boieri. Scrisori de domni* (Boyars' Letters. Princely Letters), Third Edition, Vălenii de Munte, 1932, p. 201.

4. Dumitru Ionescu, *Tratatul încheiat de Cheorghe Stefan cu rușii* (The Treaty Concluded by Gheorghe Stefan with the Russians), București, 1956.

5. I. Mitilineu, *Colecția de tratate și convenții române cu puterile străine* (Collection of Romanian Treaties and Conventions with Foreign Powers), pp. 74-77.

6. Ibid. For details, see Mircea Mușat și Ion Ardelean, *Viața politică în România, 1918-1921* (Political Life in Romania, 1918-1921), București, Editura politică, 1976.

7. "Glasul Bucovinei," I, No. 13 of November 20, 1918.

8. *Marea Adunare Națională întrunită la Alba Iulia în ziua de 1 decembrie 1918. Acte și documente* (The Great National Assembly Gathered in Alba Iulia on December 1, 1918. Papers and Documents), vol. I, pp. 14-18.

9. Nicolae Ceaușescu, *Romania on the Way of Building up the Multilaterally Developed Socialist Society*, vol. 13, Bucharest, Meridiane Publishing House, 1978, p. 46.

10. V. V. Tilea, *Acțiunea diplomatică a României* (Romania's Diplomatic Activity), Sibiu, 1925, pp. 92-113.

Constantin Olteanu

THE CONCEPT OF MILITARY POWER IN ROMANIAN HISTORY: ITS IMPACT ON SOCIETY

As a reflection of complex problems related to the emergence and the evolution of military organisms, of quantitative and qualitative changes over the centuries, the concept of military power is a mobile one, one sensitive to mutations from one social system to another, or even to mutations within the same system.

The concept of military power can be scientifically understood only on the basis of historical materialism. As it is known, Marxist-Leninist theory showed that the army's emergence was linked to the foundation and development of the society based on antagonistic classes, and of the state. In his work "The Origin of the family, of private property and of the State" Fr. Engels, referring to the Athenian States, wrote that in place of genuine "armed people" who had organized the defense of kindreds, phratries, and tribes, there emerged an armed "public force," subordinated to the State power and thus capable of being used against the people, also.[1] The setting up of a public force, separate from the people and organized as an armed force, was considered by Lenin to be as one of the characteristics of the state.[2]

In opposition to the idealistic outlook according to which the army is something isolated, removed from social, economic and political conditions,[3] historical materialism shows that the army is a social phenomenon affected directly by the laws ruling society, but at the same time, having its own law of existence and development. Consequently, an analysis of

273

problems regarding the army's genesis, character, social function, organization, equipment, doctrine and so forth must start with consideration of the character of the social system, of the various stages of society's economic, social and political development.

The theses and the appreciations included in documents of the Romanian Communist Party constitute a guide for our historians in their studying Romanian military organization through the centuries. During the years of socialist construction the problems concerning the army's emergence in our country, its evolution or the mission accomplished by it have been analyzed in the framework of economic and socio-political development. The masses' contribution in the armed struggle, the contribution of various voivodes and commanders of the army in the area of military organization, in waging wars and in the development of the martial arts have been emphasized. At the same time, Romanian Marxist historians have revealed the class character of the army, the manner in which it was occasionally used in the past by the exploiting classes on behalf of their own interests, for suppressing the great peasant revolts, for repressing the revolutionary struggles of the working class.

For a better understanding of the concept of the army and of its evolution, it seems desirable to consider certain matters related to the organization of the army during the establishment and development of the independent Romanian feudal states. The genesis of the army itself is an important issue. The establishment of the army has at least been partly motivated on the one hand the interests of the ruling class, which had organized its power in a State system, in need of an instrument for repressing internal opposition, and on the other hand, by he need of a defensive force against outside dangers.

Contemporary conditions and possibilities as well as the traditions inherited from the Geto-Dacians forerunners left their imprint on the army's organization. The Geto-Dacian army had as its main components footmen, horsemen and "war-machines;" it distinguished itself by its prowess for defending the country's borders and by its bravery and spirit of self-sacrifice in battle. Gheorghe Șincai, the chronicler, wrote with justified pride that Domitianus, the Roman Emperor, was compelled to conclude peace with Decebalus who in "military matters was very skillful, clever and did not yield easily,"[4] and to recognize him as king, give him money, craftsmen and weapons. Decebalus' great merit consists in the fact that he made good use of the time after Domitianus' defeat and took strong measures for strengthening his army, aware as he was that Rome could not tolerate a strong Dacian state on its Danubian border and that sooner or later the Roman legions would cross the river to subdue the Dacians and to transform their country into a Roman province."[5] After Dacia's conquest by the Romans the military problems changed. The Romans, who were superior to the Dacians in military matters, imposed their system of organization and means of action on the autochtonous population while borrowing something from Dacian military concepts. From the merging of Dacian and Roman concepts, Romanian military thought and art were to be born.

In the setting up of the independent feudal states, military activity assumed new dimensions and characteristics in accordance with the levels of socio-economic and political development on Romanian land. The establishment of the Romanian Country (Wallachia) as a state, in the first decades of the fourteenth century, and then of Moldavia, at the end of the sixth decade of the same century, represented a moment of paramount importance for the socio-political and military history of the Romanians. The armies played an important role in the internal life of the feudal states and in their struggle to preserve their independence. The sources prove that Basarab, commander of the army and ruling prince, participated in the fights of 1317 between certain nobles and the king of Hungary related to the ruling of the fortress of Mehadia. At the same time, the army of "the Wallachians" is mentioned as taking part in a battle between the Bulgarians and the Byzantines in 1323.[6] It is also known that the victory won by the army of Basarb I in the battle of Posada (1330) over the strong army of the Hungarian King, Carol Robert D'Anjou was of special importance for asserting Wallachia's independent status: it was the first large-scale battle fought by a Romanian army against foreign invaders.

Important for the genesis of the army is also the concept of it role. Referring to this, distinguished historians such as N. Bălcescu, A. D. Xenopol, N. Iorga and others ascertained that the establishment of the army was caused exclusively by the need to defend the country; they neglected or underestimated the army's internal role. It is known, however, that the army was used by ruling princes or by great boyars for a multitude of purposes: as an instrument of class domination, for strengthening the central power, for acquiring power, for the defense of the country, etc. "This Prince, Stephen . . . "–wrote Grigore Ureche when referring to the manner in which Stephen the Great used the army for ascending the throne of Moldavia–"rose from Wallachia with many Wallachian soldiers and other people gathered from the country and entered the country."[7]

History has shown that internal or external functions may prevail at one time or another but that both functions are integral components of the military organism. The geographic and historical conditions affecting the Romanians forced them to engage in a permanent struggle against numerous foes bent on subduing them. This situation strongly influenced the means of defending the country and, thus, determined the army's organization and equipment, military strategy, and the like. "The Romanians"–wrote Nicolae Bălcescu–"did not love the war of conquest. . . . They waged wars more in their country. . . . Defensive war, considered as part of war strategy and politics, was most splendidly waged by the Romanians."[8]

After the establishment of the feudal states and in the process of economic and socio-political development of the Romanian Countries, the army has always played a significant, positive or negative role. Headed by famous ruling princes, the Romanian army, although an instrument of the ruling classes, recorded memorable feats of arms in wars for the defense of the people's liberty and independence. President Nicolae Ceaușescu justly appreciated the significance of the army when he stated that "The valiant army of the fearless Decebalus, the legendary leader of the Dacians, the staunch soldiers of our famous voivodes and great army commanders–Mircea the Old, Ioan of Hunedoara, Vlad the Impaler, Stephen the Great, Michael the Brave, expressing the undying love of liberty of the people, heroically and valiantly defended the ancestral land, generously shed their blood for it, chose if needed heroic death rather than bow down to the enemies, never betrayed the cause of the people."[9]

The military establishment in Romania reflects the conditions and peculiarities of historic development of the Romanian states: The specific autochtonous elements are noticeable, inter alia, in differences between the Romanian army's organization, structure and strategy, and those of the armies of the states. Thus, for example, while the armies of various Western countries waged primarily offensive wars, used a relatively small number of men, were rather unweildy because of the character of the military equipment, and preferred battle in the open field, the Romanian states had light, mobile, armies suitable to wars of movement, capable of engaging defensive actions and launching lightening counterattacks. The military strategy of the armies of the Romanian Countries was determined largely by appraisal of the enemy's armament, tactics and psychology; in fact, Romanian princes displayed remarkable ability in organizing and commanding thus demonstrating that great military leaders have nearly always been able to cope with schematism and set formations used by uninspired enemies.

Until its dissolution in the eighteenth century, simultaneously with the establishment of the Turkish-Phanariot regime in Moldavia and Wallachia, the Romanian army had developed continuously in accordance with historic conditions. Thus, if at the beginng of the feudal era, the boyars' men constituted the core of the army, as time went on the prince's greater army played an ever more important role as it assumed a permanent character. Although during that period the boyar's men played a decisive part, as they provided most of the contingents, and the boyars enjoyed a large degree of autonomy, the forces had certain obligations to the prince. At the princes' summons, the boyar's men had to come with their horses, mantles and weapons. Moreover, on a certain day of each year, the boyars themselves had to come armed on horseback, at the head of their men, to be "inspected" for their combat readiness.   In this manner, the standing army emerged and gradually developed and the prince's army became one of its manin components.

It is known that in cases of great danger the peasantry and craftsmen were also called to arms; thus the country's army assumed a mass character. In this respect, it is worth noting that Stephen the Great, in the battle of Baia (1467) had at his disposal about 12,000 soldiers, mostly small-land owners, and in the battle of Vaslui (1475), when he defeated the Turks by his "skill,"[11] his army numbered some 40,000 men. Calling the peasants to arms, an action determined largely by the fact that the Ottoman Empire, the main enemy of the Romanian Countries, used such large forces as to prevent the "lesser army" from facing them successfully, represented an innovation in military organization. As long as peasants and townsmen took part in the army—until the sixteenth century—the autochtonous element was prevalent. "This army made up only of natives, having a profound homogeneity without implying any foreign elements, indestructibly linked to the country's land and soul"—wrote A. D. Xenopol referring to the army of the fifteenth century—"was very disciplined and capable of doing remarkable feats."[12] Thus, a specific feature of the Romanian Countries' army was the fact that the soldiers came from the ranks of the people.

Beginning with the sixteenth century, because of intensification of feudal exploitation, of development of the productive forces and simultaneously of armaments, the peasants' participation in the army declined; mercenaries who guaranteed the prince's personal safety and acted as an instrument of the interests of the ruling classes became more prevalent. The economic and social development of the Romanian Countries led to the improvement of the army's equipment and the acquisition of improved weapons; this brought about changes in military structure, organization and tactics. "Concurrently with the discovery of a new instrument of war, the fire arms, the army's entire internal organization necessarily changed, the relationship under which the individuals could form an army and to act as an army also changed, the relationship among various armies changed as well,"[13] emphasized Karl Marx.

The concept of military power became more complex with the setting up of the first units of the national standing army, especially after 1848 and 1859. "The Romanian uniform and the army's organization which exist now have produced much joy in our capital"—wrote *Curierul Românesc* at the beginning of the fourth decade of the last century. "It seems as if every Romanian sees his nation reviving."[14]

The problem of the army was of special concern to the revolutionaries of 1848, particularly to Nicolae Bălcescu. In his work *Puterea armată şi arta militară de la întemeierea principatului Valaheie şi pînă acum* (Military Power and Military Science from the Establishment of the Principality of Wallachia to the Present), issued in 1844, Bălcescu stressed that he preferred "to deal with military institutions before any others because these institutions are the most wonderful ones forged by our forefathers, because they had been responsible for the country's glory and power for four centuries; at last, because I am deeply convinced"—he went on to write—"that if the Romanians' country will ever take its place among the peoples of Europe it owes this fact more to the reorganization of its old military institutions."[15] The revolutionary leaders seeking to change the old economic, social and political relations, to set up the Romanian society on modern, progressive basis, paid great attention to the existing military organism, to the role that organism was to play in the preparation, development and consolidation of the victories of their movement; at the same time they were concerned with the post-revolutionary physiognomy of the army, with the place which the army was to assume in the country's defensive system. They had for a long time sought to win over many of the officers to the side of the revolutionary forces, which accounted for the fact that from the very beginning of the revolution, many of the officers assumed command of units or subunits of the revolutionary forces.

The programs of the 1848 Revolution assigned priority to the establishment of the army and setting up new defensive formations directly linked to the Revolution. Thus, one of the revendications of the 1848 revolutionaries in Wallachia, was the establishment of the national guard which was to defend the public liberties proclaimed by the revolution;[16] this measure was enacted by the decree issued by the government on June 14/26, 1848. The program of the revolutionaries in Moldavia similarly called for "the setting up of an urban and rural guard . . . for defending the country and public happiness."[17] The principal mission of the national guards was to assure the defense of the internal order; in case of an external attack they were to prevent the enemy from entering the localities where they were located. The members of the national guards were recruited from among the masses, from citizens between 20 and 50 years of age who responded enthusiastically to the call of the revolutionary leaders. In Bucharest alone, at the end of August 1848, there were five legions, ten battalions and fourty companies[18] of national guards. Gh. Magheru had remarkable merits in engendering the armed means of the Wallachian Revolution. As a minister in the Provisional Government established by the Revolution, but especially as "general captain" of the "irregular" armed forces and inspector of the national guards in the country, Gh. Magheru was concerned primarily with assuring the Revolution with a solid military basis in his capacity of organizer and commander of the camp at Rîureni-Vîlcea.

In 1848-1849 the Romanians in Transylvania also organized their own army under the leadership of Avram Iancu. Eftimie Murgu, the democratic-revolutionary thinker, a well-known leader of the 1848 revolutionary movement in Banat, expecting external intervention against the revolution in Wallachia, wrote to Nicolae Bălcescu in June 1848 that

"The first concern for you, brothers, must be the arms. As soon as possible you must have an army to be able at least to successfully repel the first attack."[19]

A significant novel element in the concept of military power devised by the revolutionaries of 1848 was the grasping of the fact that the military organism was not only the country's defender against the foreign enemies but also the defender of the achievements of the bourgeois-democratic revolution.

The development of the army, as an army of the unitary national state occurred in conjunction with the Union of the Principalities of Moldavia and Wallachia in 1859. The new elements which were incorporated then included the establishment of a General Staff, the unifying of the training, logistics and the administration of the two armies, and the appointment of a single Minister of War. The significance of these measures became evident in the execution of the mission entrusted to the army by the leaders of the newly-unified state, headed by Prince Alexandru Ioan Cuza, that the army become one of the key factors for consolidating Romania's autonomy and setting the stage for the attainment of national independence.[20] In the context of the reforms planned by the government led by M. Kogălniceanu the program of May 1860 included, also "the well-conducted and thorough organization of the armed force in accordance with the country's requirements and possibilities."[21] Nine years later, M. Kogălniceanu, as Minister for Internal Affairs, in addressing the prefects in connection with the implementation of the recruitment law, pointed out that "they must establish the eligibility of everyone, regardless of social class, to perform the legal obligation which is compulsory for everyone. It would be a monstrosity if only the working classes performed military service, if only they answered the call of the country, paid taxes in blood."[22]

During the second half of the last century, several ruling political and military personalities expressed a few interesting and occasionally progressive points of views on the role and structure of the military organism. For instance, in 1871, Ion Chica proposed a thorough study of the country's geographic features, of the possibilities for incorporating Romanian military traditions, and the setting up of military corps made up of inhabitants of the districts of Mehedințti, Gorj and Vrancea who were to become acquainted with the means and methods of defensive warfare. Once

acquainted with the valleys and narrow valleys, with the paths and hill-
ocks, with the hills and mountains—he wrote—they could provide a highly
effective resistance to the foreigners.[23] "By reorganizing local corps"—
Ion Ghica stated—"by counties or by large districts like a network covering the whole country, commanded by officers capable of conceiving and
carrying out strategic plans according to their positions and by reducing
the standing or active army, only to special corps, we could achieve general arming."[24]

As was true of other projects of that epoch, the opinions expressed
by Ion Ghica represented in their essence a solution designed to reduce
military expenditures given the state's financial situation. He failed to
grasp, however, the fact that these "corps' had to be auxiliary to the
standing army. The war waged for the winning of Romania's state independence showed that Ghica's solution was impractical. The 1877-1878
War for Independence and the hardships which the Romanian army had
to endure during the two world conflagrations in the first half of this
century provided conclusive arguments for the need of a regular army.

The War of Independence raised new problems with respect to military development. A document from that period stressed that the war
"imposes on the country the need to revise many of its organic laws.
Among these the most important one, which is henceforth very necessary, is that of the organization of the armed power, the shield of the
independence we won in battles. It [the army] cannot be the work of a
single man, even if he were a genius, because an important armed force
requires long years of perseverance, a unity of opinions, and an uninter-
rupted and unshakable continuity in ideas."[25]

For the working-class, and especially for its political party, the concept of the army assumed a new and superior meaning to that expressed
by various representatives of the ruling classes. The working-class movement in Romania from its very beginning grasped the army's class character and favored the arming of the people. Backing up these ideas a newspaper issued in Jassy wrote in 1879 that faced with a strong agressive
army, "the people would oppose it by partisan warfare."[26] In the middle
of the ninth decade of the last century, in the well-known study entitled
Ce vor socialiştii români? (What do the Romanian Socialists Want?) C.
Dobrogeanu-Gherea, in total harmony with the outstanding ideas in the
international working-class movement of the time, asked for "The dis-
solving of the standing army and the army of the people."[27]

In subsequent years the working-class press dwelt on ideas calling for
modifying the military organization of the Romanian state. Thus, *Calen-
darul pozitiviṭ* issued in Galatzi in 1892, wrote that "it's a shame that
the soldiers have to be used only as defenders of a class made up of finan-
ciers and boyars."[28] The newspaper *Lucrătorul*, a social-democratic organ,
wrote in 1892 that it had to emphasize the army's role and signficance
until the workers would grasp the necessity of arming the people.[29]

The problems concerning the army, the attitude of the working-class
movement toward the existing military organism comprised an important
part of the documents of the Congress of Reestablishment of the Social
Democratic Party of Romania (1910). The Party's program stipulated
in its twenty-first point that: "Considering the army to be only a defensive instrument of the country and not an instrument used for repressing
the working-class in its struggles for emancipation, we ask that the standing army be transformed into a national militia and until then the military
service be reduced to only one year after which the man be placed in the
reserves. [We ask] the abolishment of military law and the introduction
of compulsory tuition in barracks. . . . The standing army is the strongest
support of the monarchy and of capitalism."[30]

It has been ascertained that after the political party of the proletariat
was established and concurrently with the political-ideological matura-
tion of the working-class movement in Romania, tactical reorientation
took place characterized by a change in the attitude of the socialist movement toward the existent army. As early as January 1911 the newspaper
România muncitoare clearly explained the socialists' position in this
field: "We do not ask for the abolishment, pure and simple, of the standing armies, but for their transformation into a genuine national army as
soon as possible. Those who say that we, the Romanian social-democrats,
want the army's abolishment, do not know our program and do deliberately delude our readers."[31]

At the same time the socialist movement understood the necessity and
importance of winning the army over to the side of the masses, the significance of the revolutionary struggle. The socialists sought to promote
actions designed to secure influence over the military, sought to educate
them in the spirit of love for the people, sought to involve the army in
political life, to grant rights and democratic liberties to the army as an
organic component of the people as a whole. "The masses under colors"—

România muncitoare—"must be educated amidst the people to enjoy its own joys, to aspire to its own goals, to pulsate to the same life and trends that stir the entire society."[32]

Expressing its opinions on the military organism, the socialist movement in Romania did not fail to focus its attention on the problem of the command personnel in the army. The socialists did not underestimate the role of the officers' corp in training the soldiers, its usefulness in the stage of transformation and reorganization of the armed forces. The socialists, however, intransigently opposed the inhumane practices and methods used by certain officers and non-commissioned officers in dealing with soldiers. They also rejected the views of the ruling classes about the so-called political neutrality of the officers' corps which neutrality was designed to isolate the army form the masses' political struggles. "It's an undeniable truth"—wrote *România muncitoare* — that the best officer is the one who in becoming a military man does not cease to retain an interest in the country's social and political life, in his people's needs. The officer is a good teacher and even more than a teacher. . . because he has to come into contact with already fully grown men."[33]

The Romanian socialists consistently advised military men to join the cause of the oppressed masses from which they came themselves. In this respect the manifesto *Către concediați și rezerviști*, (To discharged and Reservists) issued in the newspaper *România muncitoare* during the 1907 peasant revolts, is most noteworthy; therein the socialist militant, M. G. Bujor urged workers and peasants in military uniform not to shoot their brothers in rebellion, but to join them.

Thus, the concept of the army encompassed an area where the class interests of the proletariat confronted those of the ruling classes. Grasping the army's class character and its utilization as an instrument of the ruling classes, the organized revolutionary movement of the proletariat, militating against the standing military force of the bourgeoisie and of the landowners, sought to transform the army into the revolutionary force of the working class while concurrently emphasizing the necessity of arming the people.

The truth is that the abolishing of the standing army and the arming of the people were of primary concern to Marx, Engels and Lenin who linked this problem to the very accomplishment of the proletariat's historic mission—the creation of the socialist society. "The social-democrats"—

wrote Lenin in 1903 in his work *Către sărăcimea satelor* (To the Village Poor)—"want the standing army abolished, replaced by a popular militia, so as to arm the entire people."[34] A little later, aware of the fact that given the military power which imperialism had at its disposal, a defense of the socialist country would be impossible without the organization of a strong standing army, Lenin renounced the general thesis on the abolishment of the standing army. That thesis was replaced by the thesis on abolishing the bourgeois army and the setting up a an army of a new type, a socialist army, a reliable defender of the people's revolutionary achievements. As a result, simultaneously with the victory of the Great October Socialist Revolution, Lenin raised the problem of the organization of the proletariat's standing army as a military organization of the new class, wholly different from the bourgeois army: thus he enriched the Marxist doctrine on war and army with an entirely new thesis—the necessity of the socialist homeland's military defense, of setting up a standing army of a new type, well-equipped and perfectly trained.

In Romania the concept of military power, ideas about its character and role, evolved scientifically only after the establishment of the Romanian Communist Party. The First Congress of the Romanian Communist Party stated the Communists' position toward the then existing army pointing out the necessity of transforming it into an army of the people. However, at that object was subordinated to the accomplishment of the socialist revolution, the Romanian Communist Party indicated that it was first necessary to carry out revolutionary activity within the army to draw the armed forces into the struggle of the masses. The Communist Party established its own military Marxist-Leninist thought, enriching it with new theses and conclusions derived from the exigencies of the times.

The theory and practice came to fruition and were fully implemented only after World War II in the Socialist Republic of Romania.

NOTES

1. Marx, Engels, *Opere*, vol. 21, Editura politică, Bucharest, 1965, p. 107.

2. In accordance with V. I. Lenin, *Statul și revoluția*, opere complete, vol. 33, Editura politică, Bucharest, 1964, p. 9.

3. The ideologists of the ruling classes dealt with the problems of the army without reference to the character of the system; they also

denied the class character of the army, and over-estimated the army's role in the life of the state. For instance, in *Enciclopedia României* published in 1938, it is said that "the Army is a national organization gathering up the entire energy of the state" (p. 655). Ignoring first of all the prevailing economic and socio-political conditions, Nicolae Iorga wrote in *Istoria armatei românești* that "the history of the military system and of Romanian battles must begin with the grasping of the natural circumstances of an unchanging and fatal character which made that system and continued those battles."

4. Gh. Șincai, *Hronica românilor*, tom I, *Opere*, vol. I, Editura pentru literatură, Bucharest, 1967, p. 5.

5. Cf. H. Daicoviciu, *Dacii*, Editura științifică, Bucharest, 1965, pp. 201-202.

6. Cf. *Istoria medie a României*, partea I, Editura didactică și pedagogică, Bucharest, 1966, p. 86.

7. Gr. Ureche, *Letopisețul Țării Moldovei*, ESPLA, Bucharest, 1955, p. 83.

8. Nicolae Bălcescu, *Opere*, vol. I, Editura Academiei Republicii Populare Române, Bucharest, 1953, pp. 26-27.

9. Nicolae Ceaușescu, *Romania on the Way of Completing Socialist Construction*, Meridiane Publishing House, Bucharest, 1969, vol. 4, p. 330.

10. *Istoria medie a României*, partea întîi, Editura Didactică și pedagogică, Bucharest, 1966, p. 227.

11. Gr. Ureche, *Letopisetul Țării Moldovei*, ESPLA, Bucharest, 1955, p. 92.

12. A. D. Xenopol, *Istoria românilor din Dacia Traiană*, vol. 3, Tipolitografia H. Goldner, Jassy, 1890, p. 28.

13. K. Marx, Fr. Engels, *Opere alese*, in 2 volumes, vol. 1, ed. II-a, Editura de stat pentru literatură politică, Bucharest, 1955, p. 73.

14. Quoted passage from V. Nădejde, *Centenarul renașterii Armatei Române (1830-1930)*, Tipografia Cultura Românească, Jassy, 1930, p. 29.

15. N. Bălcescu, *Opere*, vol. I, ESPLA, Bucharest, 1952, p. 131.

16. *Istoria României*, vol. IV, Editura Academiei Republicii Populare Române, Bucharest, 1964, p. 65.

17. M. Kogălniceanu, *Texte social-politice alese*, Editura politică, Bucharest, 1967, pp. 146-147.

18. *Studii*—revistă de istorie, no. 4, 1965, p. 885.

19. *Pagini din gîndirea militară românească, 1821-1916*, Editura militară, Bucharest, 1969, p. 45.

20. For instance, in 1863 after the secularization of the Monastic Estates when rumors of an eventual outside intervention were circulating, the ruling Prince Cuza and his government took certain measures designed to strengthen the army. Because the state did not have sufficient funds, they asked for the population's support. Thanks to this action the sum of 1,921,386 lei was secured for buying cannons. Every district offered a sum of money e!uivalent to the value of a connon (32,000 lei). Schoolboys also took part in that action (Constantin C. Giurescu, *Viaţa şi opera lui Cuza*, Editura ştiinţifică, Bucharest, 1966, p. 220). The efforts made during those years showed their effects after nearly two decades, during the War of Independence, 1877-1878.

21. M. Kogălniceanu, op. cit., p. 230.

22. Ibid., pp. 273-274.

23. I. Ghica, *Scrieri economice*, vol. II, 1937, p. 146.

24. Ibid., p. 146.

25. Arh. St. Bucureşti, fond de provenienţă personală "C", mapa no. 3, f. 13.

26. *Presa muncitorească şi socialistă din România*, vol. I, 1865-1900, Editura politică, Bucharest, 1964, p. 54.

27. Ibid., Articolul "Ce vor socialiştii români?", p. 357.

28. Ibid., pp. 273-274.

29. Ibid., p. 293.

30. *Documente din istoria mişcării muncitoreşti din România, 1910-1915*, Editura politică, Bucharest, 1968, pp. 34-35.

31. *România muncitoare*, no. 92 of January 30, 1911.

32. Ibid., no. 86 of October 21, 1913.

33. Ibid., no. 18 of July 3, 1905.

34. V. I. Lenin, *Opere complete*, vol. 7, Editura politică, Bucharest, 1962, p. 168.

CONCLUSION

The achievement of Romanian independence and unity was not the result of fortuitous political and diplomatic circumstances. It is, of course, true that the changing character of international relations pertinent to the Eastern Question and to the general balance of power which occurred in the second half of the nineteenth century and the first two decades of the twentieth century facilitated the attainment of the historic goals of the Romanian people. But it is also true that without the massive and continuous participation of the Romanian people in the centuries-long struggle for independence and unity those goals might never have been formulated and certainly now have been realized by 1918 and retained ever since.

Because of the geographic location of the lands of the ancestors of the Romanians, and later of the Romanians themselves, the course of Romanian history has been frought with constant dangers which threatened the very existence of the people and of their political and social organization. The constant struggle against external enemies, which has lasted for over 2,000 years, has not always been successful. Burebista, Decebalus, Mircea the Old, Stephen the Great, Michael the Brave and their descendants and followers were not always victorious nor able to realize their political goals in the face of foreign pressures. But they were able to devise strategies—military and diplomatic—which went to insure the maintenance of national and state integrity, the essential prerequisites for the eventual achievement of independence and unity.

Because the external enemies were invariably more formidable, from a military standpoint, then the native forces, the leaders of the ancestors of the Romanian people, and of the Romanians themselves, had to seek the best ways and means for insuring the defense of the people and of the territory. It is to the great credit of those leaders that they were able to devise exceptional military strategies that would make optimum use of the skills and determination of the people and of the terrain in staging protracted resistance against foreign foes. "The "entire people's war" was the answer to external threats.

Resistance to threats and oppression by enemies was not limited only to military action in defense of the integrity of the nation and of the state. It also manifested itself in actions directed against internal oppression. Uprisings, revolts, and revolutions such as that of Horea, Closca, and Crissan in 1784, that of Tudor Vladimirescu in 1821, and those of 1848-1849 were all expressions of disaffection with prevailing conditions which impeded the development of social and political progress.

Whether immediately successful or not, the armed struggles of the Romanians, in times of war or in times of revolution, were characterized by bravery, and determination to secure the fundamental rights to freedom and self-governance. Their struggles gained in intensity after the Crimean War with the Union of the Principalities, the prelude to the War for Independence which, in turn, was the forerunner of the ultimate national goal of Unity in an independent Romania.

Many a lesson of history is to be learned from the study of the manner in which the inhabitants of the historic lands of the Romanians have attained their historic goals. The interaction of war, revolution, and society, so thoroughly and carefully analyzed in this volume, provides the most meaningful explanation of the problems and solutions which have determined the course of the history of the Romanian people.